W9-DFS-603

Lies
Your Broker
Tells You

LIES

YOUR

BROKER

TELLS YOU

*What to Watch for
and Still Achieve
Financial Security*

THOMAS D. SALER

WALKER AND COMPANY / NEW YORK

First published in the United States of America in 1989
by Walker Publishing Company, Inc.

Published simultaneously in Canada by Thomas Allen & Son
Canada, Limited, Markham, Ontario.

Library of Congress Cataloging-in-Publication Data

Saler, Thomas D.
    Lies your broker tells you : what to watch for and still achieve financial security / Thomas
D. Saler.
        p.   cm.
    Bibliography: p.
    Includes index.
    ISBN 0-8027-1075-1
    1. Stocks.   2. Stockbrokers.   3. Finance, Personal.   I. Title.
HG4661.S25 1989
332.6—dc19   88-34207
                                                                                        CIP

Printed in the United States of America

10 9 8 7 6 5 4 3 2 1

*For my mother and father,
with love and gratitude*

Contents

Acknowledgments

How many ways are there for a grateful author to say thank you? In spite of suggestions from the definitive Roget's, there are not nearly enough ways to adequately thank the hundreds of people whose contributions helped turn this project from dream to reality. Thanks to the many brokers, branch managers, research analysts, corporate financial officers, reporters, editors, attorneys, New York Stock Exchange and government officials, professional portfolio managers, and advisory newsletter publishers who spoke candidly and courageously to me in the hope of serving the cause of truth. Special thanks to the many investors who were kind enough to share their pain so that others may learn from their misfortune. Thanks to my agent, Jane Jordan Browne, for her faith in me and my project, and for her invaluable suggestions. Thank you to Lynn Geils, whose non-user-vicious word processor turned my ramblings to print, and to K. H. Kent for his masterful graphics and endless patience. Thanks to Rick Saler, without whose assistance the timely completion of this work would not have been possible. Finally, I reserve my deepest thanks for my parents, for their unfailing support during the two long years spent writing this book and most importantly, for teaching me that being rich has nothing to do with money.

Preface

Though I had little sense of it at the time, the short paragraph I'd read from my eighth-grade history book would profoundly affect the future course of my life. The text, which described the stock market crash of 1929, had somehow caught my fancy, and I soon became a fourteen-year-old pain in the neck at brokerage offices throughout my hometown of Milwaukee, Wisconsin. Using money I had saved from odd jobs, I even opened my own brokerage account; one share of Bordens at $34. My selection of Bordens over the approximately 1,000 other candidates was based upon nothing as scientific as dividend discount models, price-earnings ratios, or consensus analyst earnings forecasts. Rather, I thought, since I had to stare at this quite homely picture of a cow over my breakfast each morning, I might as well own the company. I became *Elsie's boss*.

Elsie, it turned out, was more of a dog than a cow, and I soon unloaded Bordens in favor of more thoughtfully considered companies. In fact, during the ensuing months, I would occasionally skip school and ride the bus to the downtown office of Loewi & Company, where I would watch the ticker tape for hours without break. By the following summer I was spending nearly every minute of each business day lounging in brokerage offices: hogging the quotron, monopolizing the *Wall Street Journal*—and trading stocks. Mostly through blind luck, I'd managed to turn my original $34 investment into nearly $200. The stock market had become an all-consuming passion; quintupling my money was nice, but I found the game itself so fascinating that I'd have played with little more than penny chips.

If I was a curiosity to the brokers whose offices I regularly invaded, the feeling was certainly mutual. Except to place my buy and sell orders, I rarely spoke to any brokerage personnel, and found myself wondering exactly what it was that brokers did. I knew they made money from commissions (my commissions), but I had the impression that customers merely walked in the door, sat down at a broker's desk, and began trading stocks. Fourteen-year-olds are entitled to a few illusions.

Nearly two decades later, minus a few illusions and not considerably wealthier than the stocktrader of my youth, I again found myself inside a brokerage office—this time interviewing for the position of broker. Several years of teaching in the public schools had convinced me that a better way to make a living had to exist, a perception reinforced by a highly successful broker who was to become my brother-in-law. Unfortunately, the career options available to ex-schoolteachers (at least those unable or unwilling to "go computer") are virtually nonexistent outside of the sales profession. Though I knew by now that brokers were, in fact, glorified salesmen, the work somehow seemed classier, more intellectually challenging, and more dignified than selling encyclopedias or used cars. Besides, I thought, I'd once played the stock market and thoroughly enjoyed the experience. It seemed the perfect solution.

I was hired by the first firm I approached. Being a reasonably articulate sort and sporting the investment expertise of a fourteen-year-old, I was apparently judged to be a well-qualified investment professional. I immediately found the brokerage experience exhilarating; instead of trying to control an unruly mob of pubescent teenagers, I was wearing three-piece suits, dining at company expense in elegant restaurants, earning more while still in training than I had earned after years of teaching, and discussing economic and political issues from an impressively furnished twenty-seventh-floor office. I was treated in a first-class manner by the firm, which contrasted sharply with the substandard working conditions of the poor rural public school system from which I'd come. It seemed too good to be true: three months earlier I was making baby talk with squirrelly teens who had only the vaguest idea of who they were (or often *where* they were). Now I was discussing interesting subjects with informed adults and being paid considerably more for my trouble. I decided that I had to find a way to ensure that this kind of experience would last forever.

In order to make the experience last forever—the money, the royal treatment, the excitement, the power—I had to find a means to make the company as happy as they had made me. I soon learned there was a very simple way of doing that: sell lots of stocks and bonds. I immersed myself in the study of sales: how to reach people with money, how to give presentations, how to rebut a prospect's every objection, how to close, how to ask for referrals, how to stay out of trouble. Survival as a broker, I quickly learned, was actually very simple: *just get the sale.*

After two years of just getting the sale, my firm was reasonably happy with me; I had met their sales quotas and was working hard. But I soon noticed a disconcerting trend: though I was making more money than I'd ever earned in my life, and though my firm was making even more, my customers didn't seem to be getting their share. I had been taught to rely on the stock recommendations of my research department, but I'd found that for every winner there was at least one loser, and while the market advanced, my customers treaded water. And they weren't alone: I knew scores of brokers, both from within my firm and from without, and none seemed to possess anything more than purely superficial investment knowledge. I began to notice that often stocks would be recommended by brokers after the most amateur and shallow of office banter. I sensed that we were playing a game of investment hardball for which we were not only ill-prepared, but not even completely dedicated. Just getting the sale was all that mattered.

I wondered if perhaps the research product would prove more useful at a larger, national firm, which, after all, could afford to pay its analysts a more competitive wage. I transferred my broker's license to a well-known wirehouse and began to recommend stocks from its approved list. The research reports at my new firm *looked* more impressive—they were thicker and more elaborate, with numbers and graphs gracing almost every page—but after several months it was clear that the investment results they generated failed to match the slick appearance. When I complained to my new boss that the research seemed worthless, he replied, with an understanding smile, that his first order of business each day was to toss the entire batch of paper into the trash can. So much for research. Just get the sale.

But sell what? Investment ideas that even a firm's branch manager won't read? Stocks picked by broker-colleagues who are glorified salesmen and little more? Speculative and ill-liquid tax shelters, whose main reason for existence are their 8% brokerage commissions?

I had committed the cardinal sin for any successful broker: I had begun to ask what the brokerage industry did for my customers instead of only what it did for my life-style. And I began to ask other questions as well: What could account for the gaping discrepancy between brokerage-industry promises and results? Why doesn't brokerage research work? How does the industry define a "successful" broker? What does the industry consider to be its ultimate purpose?

This book represents the culmination of a two-year effort to understand the answers to those and other questions. The answers are not flattering to the industry I served for nearly four years. But I did not want this book to only tell investors what *not* to do, and why not to do it. I wanted also to present a fairer, more professional, and results-oriented way for millions of Americans to invest their money. *Lies Your Broker Tells You* does just that: informs, advises, and presents the real facts.

Lies
Your Broker
Tells You

SECTION ONE

CHAPTER 1

The High Price of Your Broker's Advice

Once in the dear dead days beyond recall, an out-of-town visitor was being shown the wonders of the New York financial district.

When the party arrived at the battery, one of his guides indicated some handsome ships riding at anchor.

He said, "Look, those are the bankers' and brokers' yachts."

"Where are the customers' yachts?" asked the naive visitor.[1]

I have heard the comments hundreds of times during my career in the investment business. "Everything I've done in the stock market has been wrong"; "I won't go near stocks again"; "I've won some and lost some. Overall, I'd have been better off putting my money in the bank."

What *has* been finding its way to the bank are brokerage-industry profits, ranging from $1.5 billion in "bad" times to over $5 billion in a boom market. And the nation's 70,000 brokers licensed through New York Stock Exchange member firms aren't doing badly either, averaging nearly $100,000 in annual earnings. *But how are their clients doing?* With scores of phenomenally successful alternative investments available, the time has never been more appropriate to

3

examine what the brokerage industry is delivering for its billions. Is the industry better suited to producing sales commissions than superior results for its clients? Are stockbrokers really qualified to manage the life savings of investors? Do the reams of recommendation churned out by brokerage research departments actually produce results? And has the brokerage industry become the consummate bureaucracy, existing solely to perpetuate its own existence?

It Matters Plenty

These questions should be of more than academic concern to you if you are among the seventeen million Americans identified in the latest New York Stock Exchange study as still using full-service stockbrokers. If you own $11,500 in securities—the average portfolio size, according to the NYSE—and if your broker failed to match the performance of the average stock (as measured by the Standard & Poor's 500 index) by just 3% per year, your broker would have cost you *$10,806* over the ten-year period ending 31 December 1987. If that same size underperformance were extended to cover a twenty-year period, your broker, simply by failing to match the performance of the S & P 500 index (which has averaged 15.3% since 1978), would have cost you $77,283.

Price of a 3% Underperformance
12% vs 15% on $11,500

One Year:	$ 345
Five Years:	2,864
Ten Years:	10,806
Fifteen Years:	30,631
Twenty Years:	77,283

As the data that follows will amply demonstrate, there is plenty of evidence to suggest that relying on advice from your stockbroker and/

or his firm will result in *at least* a 3% average annual underperformance of the S & P 500. And the failure of your broker to match this standard index is no longer just an expensive but moot point: besides being an accurate barometer of broad-market activity, the 500 companies comprising the index can now be purchased as a single entity without sales charges or commissions through no-load mutual funds* (see chapter eight for details). The availability of this index for purchase now *guarantees* that you will never need to endure market underperformance again, since, in effect, you can now *be* the market. Your broker, in falling behind this index, has not only displayed general incompetence through below-average performance, but has underperformed a less expensive, lower-risk, real-world alternative investment, and cost you thousands of dollars in the process. How many thousands, of course, depends upon the size and length of that underperformance; at a 5% average annual underperformance, your broker could cost you as much as $110,849 over the next twenty years.

Price of a 5% Underperformance
10% vs 15% on $11,500

One Year:	$ 575
Five Years:	4,610
Ten Years:	16,695
Fifteen Years:	45,538
Twenty Years:	110,849

The price of your broker's underperformance becomes even more expensive when compared to alternative investments that have consistently *outperformed* the S & P. (You'll find several of these alternatives discussed at length in chapters eight, nine, and ten.) Again assuming a 15% annual S & P total return and a 5% underperformance by your broker, the cost to you when compared to an investment that betters the S & P by 5% would be $10,095 after only five years, $41,376 after ten years, and an incredible $363,510 after twenty years.

*All words with an asterisk are defined in the glossary.

Price of a 10% Underperformance
10% vs 20% on $11,500

One Year:	$ 1,150
Five Years:	10,095
Ten Years:	41,376
Fifteen Years:	129,140
Twenty Years:	363,510

Adding insult to injury, of course, is the fact that while your broker could be costing you tens of thousands of dollars by underperforming readily available, guaranteed investment alternatives, he is being paid handsomely for his trouble. Because, whether you outperform the market or not, your broker's W-2 form will almost certainly outperform yours.

A Profit Machine

That your broker is nicely suited to producing commissions is beyond dispute; *Forbes* magazine, in an analysis of brokerage industry earnings, asked, "Which industry pays hundreds of people upwards of a million dollars a year and pays thousands of people $100,000 or more? We're not talking about illegal drugs."[2] They *were* talking about the brokerage business.

Between 1977 and 1988, New York Stock Exchange member firms experienced a seven-fold increase in revenues, from under $7 billion in 1977 to over $50 billion in 1988.

Despite the October 1987 stock market crash and the brokerage industry's well-known penchant for overexpansion during good times, a healthy share of that burgeoning revenue is finding its way to the bottom line, with brokerage profits holding at about $2.5 billion in 1988, up 525% since 1977.

Not surprisingly, the incomes of brokerage personnel reflect an industry awash in profits. According to data from the Labor Department's Occupational Outlook Handbook compiled by *Working Woman* magazine, three of the top-paying four, and five of the highest-paying twelve professions in America are directly related to the securities business.[3] By 1988, brokers and research analysts routinely earned over $100,000 per year, with many making over $500,000. Experienced investment bankers—brokerage personnel involved in mergers, acquisitions, and underwritings—receive an average of $300,000 in salary and bonuses; scores of investment bankers earn well in excess of $1 million per year. And partners of some of the large privately held brokerage firms earn up to $4 million annually in salary and bonuses.

Trickle Down

But again, *How are their clients doing?* Don't ask, says the brokerage industry. In preparing this book, I contacted nine of the largest U.S. brokerage firms and requested a copy of their track records, i.e., the results of all the buy and sell recommendations made over the past one, five, and ten years. The request left normally boastful firms tongue-tied. "If it existed," said a spokeswoman for one of the firms, "I wouldn't be free to give out that information." Then why should anyone use a stockbroker who has no public record instead of an alternative investment that does? I asked. "That's an interesting thesis," she admitted. Other firms were equally shy. "We track them, but I don't know that we'd share something like that," said a spokeswoman for a well-known broker. But why the hesitancy? "Probably everybody's embarrassed," conceded a candid spokesman for yet another national firm. Perrin Long, an expert on the brokerage industry for Lipper Analytical Services, concurs: "If they publish a complete track record, it might not look good." Does the industry's refusal to publish its results, even as its revenues are growing dramatically, indicate that the industry is better suited to producing sales than results? "Probably yes," he answered.[A]

For years brokerage firms have hid the results of their recommendations behind a veil of secrecy, pleased, no doubt, that no authentic record was available to the public. Without hard evidence, frustrated and disenchanted investors could only suspect that their painful lack of results was no isolated occurrence. In recent years, however, independent studies have been completed, comparing the results of brokerage-firm recommendations with other non-brokerage money managers. The comparisons are indeed damning for the brokers.

Computer Directions Advisors of Silver Spring, Maryland, ranked the performance of 147 investment advisers and brokerage firm–managed equity portfolios in 1982. Their findings, published in the *Wall Street Journal*, found that no brokerage firm ranked higher than 52nd. Three of the largest firms—Shearson/American Express Asset Management, Merrill Lynch, Pierce, Fenner & Smith, and Prudential-Bache Securities, ranked 136th, 140th, and 143rd, respectively, out of the 147 advisers tracked. Among other brokers, Dean Witter Reynolds Intercapital placed 91st, and Merrill Lynch Asset Management came in 52nd.[4]

Select Information Exchange (SIE) also began tracking the results of independent advisers and brokerage firms in 1981. Of hundreds tracked, the highest-ranking brokerage firm placed only 25th, and there were no other brokers to be found in the top 50, as of June 1985, when SIE stopped monitoring brokerage recommendations. Those ranked below 50th place were not listed in order to avoid embarrassment to the firms.

In its *1986 Investor's Guide*, *Fortune* magazine asked every major Wall Street firm to participate in its "Investment Challenge," a competition to determine which firm could most successfully manage a hypothetical $100,000 portfolio. *Fortune* observed that "hard-eyed follow-ups on how brokers' recommendations perform are at least as rare as the customers' yachts. What's almost unheard of is for brokers to assemble portfolios with a specific goal and manage them in competition with one another, taking into account such pesky realities as taxes and commissions." The challenge left even the most vainglorious of Wall Street firms cowering. "Many well-known brokerage houses and investment banks showed little appetite for having the performance of their recommendations publicly compared," said *Fortune*.[5] In the end, only four American-based firms took the challenge, yet several that refused did manage to overcome their shyness with full-page ads in the same issue. "Find out how the rich manage to get richer," advertised one firm *not* participating in the public challenge. "Now that your investments require thought, you need the services of a stockbroker whose sophistication matches the market's," trumpeted another major firm that had chosen to keep *its* sophistication *off* the record.

The results of the public challenge, announced one year later in *Fortune 1987 Investor's Guide,* provide still clearer evidence of why the brokerage industry would prefer to keep the results of its recommendations secret: While the S & P 500 index was advancing 20%, the four American-based brokers averaged a paltry 2% pre-tax return, for a total underperformance of 18%.[6] In fact, during one of the greatest bull markets in history, an investor could have more than doubled the average broker's return simply by leaving his money in a passbook savings account.

Fortune's 1987 and 1988 Investment Challenges revealed still more disappointing brokerage results. The five American firms participating in the 1987 challenge combined for an average underperformance of 9.1%[7], while the four brokers competing in the 1988 challenge underperfomed the unmanaged, "no-brainer" S & P index by an average of 9.35%.[8]

A Zacks Investment Research study, commissioned by the *Wall Street Journal,* also displayed graphically the inability of brokers to outperform simple market indexes over a long period of time. Zacks tracked the performance of stocks recommended by the ten largest brokerage firms for varying periods of time, beginning in July 1986. The most significant data, since it covers the longest time period, compared the ten brokers' picks with the S & P 500 index and the Dow Jones Industrial Average for the thirty-month period ending 31 December 1988. It found that the ten brokers underperformed the S & P 500 by an average of 1.8% and the Dow Jones Industrial Average by 4.3%, *even before paying brokerage commissions.* Assuming that the average customer of each of the firms pays just 6% a year in commissions—probably a conservative estimate—the average client of each of those ten firms would have netted a −7.8% relative to the S & P 500 and −10.3% compared to the Dow Jones Industrial Average.[9]

Investment banking, a division of the brokerage business that includes underwriting new stock and bond offerings, is among the most profitable areas for a brokerage firm. Investment banking profits can account for as much as 50% of a brokerage firm's earnings, and officials engaged in this lucrative business are routinely paid over $300,000 per year. In its 2 December 1985 issue, *Forbes* sought to determine how much of those investment banking profits were finding their way to clients' pockets. In the case of nine of the largest brokerage firms, the answer was very little. *Forbes* computed the average performance of each stock underwritten between 1975 and 1984 and compared the results to the S & P 500 index. Their findings: not one of the nine largest firms—E. F. Hutton, Merrill Lynch, Dean Witter, Paine Webber, Thomson McKinnon, Smith Barney, Shearson/American Express, Prudential-Bache, and Kidder Peabody—had even *half* its new issues outperform this standard index. Of the 432 issues underwritten by these firms, only 35.3% outperformed the S & P; overall, an investor buying each of the 432 stocks would have lose 4.6% relative to the S & P 500 average.[10]

Still another measure of brokerage house "expertise" is the performance of the mutual funds they sponsor. Once again, the results would suggest that an investor would be better served by using a dart board to pick stocks than relying on brokerage firm recommendations. Of 148 long-term growth funds tracked by *Money* magazine for the one-year period ending 1 March 1985, the twelve broker funds listed returned an average of only 9.1%, an underperformance of 11.9% compared to the S & P's 21% return. Overall, the twelve broker funds ranked 85th out of the 148 funds tracked.[11]

Broker funds showed little improvement in the 1987 *Money* rankings, which rated the performance of 111 growth funds for the three-year period ending 1 October 1987. Twelve broker funds were again included in the rankings, and once again their collective performance was dismal, averaging only 62nd among all funds while underperforming the S & P index by an average of 9.8% per year over the period.[12]

As badly as the average brokerage-firm recommendation underperforms the broad-market averages, customers relying on specific investment advice from stockbrokers are likely to be faring even worse. The reason: Your stockbroker is free to choose which stocks, if any, he uses from his firm's recommended list. Unfortunately, stockbrokers are generally even less qualified to pick stocks than their research departments. "Most research departments would have better performance records, in total, than the average broker," admitted Harold K., a securities analyst with a regional brokerage firm.[B] And if the recommendations of brokerage research departments are so embarrassing that they cannot be made public, and if individual brokers are even worse, does the industry really serve any useful purpose at all? Yes, said one highly successful mutual fund manager, his tongue firmly-in-cheek: "Listen, I need the brokers. Somebody has to be wrong. Without them, I can't make money."

With them, neither can you.

Oops

If your broker failed to provide you with useful investment counsel in the days and months immediately preceding the great stock market crash of 19 October 1987, you are probably not alone. Though prices had begun falling nearly two months earlier, many brokerage firms were still urging their customers to continue buying, or at least holding their stocks right up to the day of the crash itself. From August 25 to October 19 the market fell 37%, certainly qualifying it as a full-fledged bear market* in itself; if brokerage houses could indeed predict the future—the essential rationale for their existence—it would certainly seem reasonable to expect that a 37% drop in prices would not go unforeseen. And while unprepared clients racked up hundreds of billions of dollars in losses, brokerage houses earned huge commission dollars resulting from the panicked liquidation of stocks whose purchase they had recommended only days earlier.

Typical of brokerage advice from the period immediately preceding the crash were these two client advisories from the giant Wall Street firms of Salomon Brothers and Prudential-Bache Securities:

Salomon Brothers, 19 October 1987: "We believe that the current level of rates is not sufficient to bring the bull market in stocks, now in its sixth year, to an end. Accordingly, we recommend that investors build positions in stocks that have declined significantly in the most recent correction and where the fundamentals have remained intact or improved."[13]

Prudential-Bache Securities, 14 October 1987: "Based on the very simple logic that the bond market will not go down forever, I predict that we will see a substantial rally in the stock market between now and year end. . . . The nitpickers among you probably will want to know when this rally will start. My guess is that it will start fairly soon. . . . I believe the stock market rests on some fairly sound fundamentals, looking out over the next six to twelve months; I expect the stock market to move to new highs this year and to advance well above the old highs in 1988."[14]

Merrill Lynch, E. F. Hutton, and Drexel Burnham Lambert were even more unabashedly bullish in their forecasts in the weeks and days preceding the crash. Investors wishing to discover for themselves just what kind of investment expertise these firms were dispensing in return for their millions in commission dollars might be interested in tracking down and reading the following pre-crash recommendations:

"Investment Strategy Review," E. F. Hutton & Company, 7 October 1987.

"Research Highlights," Merrill Lynch, Pierce, Fenner & Smith, Inc., 25 September 1987.

"Research Abstracts," Drexel Burnham Lambert, Inc., 6 October 1987.

Let's Change the Subject

Since brokerage firms are, with good reason, too embarrassed to advertise their track records, the marketing efforts they employ are directed mainly at creating the proper image for their firms. Many spend tens of millions of dollars each year and retain high-powered ad agencies to assist in this noble effort. The objective is to create name recognition and a general image of legitimacy and trust, while craftily refuting any widely held negative perceptions about a firm. Merrill Lynch, for example, used a bull gracefully winding about a china shop to dispel its image as being too big, insensitive, and muscle-bound for today's markets. E. F. Hutton scored a major triumph with its "When E. F. Hutton Talks, People Listen" campaign, whose memorable commercials established easy name recognition among investors and noninvestors alike. When people listened, however, they never heard E. F. Hutton talk about results. Sometimes the attempts at imagery are more transparently manipulative; Piper Jaffray Hopwood shows an obviously well-off gentleman singing the praises of his broker while pulling out of his driveway—boat in tow. Dean Witter Reynolds follows *its* elderly couple everywhere; arm-in-arm they sing the praises of Dean Witter for making their retirement so happy and secure.

Brokerage advertising is also fond of emphasizing quantity—the quantity of "products" offered, the quantity of research analysts, the quantity of new stock or bond offerings—as if creating the issue of *quantity* would somehow make the issue of *results* disappear. Offering large quantities of products serves a dual purpose: besides creating a false issue in order to obscure a damaging one, it feeds the notion that the marketplace has become so complex that investors need the services of investment "professionals" in the brokerage business.

Brokerage image-making also tries to create the impression that a firm is in possession of valuable information upon which the futures of entire families may depend. A recent brokerage commercial is a classic example: A middle-aged man phones his broker to inform him that he had just heard the "news" that college education costs are rising dramatically. "Are we covered?" the man wonders. (The "we" is especially manipulative since it plays upon the natural parental tendency to worry about their children.) Looking equally concerned, the broker assures his client that he'll "look into it" and "not to worry." All at once, phones around the world ring off the hook, computers whir, grave-looking men speak in hushed tones as they parade through international capitals, the broker paces in his office and initiates animated consults with analysts. Finally, the word comes: All is well, no changes required. (Again, the advice that no changes are required is manipulative, designed to overcome the image of the brokerage industry as only too anxious to trade someone's account.) The man and his family live happily ever after, thanks to the concern and expertise of their broker and his firm.

In short, the advertising of the brokerage industry is as deceptive and manipulative as the sales pitches of its brokers. Too embarrassed to talk about facts, the industry settles for an approach that emphasizes everything but facts; viewers are left without one single shred of hard evidence showing why they should invest through that particular firm. This misuse of advertising is certainly not confined only to the brokerage business; beer-industry advertising is also primarily image-making. But beer cannot be quantified; its "results" to users are totally subjective. Investment results *can* be quantified; they are withheld because to announce them would defeat the purpose of the commercial. And the manipulation seems to be working. Millions of investors are remaining loyal to their brokers. According to the 1985 New York Stock Exchange share ownership study noted earlier, 37.4% of the approximately forty-seven million American stockholders still use full-service brokers to at least some extent, and 30.4% employ only full-service brokers. An equally compelling testimonial to brokerage marketing skills is the results of a study by R. H. Brusking Associates, which found that a plurality of investors—41%—rely on brokerage firms as their main source of investment information.[15]

Existence for Its Own Sake

What emerges from all the statistics and studies is a portrait of an industry far better at lining its own pockets than those of its customers, an industry that exists primarily to perpetuate its own existence. Brokerage personnel, living the good life off of their clients' money, rarely reflect on what they are actually doing to investors. Keeping their lucrative jobs is their primary concern; substituting manipulative imagery for facts is their greatest challenge.

No one can dispute that the brokerage industry has carefully crafted an image for itself that has resulted in huge earnings for its personnel. But as the statistics point out, that affluence has not flowed through to its customers. The reasons behind the industry's failure to deliver anything more than salesmanship and slogans are many and varied. Sadly, stockbrokers are little more than professional salesmen and professional friends masquerading as investment professionals, and the research on which they depend is not only tainted with conflicts of interest but is demonstrably too inaccurate to be useful. Together, these frauds and inadequacies could cost you, the average investor, tens, and possibly hundreds of thousands of dollars over a lifetime of investing.

But the high price of your broker's advice is one bill that need not necessarily be paid. Brokerage marketing skill can be overcome through a thorough knowledge of facts; understanding your broker's qualifications and the pressures under which he works is a good place to start.

CHAPTER 2

A Salesman by Every Other Name

The only direct contact you are likely to have with a brokerage firm is through a stockbroker. Brokers are the layer of industry personnel closest to the public, and they serve as the hands, feet, and mouth of the brokerage operation.

To meet a stockbroker is to be instantly put at ease. Most are smooth, polished, gregarious, impeccably tailored, and conservatively groomed—all qualities designed to put customers in a comfortable state of mind while creating an image of legitimacy and trust. The nameplate on your broker's desk will make no mention of the term "stockbroker." Instead, this genial professional is an account executive, or a financial consultant, or better still, a vice-president. He will ask about your family and inquire about financial objectives and previous investment experience. He will make no immediate recommendations; first, he will promise to consult with an array of "experts" readily available to him to design a financial plan tailored specifically to meet your individual needs. He will be the consummate professional, and indeed he is. The only question is exactly *what* he is professional at.

"Stockbrokers are salesmen, not economists. Most of what I know is what our research department tells me," one highly "successful" broker told the *Milwaukee Journal*. One might suspect that the broker, who was named one of America's "Outstanding Brokers of 1984" by *Registered Representative*, an industry trade magazine, would have an MBA or some form of business background. Instead, he was a television reporter who was assigned to the business beat because he once "received fifty shares of stock at my bar mitzvah."[16]

Few brokers, in fact, enter the field with any formal investment or business background. Many come from successful sales careers and view selling stocks and bonds as a step up in prestige over selling less glamorous products. Others come from the teaching profession, attracted by the promise of riches and seduced by their self-acknowledged "ability to communicate." Some become brokers because they enjoyed playing the market, although not necessarily with much success. "I've probably lost $500,000 trading for my own account over sixteen years," one new broker told *Forbes* magazine.[17] Many of the newer brokers are the disappointed liberal arts majors of the baby-boom generation, no longer trying to change the world and now content to become wealthy off the money of those they once scorned.

They Are Everywhere

If it sometimes seems as if stockbrokers are coming out of the woodwork, they are. According to the National Association of Securities Dealers, there are about 270,000 individuals licensed to sell stocks, bonds, and other investment securities, a figure that has been growing at about a 10% annual rate, nearly four times faster than the overall economy. About 70,000 of these salesmen are full-time stockbrokers licensed through New York Stock Exchange member firms; the remaining 200,000 are mostly part-time brokers licensed through insurance companies, financial planning firms, the NASD, and other exchanges.

The effects of 270,000 salesmen all pushing essentially the same things are nearly impossible to ignore. Many investors, especially those living in high-income neighborhoods, report receiving at least 5 "cold-calls"—unannounced and uninvited telephone solicitations—each week. Business executives, whose names often appear on lists such as the "Manufacturers Directory," receive from three to five cold-calls *every day*. That's over 500 solicitations each year, in addition to direct-mail, radio, television, or newspaper advertising. The fact that most prospects already have at least two brokers seems not to deter the onslaught.

In many areas of the economy, increased competition is a boon to the consumer. In the area of investments, however, the dog-eat-dog competition among brokers and firms can damage the quality of the advice you receive. In an overly competitive industry, the only means of survival for a broker is to excel at *marketing* or *selling* himself. "You can be the best broker in the world, but if you can't sell, forget it," said broker K. H. Kent. "Most of the brokers I've met know very little about the market. What they were most concerned with was 'Who can I call on the phone today to set the hook.' "[c]

Once on the phone, brokers grope for ways to stand out from among the hundreds of other brokers a prospect will hear from each year. One of the ways to stand out, of course, is to appeal to the greed factor present in nearly all of us. In order to lure customers away from the competition, brokers often set unattainable goals, goals that would be beyond the reach of even qualified money managers. The sorry spectacle of a blind man trying to hit home runs has a predictable ending: lots of strikeouts.

The rapid expansion of the brokerage industry has its roots in demographic patterns dating from the post–World War II baby boom. The prime age for new brokers to enter the business is twenty-five to forty years of age. Brokerage officials are leery of hiring brokers directly off of college campuses: an overly youthful appearance would not convey the proper *image*. Besides, the industry would like to see a record of successful work experience, preferably, but not necessarily, in sales. Recruits face the prospect of several lean years before making a large income; by the age of forty most individuals have family responsibilities that would preclude an even temporary cut in salary. Thus the perfect candidate to become a broker lies somewhere in the twenty-five to forty age group. It happens that nature has supplied a more than abundant array of candidates: between 1946 and 1960, fifty-six million Americans were born, accounting for nearly 25% of the entire U.S. population. This age group, now about twenty-six to forty years old, also happens to include a high percentage of career women, another choice recruiting area for the brokerage industry.

Meet Joe, Your New "Financial Consultant"

Since few people attend college with the expressed intent of becoming a stockbroker, most baby-boomers become brokers almost by accident. A typical scenario: An individual, let's call him "Joe," is growing up in the fifties and sixties. Joe is not sure if he wants to go to college, but he is sure that he doesn't want to be drafted. Reluctantly, he enrolls in a nearby university, pursues whatever "major" is convenient, graduates when the coast is clear, then struggles to earn a living with a nearly worthless degree in an overly competitive field in which he has no interest. Finally, growing tired of poverty and boredom, Joe joins the ultimate catch-all profession: *sales*. It is often noted that hard work and dedication, not necessarily intelligence and knowledge, are the most important ingredients to success in sales. Since nothing motivates quite like poverty, Joe turns into quite a salesman, earning a good living and enjoying the material rewards so long denied him. But after a few years Joe notices that his income has "plateaued"—a dreaded word in the sales lexicon—and that the travel is beginning to seem tedious. Now Joe is wondering how he can stay in sales—he is learning to like this good life—yet increase his income and cut down on his travel. He remembers an old college buddy who became a stockbroker; his buddy said the job was great and he made tons of money. Better still, he never had to introduce himself as "just a salesman" to anyone. Joe likes that idea, even if he doesn't really know what stockbrokers *do*. Joe also doesn't know anything about investments, but that did not stop his buddy, either.

So Joe phones several of the better-known brokerage firms (mostly those he has seen advertise on television) and sets interviews with each. All are impressed with Joe's easygoing friendly manner and especially with his record of sales success. No one seems concerned that Joe thinks a municipal bond is a justice-of-the-peace wedding; this is one "financial consultant" who is going to be a profitable addition to the staff of investment "professionals." Joe is welcomed aboard, paid a small bonus, and sent directly to "training."

There are literally tens of thousands of "Joes" in the brokerage business, sitting behind large desks in impressively furnished offices, working for firms whose names we all recognize, and managing the life savings of individuals drawn to them by charm, persuasion, and a heavy advertising budget. But Joe doesn't seem concerned that his central role in a capitalist marketplace is a bit incongruous with his past; in fact, he doesn't even seem to notice. He does notice, however, that now he can afford many of the things he has always wanted, and he is surprised at how much he wants. To get what he wants, he is going to have to work hard, he is going to have to work the phones. He's going to have to become an even better salesman.

But another accident of nature will make that job tougher for Joe and for all brokers. Because of the Great Depression and World War II, there was a relatively low number of births between 1930 and 1945. This group, now about forty-five to sixty years old, represents the prime investment age group, the chief prospecting target for brokers. Yet there are nearly twice as many Americans aged twenty-five to forty as forty-five to sixty. Joe had *better* learn how to sell.

Learning to Tell a Good Story

Each brokerage firm is responsible for training the new brokers it hires. The training program recognizes a fundamental reality: no broker can sell securities without a federal license; in order to obtain that license the prospective broker must pass an exam called the General Securities Registered Representative Exam, better known as the Series 7. The majority of the four to six months each broker spends in training is devoted to passing the Series 7, essentially a bureaucratic trivia test designed to measure a candidate's ability to retain huge quantities of largely irrelevant federal regulations. The 250-question exam tests a candidate's knowledge about such mundane subjects as settlement dates, accrued interest calculations, margin requirements, compliance dos and don'ts, and myriad of other regulatory trivia. Though not difficult in itself, even the brightest of prospective brokers find the sheer quantity of information to be digested supremely challenging. The test, given once each month in several major cities, consumes nearly eight hours, after which drained brokers-to-be drag themselves and their blunted pencils and nearly zapped calculators from the examination room feeling tired, relieved, and unfortunately, knowledgeable. The problem is that the test does not measure investment expertise, only bureaucratic razzle-dazzle. The ability to precisely calculate the accrued interest on a corporate bond, taking into account holidays, weekends, and leap years is certainly a skill that could make any new broker a smash attraction at a Wall Street cocktail party; its exact relationship to investment expertise, however, is doubtful.

David Uthe, a senior analyst for the Qualifications Department of the National Association of Securities Dealers, which administers the Series 7, admitted the test does not prove investment expertise. "The Series 7 is technically an entry-level, minimal-competency exam. It focuses on the mechanics of the marketplace in terms of executing orders, the nuts and bolts of the various securities products and their relationships to each other in terms of risk and utility and capital formation, as well as industry regulations regarding the handling of customer accounts. While a Series 7 registered representative is qualified to competently function under supervision, passing the Series 7 is not a substitute for a proven track record, and industry rules prohibit it from being used to advertise 'investment expertise.' " In sum, the test assures that each broker knows enough to keep himself out of legal trouble, not whether he can keep you out of financial trouble. □

In addition to the federal licensing test, there are two other main areas of study for new brokers: sales skills and product knowledge. The attention paid to acquiring sales skills has increased in direct proportion to the competition among brokers and firms. Many brokerage firms now employ psychologists to interview, test, and ultimately screen out would-be brokers lacking the correct salesman profile. Trainees attend motivational lectures and sales seminars, listen to sales-oriented tapes, role-play with fellow trainees, tape record and analyze sales presentations, and generally elevate the practice of manipulating people to an art form. Some trainees become quite adept: at one role-playing session, a trainee gave such a convincing sales presentation to his boss (a brokerage firm vice-president) that the official, who frequently boasted of never having owned a single share of stock in his life, bought 100 shares of the stock the trainee was hustling. The story has a bittersweet ending: the stock proceeded to dive nearly 50% over the next twelve months, but the firm had added another producer to its stable of investment "professionals."

When not preparing for the Series 7 exam or sharpening manipulative skills, the broker-in-training is usually attending classes designed to imbue him with "product knowledge." Brokerage firms argue that it is this area of each broker's training that turns completely raw salesmen into professional investors. Unfortunately, the facts argue otherwise.

Most brokerage firms offer scores of "products" to investors (often as many as 100). As noted in chapter one, the reason for the large quantity of offerings relates to a fundamental law of good marketing: raise a false issue in order to obscure a damaging one. In other words, by dwelling on the *quantity* of products available to investors, the brokerage industry is able to submerge the more crucial issue: *results*— as well as overwhelming clients by the number of investment choices available to them, and thus justifying the need for the broker. This large quantity of products represents a sizable learning problem for new brokers. In fact, most brokers admit they neither fully understand or use all their firms' offerings. As in the case of the Series 7 test, the broker will study (memorize) a largely academic plethora of information, such as what each offering invests in, the liquidity features, tax ramifications, fee structures, and pay-in schedules. He will also learn detailed rebuttals to every possible objection that you or any other prospect could raise to a given product. Unfortunately, the road to becoming an investment professional is considerably longer than simply being able to perform a flawless recital of academic information about a product—information that *any* person with the time to read the prospectus could obtain for themselves.

For the remainder of his training, your future "financial consultant" will be encouraged to talk with veteran salespeople/brokers who have become "successful"—i.e., big producers—to learn their secrets. For broker Kent, these chats were eye-openers: "When I looked around at the people the firm considered successful, it seemed that they were those who were the best talkers, but that their success had no relationship to making clients money. It was just that they could tell a good story."

The "Successful" Broker

It is upon this ability to "tell a good story" that the future of each new broker will depend, since success in the brokerage business is measured totally in terms of commissions generated, not results for clients. Few brokerage firms even bother to track the results of their own research departments' recommendations, much less the recommendations of individual brokers. Yet the commission totals of each broker receive daily scrutiny. Your broker will never find himself in trouble with his firm as a result of any recommendation that caused you to either lose money or to underperform the overall market. He will find himself in trouble, however, if you and other clients fail to generate sufficient activity, even if that inaction results in outperformance of the broad market by his clients' portfolios. Whether you do or do not earn superlative investment results is of no interest to your broker's superiors; they will judge his performance entirely upon what you do for him, not on what he does for you.

When a broker reports to work each morning, he is usually greeted with a summary of the previous day's "sheared sheep"—the daily commission run, a ranking of each broker's production the day before. The office manager also receives and reviews the daily production totals of each salesperson. Weekly and monthly commission reports are also issued, with each broker given a numerical ranking of his production versus other brokers in the firm. At many brokerage houses, these daily and monthly commission reports are passed among all the brokers to inspect and initial. Thus the broker feels pressure to produce commissions not only from his branch manager but from his peers as well.

It is interesting and revealing to note that nowhere in its discussion of the "Outstanding Brokers of 1984" did *Registered Representative* make any mention of results for clients, only of commissions generated. In fact, these "outstanding" brokers were added to the list *totally* on the basis of sales production. Similarly, titles such as "vice-president" are issued to brokers solely on the basis of gross commissions; at many firms, production of $150,000 in gross commissions per year will earn the broker the title of vice-president. As production increases, additional titles are forthcoming, such as first vice-president or senior vice-president. The advantages to a broker in calling herself a vice-president are obvious: it is a more impressive, dignified, and nonthreatening title than *salesperson*. That the broker actually earned her title completely through salesmanship is still another example of brokerage image-making obliterating every fact in its path.

With the intense pressure to produce commissions, it is hardly surprising that brokers are frequently preoccupied with their monthly commission totals. "How is your month going?" is perhaps the most frequently asked question among brokers. ("How is your client's month going?" is rarely asked.) Since the average income of the nation's full-time brokers is nearly $100,000, the answer to the first question would usually seem to be, "Quite well, thank you." And the $100,000 average broker income becomes even more astounding in light of the pay-out structure that most brokers face. Brokers receive only 30 to 50% of all commissions generated, depending upon the type of product sold, with the remaining amount retained by the firm. Sales of stocks and bonds usually earn the broker from 30 to 40% of the total commission; sales of tax shelters, annuities, and other "special" products (which carry a considerably higher commission to begin with) pay the broker from 40 to 50% of the gross commission. A quick tabulation shows just how much selling is required for a broker to earn $100,000 per year: Assuming an average pay-out of 38%, a broker must generate $264,000 in gross commission each year. At an average commission of 3% per sale, the broker must sell more than $8,800,000 of securities each year to gross $264,000 in commissions.

$8,800,000	Total Securities Sold	
×	3%	Average Commission
$ 264,000	Gross Commissions	
×	38%	Average Broker Pay-out
$ 100,320	Average Broker Income	

To put these numbers in a clearer perspective, a broker would have to sell *456,896 shares* of AT&T stock at $29 per share to earn $100,000. Indeed, phenomenal salesmanship is required to even be considered a "failure" by brokerage-industry standards. A broker earning "only" $25,000 per year will soon be called into his manager's office and asked, "Do you really like this business?" Regardless of the broker's answer, the manager will likely reply that it hurts him deeply to see any person "fail" and that perhaps it would be best (for the firm) if the broker found another line of work. Assuming a 38% average pay-out and a 3% average commission, that broker will have sold $2,212,500 worth of securities per year. *And failed.*

Most firms have responded to the intense competition for clients by slapping sales quotas on their brokers. Two of the largest Wall Street houses reportedly will fire any salesperson not generating $250,000 in total commissions after five years in the business. Smaller regional firms are less severe, but any broker grossing less than $100,000 after five years will usually be fired. Quotas can also be informal: brokers below a certain production level are subject to a cut in their pay-out rate; the objective is to force the broker to quit, thus saving the company the expense of paying unemployment benefits.

Paul H., a branch manager with a national brokerage house, agrees that quotas eventually hurt customers by rewarding brokers who are the best *salespeople*, not the best investors. "Most firms don't have the patience to let brokers build accounts in an orderly fashion, therefore they put big pressure on them," Paul said. "They give them quotas and they want to quickly see who is going to do it and who isn't. In the process they are losing some people who are not that aggressive as pushers but might be better for the client." And the ultimate effect of quotas? "What you get is a lot more of the pushers remaining because they can make the quotas," notes Paul.[E]

Needless to say, selling close to $9 million of securities in one year is a full-time job. Most brokers work fifty to sixty hours per week, eat lunch at their desks or with clients, and spend almost the entire day selling, the telephone nearly glued to their ear. There is virtually no time for even the most rudimentary study of the financial markets. Brokers stack the reams of research reports they receive each day on a portion of their desks unread. Just when the stack assumes monstrous proportions, it suddenly disappears, usually into the circular file. The payment structure in the brokerage business simply leaves no room for any activity except *sales*; the intense competition among firms leaves no room for any other type of broker except supersalesman. And it is perhaps the ultimate reflection of the supersalesman's ability to sell that he can actually convince otherwise intelligent people that he is qualified to manage their life savings.

But few are. "We have various awards for people [brokers] doing so much in gross commissions," said branch manager Paul, "and some of the people who make the greatest number of commissions probably do very poorly, or very ordinarily, for their clients."

Notes Ray Wax, a stockbroker interviewed at length in Studs Terkel's classic, *Working*: "The average broker lives to generate commissions and he goes home as though he were selling shoelaces or ties. He doesn't carry the goddamn market with him."[18] He doesn't have to; it should be clear that an "outstanding" or "successful" stockbroker is one who generates large commissions, and nothing more.

Faced with the reality of having virtually no investment expertise, no real investment training, and the requirement to sell about $4 million of securities each year to keep their jobs, it should come as no surprise that brokers experience large amounts of frustration in trying to make clients money. Said broker Wax, in *Working*: "Can you imagine? I really felt I could buck this machine. When I began, I was so sure that I could win. I no longer have that confidence. What's happening is so extraordinary. It's so much bigger than I am. Too many things that I can't control are happening. I can tell you what happened after the fact, but it's very difficult to tell you before the fact."[19] Of course, the entire brokerage industry is built on the ruse that it *can* tell clients what will happen before the fact, in spite of overwhelming evidence to the contrary (see chapter three). But few brokers are as honest as Ray Wax. Comparing his previous experience as a builder to the task of predicting the gyrations of the financial markets, Wax sums up the broker's experience: "When I built the houses, I hired the bricklayer, I hired the roofer, I determined who put the goddamned thing together. And when I handed somebody a key, the house was whole. I made it happen. I can't do it in the market. I'm just being manipulated and moved around and I keep pretending I can understand it, that I can somehow cope with it. The truth is I can't."[20]

Does the broker really know anything more about investments than the average investor? Broker Kent doubts it. "No, probably less," he said. "Plus, a broker has all these reasons why he is calling you, and the main one is he needs to put food on his table. He can't make a fair judgment about what's right or wrong. Studies have shown that when a broker invests his own money, he does very poorly; they are just not capable." Then is the industry better at producing sales than results? "In general, yes," admits broker Paul. "You have far more salespeople than you have knowledgeable market participants in the people who are licensed to sell securities. You can produce sales much easier than you can produce results." Paul points out that brokers lack considerably more than investment expertise: "The average broker has neither the interest nor the inclination to do the tremendous amount of reading and work required to discover situations to purchase."

Personality type may also play a role in the inability of brokers to produce results for clients. Stockbrokers are essentially self-employed businessmen; they could accurately be called entrepreneurs. And as analyst Harold K., a research analyst with a large regional firm points out, entrepreneurs have a distinct personality that often influences the way they manage money. "An entrepreneur is different than a professional management type. Most entrepreneurs tend to be more emotional, change faster, change course more in midstream, than someone in professional management. Most research departments would have a better performance record, in total, than the average broker." Why? According to Harold, "One of the precepts of investing is to let your winners run and cut your losses short. Most brokers do the reverse; they cut their winners short and let their losses run. I've talked to my counterparts at ten or fifteen brokerage firms and that turns out to be the case."

Harold provided a typical example: "Let's say a broker recommends ten stocks to a person, and five go up and five go down. The losers stay in the portfolio longer because with the same percentage move, the typical broker will sell out the winner and double up on the loser. The client takes money out of winners to double up on the losers," creating, of course, substantial commissions in the process. Indeed, in analyzing the shortcomings of stockbrokers, it is often difficult to determine where incompetence ends and greed begins. Harold points out that the tendency to cut gains and double up on losers is not confined exclusively to brokers; clients make the same error. It is a classic example of the blind leading the blind. Understandably, with their money at stake, many investors make emotional rather than rational decisions; they prefer to lock up profits before the market "changes its mind" on their stock, and refuse to close the book on a loss, as if to do so would somehow legitimize that loss. At these times, when professional investment counsel is needed most, the client turns to a broker who knows little more about investing than the client does, and who perceives an opportunity to earn a double commission by merely reinforcing the investor's anxieties.

Conflicts of Interest

Besides being unqualified to manage money, brokers face a conflict of interest arising from their need to generate large commissions. "The brokerage business has a natural conflict of interest," admits branch manager Paul. "If you buy a stock, I make money; if you don't buy a stock, I don't make money. You won't find a broker who will do you much good until he doesn't need your next transaction. If he needs income to live on, he's not going to be acting in your best interest."

Between the need to sell $4 million of securities each year just to keep their jobs and the widely acknowledged tendency of brokers toward a consumptive life-style, nearly *all* brokers need your next transaction. It follows then that few, if any, brokers are truly acting in the best interests of their customers, assuming, of course, that they were even qualified to define that best interest. The dilemma is enough to drive some of the newer brokers to an early retirement. "I wanted to act as a financial adviser, not salesman," one former broker told *Changing Times* magazine. "What's in the best interest of the company was not always in the best interest of my clients."[21]

As Paul points out, a stockbroker earns a commission only if a client *acts*, either buying or selling securities. Thus the broker's life becomes a constant search for a rationale to justify action. But the conflicts of interest brokers face go far beyond mere action versus inaction. Even assuming your broker can convince you to act, the product he recommends to you may be more a function of the differing amounts of commission paid by each product than the product's investment merits or suitability for your situation. For example, a stock listed on the New York Stock Exchange may produce only a 2% total commission for a broker; an over-the-counter stock in which his firm is a market maker (sells from its inventory) yields up to a 5% commission. In addition, the pay-out to the broker is also higher on the market-maker stocks, as brokerage firms attempt to encourage their brokers to push "house" products. Thus the broker stands to earn at least three times more commission by selling you the stock of a small company out of his firm's inventory than a high-quality company such as IBM. The dollar difference in commission is even greater over time, since the broker will "earn" the same higher commission when you sell the stock. The following table shows the difference in commission structure between a listed New York Stock Exchange company and a small over-the-counter company sold from broker inventory.

Exchange	Quantity	Gross Comm.[†]	Pay-out	Net to Broker
NYSE	100 @ $30	$ 60 (2%)	33%	$20
OTC	100 @ $30	$150 (5%)	40%	$60

†Table uses standard gross commission and pay-out rates.

The same conflict of interest appears in the commission structure of bonds. Listed bonds, such as those on the New York Bond Exchange, will generate only a 1 to 2% commission for the broker. For that reason, most brokers feign ignorance of the listed bond market's existence, preferring instead to peddle bonds out of their firm's inventory, while earning from 3 to 5% commission. Like stocks sold from company inventory, the client is shown only a "net" price, totally obscuring the size of the commission.

Broker Kent gives a practical example of how this conflict of interest can affect you: "A broker has to sell a bond today, and he has two types of bonds in his inventory; one will pay him 5% and the other will pay him 3%. Now he's talking to a customer, and the 3%-commission bond is really conservative and it, is right for the client; the 5% bond is more speculative. He will sell the bond with the 5% commission because he will make more money on it, and he will have to answer to someone at the end of the week on how much he sold. This goes on every day. Brokers say, 'I'm going to sell the highest load [sales charge] that I can so that I make the most money for myself.' For most brokers, the bottom line is the dollar. They'd sell their mothers to make a buck."

Carol J., a former broker with a Wall Street house, remembers how the size of a product's commission often influenced the choice of investments recommended to her firm's customers. "The branch manager wanted you to push the funds that would pay a higher commission because he would get a cut of whatever commission you generated," Carol said. "I remember one broker had latched onto an older lady. She was retired and wanted safety, not necessarily the highest return. The branch manager told the broker to push a certain fund because we were having some sort of sales drive on that fund. Whoever could get the most orders for this particular high-yield fund would get some sort of prize. This went on all the time. They would always try to discreetly and tactfully persuade you to do what was best for the managers, not necessarily for yourself or your customers."

Carol decided to leave the brokerage business after one particularly gruesome display of managerial insensitivity. "A prospect had rejected what a broker from my firm was pushing and instead put $50,000 into an annuity through another firm. But just a few days after receiving his first monthly annuity payment, the customer's husband died, and since they had chosen the settlement option that provided a high monthly payment only for as long as he lived, his widow received nothing of the $50,000. It was just gone. Well, when my branch manager heard about it he laughed so hard he had to sit down at the end of the table. He called them 'stupid jerks,' and went on about how glad he was that it happened since they didn't put their money with us. Right then I knew this was not the place for me. All along the manager had been saying that the most important thing was our customers, and then I found out it was all a lie, it wasn't real. It seemed to me that what they really wanted was to get us to push some program on somebody."[F]

The differences in commission rates among the various stocks, bonds, and funds are small potatoes compared to those to be earned in the "special products," the term used by brokers to describe such investments as annuities and limited partnerships*. Brokers can earn from 4 to 8% on these investments, explaining, perhaps, what makes these products so "special." (Investors in the Baldwin-United annuities or the Petro-Lewis oil and gas partnerships learned from experience that there was very little special about the investments themselves.) Because of the high original commission charges, brokerage firms want to encourage their salespeople to push these products, offering a 40 to 50% pay-out rate as incentive. So profitable are the "special products," that many brokers view stock and bond business as significant only to the extent that it can serve as an entree to a client's "serious" money—money intended for big-commission items such as tax shelters. Since the average purchase size of a limited partnership is generally higher than for a stock or bond, and since the commission and pay-out rates are also higher, a broker stands to earn up to five times more commission on limited partnerships than on, say, government bonds.

This conflict of interest is of more than academic concern to investors such as Sandra H. Dennis, whose story is an all-too-typical example of what can happen when brokers smell the potential for a huge pay-off and see an uninformed, trusting prospect as easy prey.

In August 1983, Sandra was unemployed, widowed, and without health insurance. She had recently sold her home for about $40,000; that money, plus approximately $25,000 in savings, represented her total net worth. Badly in need of income, she walked into a brokerage office in hope of generating a reliable monthly income to offset living expenses. What she got was a rude indoctrination to brokerage-industry incompetence and conflicts of interest.

"I was new to the area, unemployed, and I was downtown filling out job applications," Sandra recalled. "I had proceeds from the sale of my house in my checking account. I was extremely depressed; I couldn't find a job and I saw the brokerage office. I thought I'd go in and get this money safely put away and earn some income since I wasn't working."

Once inside the brokerage office, Sandra was introduced to the "Broker of the Day," the salesperson assigned to handle all walk-in and call-in business for that day. To her delight, she was introduced to a woman broker; she felt instantly at ease. "Honest to God, I trusted her. I thought, 'How neat, I have a woman to work with.' "

The broker asked Sandra about her current situation, investment background, and objectives. As she spoke the broker listened attentively, occasionally nodding gravely, all the while playing the role of the concerned, empathetic investment professional to complete perfection. "I told her I'd just sold my house and needed income. I needed income," Sandra emphasized.

The seduction tango was working; lured into the office by name recognition, comforted by an empathetic-appearing broker, and put at ease by the professional, conservative aura of the office, Sandra decided she had come to the right place; she *bought the image*. She was soon to find out that behind the slick veneer was a perverted industry, too incompetent to make money for her and too drunk with greed to care.

After listening to Sandra's needs, the broker made three recommendations: $25,000 was to be invested in an oil and gas limited partnership; $10,000 would be invested in a real estate limited partnership; and $5,000 would be invested in government securities (GNMAs). The limited partnerships were supposed to generate 8% interest the first year, then increase by 1% each year before peaking at 14% in the seventh year. The partnerships would then be dissolved. The government securities would pay a consistent yield of 12.5%. Trusting the broker and her firm, Sandra agreed to the recommendations and wrote a check for $40,000. Her nightmare was about to begin.

Shortly after Sandra's investment, the oil and gas partnership went "public," meaning that its units were now traded daily among any investors willing to buy or sell them. The daily value of the units were now quoted in most newspapers, and Sandra soon noticed the numbers didn't add up. Based upon the number of units she had purchased and the current resale price she had seen in the newspaper, Sandra calculated that the value of her $25,000 investment had dropped to about $7,000. Angry, she confronted her broker: "You mean to tell me that my $25,000 is now valued at $7,000?" she asked. The broker's reply is a classic example of broker double-talk: "Yes, but wouldn't you rather have a management team handle the funds that is prudent and wise and are paying attention to what is happening to the market? They're trying to preserve the funds. Should we have some flare-up in the Middle East it is really going to be valuable," her broker explained.

Sandra had just seen nearly 25% of her total net worth destroyed and was being told that it was all okay since the people who were doing the destroying were "prudent." "She gave me a runaround, a sales pitch," said Sandra. "She didn't give me any honesty. I realize she is a saleswoman, but we are talking about my bread here."

Soon even the income that had been promised began to disappear. Instead of the promised 8% yield, the partnerships were yielding only 4%. Sandra had been given the clear impression that the income level and the resale price of the partnerships were guaranteed. "I thought I was buying a contract, where if I agreed to buy this, they agreed to pay that. I would never have agreed to this." Lacking the investment knowledge necessary to ask informed questions, Dennis had relied upon the broker to volunteer information about potential risks. When staring at a commission of over $1,000, most brokers will remain silent, neither overtly lying about the product nor doing anything to uncover possible misunderstandings that a client may harbor. The broker sees an opportunity to exploit a prospect for the highest commission possible; perhaps, the broker reasons, the investment will work out, too.

"She never told me this [investment] was high risk, either high risk for the income or for the original investment," Sandra said bitterly. "All she said was how in 1973 everybody who did business with the oil companies tripled their money."

Based upon the income levels she thought were guaranteed, Sandra used the $20,000 remaining from her savings and bought a duplex. "Now I'm committed to $475 a month, and in order to make those mortgage payments and pay the heat, I have to cut back on food."

The case of a widowed, unemployed woman losing 25% of her money and earning less than a simple passbook savings account on her remaining investment is tragedy enough. What makes the situation even more grotesque is how easily it all could have been avoided.

Sandra's investment needs were safety, liquidity, and a *predictable* monthly income. No reasonable broker could possibly conclude that the two limited partnerships recommended met those objectives. In fact, limited partnerships are among the highest risk, least liquid, and most unpredictable of all investments. A GNMA Fund, or other government bond fund, which yielded 12.5% (at the time), would have been a perfect, obvious solution for the *full* $40,000. At 12.5%, Sandra could have counted on receiving about $416 each month for as long as she wanted. Instead, she was receiving barely $150.

Why didn't the broker recommend government bonds for the full $40,000? A close look at the commission structure of the recommendations may yield a clue.

Investment	Amt. Inv.		Total Comm.		Pay-out		
Oil & Gas Partnership	$25,000	×	8%	×	40%	=	
Real Estate Partnership	$10,000	×	8%	×	40%	=	$ 32u
GNMA Fund	$ 5,000	×	2%	×	35%	=	$ 35
Total							$1155

If, on the other hand, the broker had invested the full $40,000 in the GNMA Fund, she would have earned only about a $280 commission, of $875 less.

Investment	Amt. Inv.		Total Comm.		Pay-out		Net to Broker
GNMA Fund	$40,000	×	2%	×	35%	=	$280

The bottom line: a broker earns a $1,100 commission from an uninformed, unemployed, unskilled investor who needs income and safety, and gets neither. What Sandra did get was a real-life education on the gap between brokerage-industry results and image. "I thought she could completely understand my situation and take care of me," said Sandra. Now she knows differently. "I thought this was a trusted position [stockbroker], but they're just salesmen; I can't believe they could be handling people's money."[G]

Dialing for Dollars

While there are hundreds of Sandras walking into brokerage offices across the country each day, brokers know they can't rely on walk-in or call-in business alone to make a living. Most of the time brokers must aggressively solicit business, and the process usually begins from scratch: a broker contacts an individual suspected of being an investor; that individual neither asked to be contacted nor knows the broker. This process is known among brokers as "prospecting"—"The lifeblood of our business," as one broker called it—and all salespeople know that their futures in the securities business will depend upon how hard and how well they master that process.

By far the most popular form of prospecting is the "cold-call,*" in which a broker telephones an individual at home or work, and offers an investment "opportunity." Nearly all brokers have tried cold-calling; at least half use it as their primary source of prospecting. Brokers use lists to reach specific target groups: the Manufacturers Directory to reach high-level business executives, the Bresser's Street Directory to reach wealthy neighborhoods, the yellow pages to reach doctors, lawyers, and CPAs, and the daily newspaper for names of people recently promoted or relocating.

Often brokers will purchase lists advertised as supplying names, addresses, and phone numbers of investors. Some list merchants claim to break down leads into product preferences, such as stock investors, bond investors, or tax-shelter investors. Armed with thousands of such names, the phoning begins; many salespeople will make up to thirty cold-calls per day. While not an especially impressive number in itself, thirty completed cold-calls will require the broker to dial the phone about 150 times—only one out of five people will be available. That is nearly 3,000 phone calls each month, during which a broker will experience both highs and lows, but mostly lows: one solid prospect out of ten completed calls is considered good. It will require about three solid prospects to yield one client, and even that one client will require an average of five phone calls before doing any business. There will be hang-ups—"slam dunks," as they are known in the business— put-offs, every conceivable excuse, and the inevitable calls to investors long since departed for a more celestial marketplace.

Having suffered approximately thirty rejections for each success and after having dialed the phone 150 times to receive those thirty rejections, plus finding themselves under pressure to sell $4 million of securities each year to remain in their job, should it be any surprise that brokers have virtually no time for any other activity in their day except *selling*. The process of cold-calling, sending information to prospects, and following up again and again is so tedious that even in those rare circumstances when a broker actually brings investment expertise to his job, he has neither the time nor the energy to adequately keep pace with the rapidly changing financial markets.

The broker who survives this process is only one thing: *a selling machine*.

"We are salesmen, and there is a greed thing involved," admits broker Kent. "The broker calls a customer and says, 'I have something that is really good.' The broker doesn't know if it is good; it was just the customer's turn to be called. It wasn't any more good today than it was yesterday."

Once on the phone, brokers often introduce themselves as specialists in a certain type of product, usually whatever product happens to be popular at the time. Most brokers, in fact, will change their product specialty based on market activity and the direction of interest rates every six or twelve months. In other words, when interest rates are declining and stocks are moving higher, brokers will introduce themselves as specialists in stock picking; when interest rates are rising and stocks and bonds are out of favor, brokers will call themselves specialists in annuities, or real estate or oil and gas partnerships. The only true specialties of brokers, of course, are selling and opportunism.

Most cold-calls are scripted, meaning the broker repeats a short, prepackaged speech to each prospect, usually making adjustments for his own speech patterns. The broker relies heavily on the name recognition of his firm to get a prospect's ear, as if frequent television advertising somehow proves investment expertise. Once he has the prospect's attention, the broker will try to find his prey's "hot button," i.e., the approach that seems to most interest the person. If the broker finds that a prospect likes to speculate, he will announce that he has an "excellent opportunity" for an aggressive investor. If the prospect is conservative, the broker will sound empathetic, allowing as how he "understands how painful it can be to lose money in the stock market" and, of course, "that's why I specialize in government bonds."

Since cold-calling is so crucial to brokers, it was inevitable that outside "consultants" would pop up to assist brokers in this valuable undertaking. "Cold-Call Clinics" are held throughout the United States, often employing motivational speakers, sales consultants, telephone marketing experts, and even psychologists. One such clinic, "How to Sound Like a Million Dollars on the Phone," advertised in *Registered Representative* that it would provide brokers the opportunity to learn all the proven cold-call techniques that the top producers use, including how to develop each broker's voice potential "without sounding phony."[22]

So specialized has the process of manipulating people become that *Registered Representative* also published an article profiling a "voice doctor," who teaches brokers and other salespeople how to effectively use their voices in sales presentations. The basic assumption behind such a calculated approach to selling is that consumers react more to the *sound* of a salesperson's voice than to the actual content of the sales message.[23]

The importance of name recognition, public exposure, and voice quality has given rise to the golden-throated radio broker. Many radio stations broadcast periodic stock market updates, usually once each morning and afternoon. Rather than hire an announcer to read the spots, a station will often employ the best-sounding stockbroker from among many who aggressively campaign for the job. For the broker, the radio time is priceless; here is the perfect opportunity to appear knowledgeable and get exposure before tens of thousands of potential investors, while carefully orchestrating a nonthreatening, nonsalesman, *image*, as well as obtaining somewhat of a celebrity status. In reality, the broker's "knowledge" consists of reading, usually verbatim, from the Dow Jones Financial News Tape. As for the nonselling, brokers offer quotes of selected stocks; often they are stocks in which their firm is a market maker or are otherwise pushing.

The goal of appearing knowledgeable and nonthreatening is also behind the latest marketing fad used by brokers: the educational seminar. Brokers will advertise a seminar to be held on a certain subject, such as tax shelters, or tax-exempt bonds. Rarely are seminars advertised as pushing any specific product; to do so would destroy the "educational" image of the ploy. Brokers tend to exploit the desires of investors to pay less taxes, advertising "ideas" that will allow investors to "keep more of what they earn." The seminars are usually held in impressive hotel ballrooms, with snacks, coffee, and drinks—but only *after* registration. Attendees are required to sign in as they enter, usually under the lame excuse that only those with reservations can be admitted. The true purpose of registration, of course, is to allow the broker to contact each person later on.

The seminar begins with the broker introducing himself (usually more than once) and then turning the seminar over to guest speakers. Each guest speaker will try to prove his expertise by providing at least one convoluted scheme to pay less taxes; the fact that the scheme applies to virtually no one doesn't matter. What does matter is that the impression be left among the investors that this speaker knows even *more* ways to save on taxes. Often the speaker turns out to be a "wholesaler," a representative of a limited partnership whose objectives are in concert with the subject of the seminar. Investors receive a prospectus (with the broker's card neatly stapled inside and the subscription agreement already filled out) and a nonthreatening overview of the product being hustled. Rarely does the broker sponsoring the seminar say anything except introductions and thank yous; this is, after all, an educational seminar. The broker will reappear soon, however, calling each attendee to personally thank her for coming and asking earnestly if she has any questions—or *money*.

Besides cold-calls and seminars, direct-mail advertising is another widely used prospecting technique of brokers, who send information about a particular investment by the thousands to carefully selected neighborhoods. The information will usually trumpet a high yield or return, such as "12% Tax Free—GUARANTEED!" in order to grab investors' attention. Direct-mail advertising, however, is falling into disfavor among brokers and firms; brokers report a less than 1% return rate, and firms view the increasing postage costs as prohibitive. It is likely that the junk mail bombardment of individual homes by all types of businesses has reached the saturation point.

The overselling of America has forced brokers to find other, less direct, methods of prospecting. Unquestionably the most successful of these is the "Professional Friend" approach. Under this strategy, the broker cultivates relationships with CPAs, attorneys, financial planners, or any person who can serve as a "center of influence," i.e., lead the broker to people with money. The broker never tries to sell any products to these "friends," only to provide information, service, a sympathetic ear, and occasionally, a free lunch. As the friendship grows, mutual referrals begin, referrals based not upon expertise, but upon an "I'll scratch your back, you scratch mine" reciprocity. In a business that reeks with the narrow pursuit of self-interest, no single abuse of public confidence stands out as more glaring than the exploitation of the *buddy system.*

Pavlov's Prospect

Once a broker has identified a serious prospect, he shifts his attention from prospecting to selling. For even the most successful of brokers, two out of three serious prospects will slip away without becoming clients; for average brokers, four out of five will escape with their finances intact. Few brokers attempt to close a sale on the initial call; first there is an elaborate mating-like ritual that will take weeks or months. One broker wondered if clients didn't buy from him on his first call out of fear that he "wouldn't respect them in the morning." Whatever the reason, opening an account takes time; the industry average is nearly five calls before a prospect becomes a client.

The delay stems primarily from the tendency of investors to procrastinate; investors fear making mistakes with their money and put off making decisions because those decisions are risky and unpleasant. This very human tendency to procrastinate goes to core of the salesman's job: "The most important function of a salesman is to convince a prospect to stop procrastinating," Professor Joseph Delph of Indiana University told the *Wall Street Journal.*[24] Whether the salesperson is selling used cars, TVs, stereos, or securities, there is only one antidote for procrastination: *create urgency.*

Creating urgency implies establishing a deadline: if the prospect doesn't buy the product by a specified date, he will have to pay more for it later. The TV or stereo salesman has the perfect solution: put the item *on sale.* Now if a prospect is truly interested in the merchandise, he has a compelling reason to *act now*, or else face a guaranteed higher price later. For the securities salesman, the "on sale" strategy is dependent upon convincing the client that the broker can actually *know* that the future price will be higher. In other words, the salesman/ broker overcomes procrastination by pretending that he or his firm can predict the future, and therefore know that an item is on sale *now*.

One of the primary arguments brokers use in selling the idea that they can predict the future involves the broker's research department. Even if the prospect understands that the broker is only a salesman, the broker will merely point out that he relies on his research department for his strategies, anyway. He then supplies the potential investor with thick, number-filled research reports on the stock he is pushing. The message is clear: The broker and his research department believe his item is *on sale* now, because they can look into the future and they see a higher price. *Buy it now before it is too late.*

Unfortunately, the implication that brokerage research analysts can accurately predict the future is yet another example of a carefully crafted image not quite squaring with the facts. Volumes of academic research have been published on the subject of research department forecasting accuracy, and the conclusions are perhaps best summed up by Anthony Hitschler, vice-president of Provident Capital Management, Inc., writing in the *Financial Analysts Journal*: "Most empirical evidence supports the conclusion that [research] analysts cannot forecast earnings with enough accuracy to improve upon an extrapolation of past growth rates, which is itself not a useful predictor."[25]

After several unhappy experiences with brokerage research recommendations, investors begin to learn the wisdom of Mr. Hitschler's observations. Clearly, the "Buy it now because my research department says so" strategy will not work on these prospects. And if the broker cannot create *urgency* through his research department, just what manipulative tool can he use to get a prospect to stop procrastinating?

Using the "If you can't convince 'em, confuse 'em" approach, many brokers turn to the "black magic" of the securities business: technical analysis. Technical analysis is built on the theory that by carefully studying the trading patterns of a stock, a wise interpreter can accurately predict the future performance of that stock. Many professional money managers, of course, do use technical analysis to varying degrees as part of their stock-selection process, but its profitable application requires extraordinary skill and experience, qualities noticeably lacking on most brokers' resumes. And while professional money managers use technical analysis as an early warning signal of long-term trend changes (a completely worthy and possible objective), most brokers use its arcane terminology only as a manipulative weapon to induce short-term trading. Figuring, perhaps, that since some people believe that their futures can be seen in the stars, brokers sell the idea that the short-term future of the stock they are pushing can be seen in the charts. Like reading stars, reading charts requires a "special" insight, which, of course, the broker supposedly has and the client hopefully doesn't fully understand. Based upon their careful reading of the chart pattern, brokers will urge clients to act *now*—before it is too late.

The ultimate goal of technical analysis, as practiced by the salesman/broker, is to create the impression in a prospect's mind that through an expert reading of trading patterns, a broker can predict the near-term performance of any stock. The broker simply informs the prospect that the chart indicates a dramatic price movement is imminent; therefore, it is essential to act *now*. The broker will buttress his case for immediate action by referring to vague chart patterns such as head-and-shoulders formations*, trend channels*, double bottoms*, reversal patterns* (at last count there were eighteen, including the triple bottom*—just in case the broker misinterpreted the earlier double bottom), and gaps* (including the all-new "overnight" gap*). The more complex the process can be made to sound, the more expert, and therefore indispensable, the broker appears.

No single sales trick in a broker's arsenal of manipulative skills can create a sense of urgency in a client more effectively than the misuse of technical analysis. When in need of a commission, a broker can simply phone a client whose stock has been rising and inform him that a head-and-shoulders pattern is developing and that it is imperative that the stock be sold immediately, before the price "breaks the neckline" of the formation and plunges to unimaginable depths. Investor Peter R. was the victim of one such scam in 1984. Peter was holding a stock that was performing nicely when he received an alarming call from his broker. "He told me to sell out immediately, that the stock was going to drop ten or fifteen points within the next day or two," recalled Peter. "I sold, and lost the dividend, which was $1,500, and the bloody stock just kept on going up." Does he think the broker just wanted a commission, perhaps a *double* commission by reinvesting the proceeds? "That was the answer, sure," he said. And his feelings toward the broker? "I won't forget him."[H]

In short, no matter what action a broker wants to justify, there is a pattern just for him. "You could generate a series of prices from some dice and put them in front of a technician, and he'd draw a trend line and a head-and-shoulders," said Tony Estep of Salomon Brothers, to *Forbes* magazine.[26] The broker would also draw a commission from the resulting transaction, and in the final analysis, *that* is what the brokerage business is all about. "The function of a broker is to try to get his account to trade," said broker Wax in *Working*. "A broker's lifeblood, the only money he makes is generating commissions. Most money is made by getting people to turn their portfolios, their stocks, over three, four, five times a year. If you're really unethical—cynical, the milder word—you may get 'em to turn their stocks over ten times a year or fifteen times. There's a name for it."[27] (The name is *churning**; you'll find ways to protect yourself from it in chapter seven.)

No discussion of the "Sales Professional" would be complete without a brief rundown of some of the specific manipulative tricks most salespeople employ in their presentations. If you have already been using a broker, some of the lines will no doubt have a familiar ring; if a broker is in your future, knowing the corner you are being boxed into could help you avoid the kind of impulse buying the broker is seeking to create. These manipulative skills can be learned through experience but are acquired mostly by brokers through reading any of the scores of "How To Sell" books, attending sales seminars, or listening to cassette tapes. As nearly every industry becomes more competitive, salespeople in all fields are turning in large numbers to these sales "experts" to gain an edge. Many of the tricks are transparently manipulative in print; however, in the hands of a smooth and polished salesperson they often go undetected by customers. A small sample:

MANIPULATIVE TRICK OR STATEMENT	WHAT'S REALLY HAPPENING
"Our research indicates XYZ Corp. will go up 50% over the next twelve months. You'd like to earn 50% on your money, wouldn't you, Mr. Jones?"	The salesman asks an obvious question guaranteed to elicit a "yes" response in order to obscure the more basic issue—no one can say with any degree of certainty what a stock will do.
"If I could show you a way to earn 20% on your money, you'd be interested, wouldn't you, Mr. Jones?"	The salesman is trying to make a prospect's desire to make money the issue, instead of whether the broker is actually qualified to do it.
"I'll be in your area tomorrow. Would it be convenient for me to see you at nine A.M. or would one P.M. be better?"	The salesperson likely will "be in the area tomorrow" only if the prospect agrees to the appointment, but aside from the lie, the salesperson is not giving the prospect the opportunity to say "no," only to agree to a choice of times.
"Your receptionist is so friendly Mr. Jones. You must take great care in the hiring of your employees."	Salesmen are taught to start each presentation with a "sales starter," i.e., praise of some aspect of the prospect's business. This trick is calculated to get a prospect in a positive, talkative mood while making the salesman appear friendly and unthreatening.
"Would you like the account opened in your name, or jointly with your wife?"	Instead of asking, "Are you going to buy the stock or not, Mr. Jones?" many brokers ask one or more indirect questions designed to *ease* the prospect into a buying decision.

"Would you like 1,000 or 2,000 shares, Mr. Jones?"	Brokers will often suggest that a prospect buy an absurdly high quantity in order to make a smaller quantity appear less risky. "No, I only want 100 shares," the prospect should reply. Account opened.
Ignore "no's"	Brokers are taught to ignore a "no" from a prospect and continue with the sales presentation. Some sales trainers recommend that salesmen continue until at least three "no's" are given. Brokers are trained to never disagree with a prospect, but to answer every objection with, "I can understand how you feel about that Mr. Jones. Would you like 1,000 or 2,000 shares?"
Sell the Sizzle, not the Steak	Since presenting a prospect with facts regarding an investment might ruin the chances for a sale, brokers are encouraged to limit their presentations to areas that have flash, or sex appeal. *KISS*—Keep It Simple Stupid—is the goal for every presentation.

Clearly, what was once the *art* of selling has become the *science* of selling, with every spoken word neatly calculated to draw a preconditioned response. This institutionalized phoniness is an inevitable result of the "formula-tested" approach to selling so popular in this overly competitive era. And it also serves to call into question what relationship there could possibly be between the mastering of such "skills" and the ability to successfully manage money.

Most brokers will freely admit they are professional salespeople, not investment professionals. But they argue that behind them stand a large and supposedly qualified group of true investment experts—their research departments. "Most of what I know is what our research department tells me," concedes one of *Registered Representative's* "outstanding" brokers of 1984. Unfortunately, that can often mean big trouble for you and your investments.

CHAPTER 3

Thou Shalt Not Sell

If the stockbroker represents the limbs of the brokerage operation, the research department is its heart. Most of your stockbroker's recommendations begin there, and most of what is commonly referred to as "full-service" brokerage describes the availability of the research product to the client. Ostensibly, research is the reason for the drastically higher commissions charged by full-service brokers.

With over 10,000 securities analysts in the United States alone, there is plenty of research to be had. A small regional brokerage firm may employ as few as 5 analysts while a major Wall Street firm may have over 50. They are among the highest-paid group in the financial-services industry, with an average annual income in excess of $100,000. Many of the superstar analysts earn over $500,000.

Highly Educated Coin-Flippers

By training, background, and expertise, the securities analyst is by far the most professional and knowledgeable of all brokerage-industry personnel. Most have MBA or Finance degrees and work long and hard at understanding their field. An analyst is usually assigned by his firm to cover a specific industry, such as computers or electronics, or perhaps a certain class of companies, such as small, emerging "growth" companies. They then pore over balance sheets, economic forecasts, press releases, and quarterly updates, and keep close personal contact with each company's management in order to fulfill their most fundamental responsibility: to project accurately the future earnings (profits) of a company. Your broker will then use those projections to tout the stock or bond he is trying to convince you to buy. It is upon these forecasts that you will make investment decisions that could cost you thousands of dollars. That is why it is important to understand what goes into a brokerage report and how much credence should be assigned to the recommendations it contains.

Even after their exhaustive study of all available information, analysts still must rely heavily on the management of each company they follow to hone in on the eventual earnings. Unfortunately, when looking into the future, company management is itself often unsure of what its own earnings will be and is forbidden from disclosing its figures to an analyst, anyway. "The law prevents companies from disclosing earnings in a selective way," says James Haering, former manager of investor relations at Bethlehem Steel. "If you were to tell one or two analysts and not tell everybody, that would give them an unfair advantage. If you are going to give an earnings estimate, you must give it in a broad way so as not to give any investor a specific advantage."[1]

Jerry Remmel, vice-president of finance at Wisconsin Electric Power, describes a typical conversation with an analyst fishing for an earnings estimate: "An analyst will call me up and say, 'Hey, I got a number for the year that's $4.50.' I'll respond in general terms by saying, 'I think you are out in left field,' or, 'I think you are in the ballpark.' I might give some reasons why, or things they ought to look at if they want to to review their estimate. I might say, 'Hey, pay attention to the fact that we've had a cold winter, or hot summer, or industrial load is down'—things that should have been detectable by them if they were looking in the right places. The bottom line is we can't tell an analyst anything that we can't tell any potential investor."[1]

Too Inaccurate to Be Useful

So how good are analysts at predicting earnings? "I don't want to get involved in trying to rate any of these people [analysts]. . . . We have to deal with them on a daily basis," said one management official who asked not to be identified. "While I might have some opinions, I'd hold them to myself." Said another official, who also requested anonymity, "Analysts tend not to go into enough depth. They don't have enough time to spend analyzing a company. Sometimes you get a report and say 'Geez, this guy's looked upon as an expert. I can't believe what's coming out in print.' "

Over the past two decades scores of independent studies have been conducted in an attempt to measure analysts' forecasting accuracy and understand the implications of that accuracy—or inaccuracy—in reaching useful investment decisions. Anthony Hitschler's comments, published in the *Financial Analysts Journal* and mentioned previously in chapter two, succinctly summarize the overwhelming bulk of data and bear repeating: "Most empirical evidence supports the conclusion that [research] analysts cannot forecast earnings with enough accuracy to improve upon an extrapolation of past growth rates, which is itself not a useful predictor."[28]

An exhaustive study by Professors Philip Brown, George Foster, and Eric Noreen, published by the American Accounting Association, examined over 21,000 earnings estimates made by security analysts over a five-year period, from January 1976, through December 1980. The study found *an average forecast error of 28.5%* for forecasts made one year in advance. Forecasts made eighteen months in advance were even worse, with an average error of 42.8%. Analysts even made an average error of 18.3% in their forecasts made only six months in advance.[29]

SIZE OF ANALYST ERRORS

Months in Advance	Average Error
6	18.3%
8	20.3%
10	23.1%
12	28.5%
14	32.9%
16	39.1%
18	42.8%

Source: Studies in Accounting Research #21

Edwin Elton, Martin Gruber, and Mustafa Gultekin, writing in *Management Science,* also studied the size of analyst errors. The study asked, "How large is the misestimate of actual earnings growth by the analysts? In March [nine months in advance] the average error for the 30% of the companies for which earnings were most underestimated was 63.6% while the average error for the 30% of the companies for which growth was most overestimated was 38.9%." Given the size of these errors, can an investor expect to earn excess returns on the basis of consensus analysts' forecasts? "The answer is no," the study concluded. "In some months the stocks for which high growth was forecasted had positive . . . returns; in other months they had negative ones."[30]

The size of analyst errors becomes even more interesting in light of guidelines set by the Securities and Exchange Commission to govern the forecasts of corporate management concerning its own earnings. A 1976 SEC directive forbids management from making earnings estimates within a range so broad "as to make the disclosure meaningless." What size error would make the disclosure meaningless? According to the SEC, an error greater than 10% would be a "material" error. In the words of David Dreman, writing in *Barron's,* if the SEC ever insisted on analysts' forecasting errors not exceeding 10%, "much of corporate America might find itself in the defendant's chair."[31]

Still another study by Elton, Gruber, and Gultekin, published in 1982 by the New York University School of Business Administration, studied analyst forecasts covering 414 firms for each of the years 1976, 1977, and 1978. The study concludes that "the vast majority of forecast error arises from misestimates of industry performance and company performance. The percentage of error due to industry mis- estimates starts at 37.3%, [twelve months in advance] and declines continuously over time to 15.5%."[32]

R. Malcolm Richards, James J. Benjamin, and Robert H. Strawser evaluated analyst estimates for ninety-two New York Stock Exchange companies, covering the years 1972–1976. Estimates for fifty of these companies were also studied for 1969–1972. Their findings, published in *Financial Management*, showed an annual forecast error of 23.1% for the nine periods studied.[33]

SIZE OF ANALYST ERRORS

Year	Mean Error
1969	8.3%
1970	43.1%
1971	12.8%
1972	8.0%
Average Annual Error on 50 Companies	18.1%
1972	7.8%
1973	13.7%
1974	59.6%
1975	22.5%
1976	16.7%
Average Annual Error on 92 Companies	24.1%
Total Average Error	21.3%

Source: *Financial Management*, Fall 1977

The same Richards, Benjamin, and Strawser study also identified analyst forecasting errors by industry and found an average error of 26.2%, including a 46.7% error in retail stores and a 88.8% error in the office equipment and computers industry.

ANALYST FORECASTS BY INDUSTRY

Industry	Average Yearly Error (1972–1976)
Banking	4.9%
Building	23.6%
Chemical	20.8%
Drugs	7.8%
Electrical Equipment	18.0%
Electrical Utilities	8.9%
Office Equipment & Computers	88.8%
Paper	19.6%
Petroleum	23.3%
Retail Stores	46.7%
Average Error	26.2%

Source: *Financial Management*, Fall 1977

As poor as their forecasting record has been, perhaps the ultimate indictment of brokerage-industry research is the finding that analyst projections are generally no more accurate than those that could be achieved by you or any other investor on your own simply by extrapolating from past trends. William Ruland, an assistant professor of accounting at the University of Kansas, compared analyst forecasts with projections made by a simple time model. Ruland, writing in the *Accounting Review*, found that "analyst forecasts reported prior to the announcement of management forecasts were not significantly more accurate than those of [a] simple naive model." In other words, the analyst forecasts "do not appear to be more accurate than those which investors could make for themselves using publicly available information."[34]

J. G. Cragg of the University of British Columbia, and Burton G. Malkiel of Princeton University, also compared analyst forecasts with a simple time-series model. Their study, published in the *Journal of Finance*, called the overall forecasting performance of the analysts "rather poor," and came to the "remarkable conclusion . . . that the careful estimates of security analysts . . . perform little better [than simply extrapolating from] past growth rates."[35]

The results of these studies raise a perplexing question: why, in spite of their training, knowledge, and dedication, are analysts so inaccurate? As Bethlehem Steel's Haering says, "Analysts are professionals and they're doing the best they can." Clearly, the best is not good enough to provide clients with investment returns superior to those that could be achieved by a purely random selection process, but why?

Conflicts of Interest

Any analysis of the reasons for the inaccuracy of brokerage-industry research must include a review of the myriad conflicts of interest under which analysts labor daily. Unlike your salesman/broker, who is paid only if you buy or sell securities, a research analyst is a salaried employee whose conflicts of interest are more subtle, yet no less dangerous to your financial well-being.

Many brokerage firms engage in investment banking, which includes underwriting stock and bond offerings and advising management on mergers and acquisitions. Investment banking is among the most lucrative areas of the brokerage business, generating profits that far surpass those earned on small stock and bond trades. Because of its importance to the bottom line, the brokerage industry is increasingly coming to view its research analysts as, above all, a magnet to attract investment banking business to the firm; if the analyst also happens occasionally to recommend a stock that outperforms the S & P 500 index, well, that's great, too. "Analysts need not be right about stocks even half the time in order to fulfill the goals this firm sets out. All we ask is that they bring some [investment banking] business in the door," one research department director told *Fortune* magazine.[36] A corporate financial officer who deals with analysts daily commented: "There is no question that one thing an analyst brings to his firm is an entree to investment banking business, which is very, very important to his firm's profitability, to the extent that they're good and know the industry, that could be a factor in a company using that firm for investment banking business."

We already know that analysts are not very good at predicting earnings, but that is clearly not the issue here. An analyst must only be good at *being good* to the management whose investment banking business he is trying to attract. An analyst under pressure to get lucrative investment banking business for his firm will often tout the stock of a company he is trying to seduce. This not only endears him and his firm to the company's management, but could also have the effect of driving up the stock price, making an equity offering even more likely. "If the brokerage firm has an investment banking relationship with a company, I personally wouldn't put that much confidence in the analyst's 'buy-hold-sell' recommendations," admitted analyst Harold K. "There is a bias toward the positive" in investment banker relationships.

The upshot of a brokerage firm's need to maintain a positive relationship with investment banking customers is to make "sell" the dirtiest four-letter word on Wall Street. "To give an outright sell on a company that you have an investment banking relationship with . . . might really tick them off. They might have a need to raise some money and they have a debenture issue or something that you would normally handle for them, and now they'll go to another investment banker," notes Paul H., the regional brokerage firm vice president. "Those relationships are such that bad news gets soft-pedaled."

Even without an investment banking conflict of interest a negative recommendation by an analyst could result in his being cut off from a company's management, making it nearly impossible to do his job. Harold K. confirms that his firm has experienced hostile reactions from companies whose stock has been downgraded. "We've gotten nasty letters from management saying, 'How can you sell my stock off? The fundamentals are going along fine.' "

These political pressures put the brokerage industry in a quandary, resulting in a kind of diplomatic code with which analysts and brokers disguise their real messages. "Short-Term Neutral/Long-Term Buy"; "Buy/OK to Hold"; "Neutral/OK to Raise Cash"; "Accumulate/Strong Hold." Even brokers admit they are confused. "Accumulate? What does that mean? Does it mean buy? Does it mean maybe buy? Does it mean buy if you feel like it?" complained investment executive Doyle Butkiewicz.[K] Others are equally perplexed. "My firm often calls stocks

a 'strong hold.' It sounds more like a wrestling term," said another broker.

Besides protecting valuable investment banking relationships, vagueness has another advantage: "If nobody knows what you meant, they can't say you were wrong," one portfolio manager told *Fortune*.[37]

To the brokerage industry, the bottom line is simply that preserving investment banking business and access to company management is more profitable, and therefore more important, than helping the average investor earn superior returns. When reading your broker's latest recommendation, keep in mind that not only are the earnings estimates unreliable, but the specific "Buy-Hold-Sell" advice, perverted by intense conflicts of interest, is even worse. "A company practically has to be in bankruptcy proceedings before most analysts will even lower their ratings from a buy to a hold," notes Stan Weinstein, the highly respected editor of the *Professional Tape Reader*, in *Money*.[38] In fact, some analysts never can bring themselves to utter that nasty four-letter word; one brokerage firm issued a negative report on a company but stopped short of recommending that the stock be sold. Instead, it instructed clients to use the stock "as a source of funds."[39] In the underground jargon of the securities analyst, buy means hold, hold means sell, and sell means the company just went Chapter 11.

The growing domination of large institutional investors such as banks, pension funds, and life insurance companies, has led to still another conflict of interest for analysts. In 1965, such institutions accounted for only 10% of volume on the New York Stock Exchange. Twenty years later, that figure had grown to over 90%, with individual investors now directly representing less than 10% of daily volume. In fact, block trades of 10,000 shares or more now account for over one-half of all New York Stock Exchange trading. The economic consequences to a brokerage firm are obvious: a typical individual investor purchase of 100 shares of AT&T would generate a commission of about $58; a typical institutional trade of 100,000 shares of AT&T would produce a commission of nearly $8,000, or 137 *times more*. With institutions providing most of the activity and most of the profits, it is only logical that analysts and brokers cater to them. Institutions not only get the best information and get it first, they are also positioned to act more quickly than individual investors. By the time the small investor learns of an important development, institutions have already acted, either driving up or pushing down the price of the stock and leaving little profit opportunity for the individual. As in the case of investment banking, the institutional client is simply more important to the brokerage firm than the individual investor.

The task of keeping institutional clients happy can also lead to some unsavory business practices. An institutional client, wishing to unload a large block of shares without depressing the market, may ask the brokerage firm's trading department to take care of the "problem" for them. The only method of disposing of a large block of a thinly traded stock without adversely affecting the market price is to sell the stock gradually, in small increments. In these cases, the small investor's portfolio can serve as the perfect garbage can for the institutional client's unwanted stock. Lawrence Stranghoener, manager of corporate planning at Honeywell and a former brokerage firm analyst, told *Money* that once "an over-the-counter trader called to ask if I'd send a favorable communiqué to retail brokers on a certain stock. Why? He had 10,000 shares that he wanted to move out."[40] Stranghoener refused.

In fact, trading departments often bypass analysts entirely in trying to peddle unwanted stock. Brokers report near daily "blue-light specials" from their trading departments—stock available at an attractive price with a large commission "built in," i.e., hidden from the public. These "specials" are usually available on stocks in which the brokerage firm is a "market maker" and can offer to a customer at a net price, totally disguising the size of the commission. All that need be done for the broker to earn that commission is to pick up the telephone and employ some of his finely honed sales skills.

Besides investment banking and institutional business, trading activity represents an important component of brokerage-industry profitability. Brokerage firms often buy and sell stocks and bonds for their own accounts, much as individuals and institutions do. The objective, of course, is to make money. Not surprisingly, wrong trading decisions often occur, creating the potential for the type of conflict of interest that former analyst Stranghoener described. In the final analysis, your stock and bond business will rank behind investment banking, institutional business, and trading activity as a source of profits for the brokerage firm. You will be treated accordingly.

In addition to inaccurate earnings projections and conflicts of interest, analysts are bedeviled by a host of other problems and bad habits that will impact their ability to help you earn—and keep—superior investment returns. Conflicts of interest aside, analysts are simply not very good at knowing when it is time to sell a stock.

Falling in Love

There are two major reasons for issuing a "sell" recommendation. One, fundamental earnings projections are fulfilled and the stock moves from an undervalued to an overvalued position, or two, the fundamental earnings projections deteriorate faster than the price of the stock, leaving the stock at least temporarily overvalued. "In most cases, brokerage firms never put a sell out on a price basis, and by the time they get around to putting a sell out on a fundamental short-fall basis, it's so late the stock is already down 80 to 90%," said analyst Harold K. He also believes that analysts generally "stay with stocks too long while fundamentals are deteriorating" and tend to "fall in love with a stock and stay with the stock while it gets overpriced."

One of the occupational hazards analysts face is the necessity of developing a rapport with the management of each company they follow. To get reliable information from a company requires at least some degree of professional closeness; often however, that closeness can work to the disadvantage of the analyst and, therefore, you, the eventual investor. Example: one analyst from a major Wall Street firm who enthusiastically promoted Baldwin-United's stock was a regular guest of Baldwin's chief executive officer aboard the company jet, according to *Fortune*.[41] Hugh Denison, former director of research at the Milwaukee Company, confirms that "it is unusual for us to recommend a company without a personal visit by a member of our research department."[L] The danger, however, is that analysts "will get wooed by management. With people that they really like they will color the firm in a better light than they ought to objectively," warns Paul. Analyst Harold notes that his professional closeness is one reason behind the dearth of "sell" recommendations: "You've grown close to management, you tend to like them. It's working out, so you don't want to replace this issue and say 'sell.' " (Baldwin filed for bankruptcy under Chapter 11 of the Federal Bankruptcy Code on 26 Sept. 1983.)

Professional closeness may also be a factor in what is generally regarded as still another analyst weakness: the tendency to be overly optimistic. "The bias is toward being more positive than negative," admitted D. Larry Smith, director of research at Smith Barney, in *Money*.[42] Tom Czech, investment strategist at Blunt Ellis & Loewi, also notes that excess optimism "is something we run into when we look to see estimates made by other analysts." But why? "The analyst finds it necessary to be very, very optimistic because the brokers want something they can't have—a sure thing," claims Czech.[M]

Another possible explanation for the overoptimism may lie in the compensation system of analysts. All analysts receive a base salary, but many also receive a bonus related to the volume of stock traded in companies they follow. Obviously, an optimistic report will generate more business than a neutral or negative one, and consequently a larger bonus for the analyst.

Whatever the reasons, the tendency of analysts to be overly optimistic is confirmed in the American Accounting Association study by Brown, Foster, and Noreen. The authors found that "the average magnitude of forecast overestimates exceeds the average magnitude of forecast underestimates."[43] This propensity for excessive optimism is especially noteworthy since errors of overoptimism can hurt an investor far worse than any other type of error an analyst may make.

Mission: Impossible

Even without the many conflicts of interest, problems of the market-place and human nature, a broader question need be asked: can anyone really predict the future, anyway? Often the management of a company has no idea what its *own* earnings will be. If management doesn't know, how can an analyst possibly know? "I couldn't tell you what our current quarter is going to be within a reasonable number, because it's so sensitive to weather," admits B. William Kostecke, former vice-president and treasurer of Wicor, a utility holding company.[M-1] "They don't have clairvoyant vision either, and they tend to be optimistic," said one brokerage official about company management. The bottom line: nobody really knows what the future will be, but it is in the best interest of the brokerage industry to convince the investing public that somehow it does.

Former Bethlehem Steel vice-president Jim Haering best summed up the futility of predictions when he said, "Forecasting the future fortunes of a company is an extremely difficult task that nobody can really do with very much accuracy. Forecasting that kind of thing is similar to economists trying to forecast interest rates: they simply can't do it, which doesn't seem to deter them from continually trying. But their track record is terrible, whether it's interest rates or the direction of the economy. It's the same thing with securities analysts: nobody can really predict earnings or predict how a company's going to do with any consistency." Commented one broker: "If someone really knew the answer to that [a company's future earnings], they wouldn't be researching anymore. They'd be millionaires and retired."

Further clouding the analysts' crystal balls is the difficulty of projecting an obvious and key determinate in individual company earnings: the performance of the overall economy. Without correct assumptions regarding interest rates, gross national product, monetary and fiscal policy, tax code changes, inflation, and unemployment, the best of industry and company analyses become worthless. Unfortunately, the track record of the dismal science in projecting accurately the performance of the economy is dismal indeed.

Four leading authorities on the subject of economic forecasting have spoken with *Time* magazine.[44] All expressed serious doubts about the ability of economists to predict the future. Said Martin Feldstein, professor of economics at Harvard and former chairman of President Reagan's Council of Economic Advisers: "One of the great mistakes of the past thirty years of economic policy has been an excessive belief in the ability to forecast." Milton Friedman, the 1976 economics Nobel laureate, admitted, "We have often claimed more than we can deliver." Friedrich A. von Hayek, winner of the Nobel Prize for Economics in 1974, told *Time* that "not even a computer can keep track of the daily information that is dispersed among hundreds and thousands of people about their real intentions to buy, sell, and invest. They signal them through prices. They often won't say what they intend and don't even know themselves until the moment they find out the price is right." Donald Regan, former chairman of Merrill Lynch and Treasury Secretary in the Reagan Administration, puts it more bluntly: "If you believe them [forecasts], then you also believe in the tooth fairy."

Understandably, economists come closest to being accurate during periods of relative stability in the economy. But even in those periods, their accuracy can be abysmal. For example, in 1983 most economists had predicted 1984 to be a period of only moderate growth with rising inflation. Instead, gross national product grew at a nearly 7% pace, almost three times faster than the post–World War II average. Inflation, meanwhile, fell to its lowest level in more than a decade.

Pre-crash predictions do not apply here, since the topic in this section is *economic*, not financial market, predictions. In fact, economists turned out to be *right* (i.e., no recession) before the crash; the markets, on the other hand, incorrectly forecasted a recession, or worse.

Beware the Negative Surprise

More dangerous to investors has been the inability of economists to correctly predict recessions. Virtually without exception, economists have missed every major economic downturn in the past twenty years, including the 1981–1982 recession, the worst slump since the Great

Depression. Failing to recognize an approaching recession obviously results in overly optimistic economic forecasts, forecasts on which securities analysts depend in making their earnings projections for individual stocks.

Forecasting recessions, of course, requires the ability to foresee changes in the underlying economic trend, something at which economists, and therefore analysts, are notoriously poor. "There are indeed instances of analysts anticipating changes in trends correctly, [but] this is a rare event. . . . The true mark of maturity in an analyst is to recognize how much he doesn't know," writes Anthony Hitschler in his essay, "To Know What We Don't Know," published by the *Financial Analysts Journal*.[45]

Unfortunately, what the analyst doesn't know (yet pretends otherwise) can have devastating consequences for you. Errors of overly optimistic securities analysts—errors resulting from an inability to detect an approaching recession—are especially deadly. The reason: stock prices at any moment reflect the consensus earnings forecasts of analysts; when the eventual reality turns out to be below expectations, the result can be a virtual bloodbath for investors. An example: The Richards, Benjamin, and Strawser study, published in *Financial Management*, found that analysts' earnings projections for 1974, a recession year, were too high by an astounding 59.6%.[46] Individuals encouraged to buy stocks as a result of these overly optimistic forecasts would have lost about 50% of their money in the bear market of 1973–1974.

However, in the case of the October 1987 crash economists were generally correct in their assumptions; thus they were not overly optimistic, as in 1973–1974. The crash was *not* the result of economic forecasting errors, but rather of excessive market valuations of stocks as a result of rampant speculation.

Analysts' headaches do not end with conflicts of interest and the impossibility of long-range predictions. Even in those rare instances when an analyst's earnings forecast is accurate, the company's stock may behave in a seemingly inexplicable way. The stock of a rapidly growing company often goes down; the stock of company teetering on the verge of bankruptcy frequently goes up. It is a phenomenon that literally has analysts climbing the walls. "On any stock, you can pound the table and insist that technically you are right. But the market doesn't give a damn," said one frustrated analyst to *Fortune* magazine.[47]

Anthony Hitschler perhaps best expressed the frustrations that analysts must feel when he wrote in the *Financial Analysts Journal*, that "many analysts doubtless believe they are the victim of some devious and unfair plot against them, since when they are right, it doesn't seem to matter to the stock price and when they are wrong, it matters very much."[48]

This *Good Company/Bad Stock* syndrome is at the heart of why so many investors experience only frustration in trying to make money through a brokerage firm. The reasons for the syndrome have been explained in numerous studies, and they all point to the same culprit: the "efficient" marketplace.

Essentially, the theory of the "efficient" marketplace holds that in this era of high technology and rapid dissemination of information, all the market players that truly matter—the institutions—have the same information at exactly the same time. The Institutional Brokerage Estimate System (IBES) published by Lynch, Jones, & Ryan, compiles over 80,000 earnings forecasts from analysts representing more than 100 Wall Street and regional brokerage houses, each month. This data assures that every major institutional investor knows exactly what each analyst is projecting.

The IBES also publishes a consensus earnings forecast for each company. Studies have shown conclusively that *earnings forecasts are already embedded in stock prices.* A well-known study by Leonard Zacks, published in the *Financial Analysts Journal*, found that "forecast data are fully incorporated into stock price by the time they become measurable."[49] Elton, Gruber, and Gultekin confirmed that "prices reflect consensus forecasts."[50] In other words, at any given moment, the price of a stock already fully takes into account (discounts) the consensus earnings forecast. The future performance of that stock relative to the overall market will depend not upon whether its earnings growth is good or bad, but upon whether its earnings growth is better or worse than *expected*. Better than expected growth is a *positive surprise*; earnings growth below expectations is a *negative surprise*.

From this data it is easy to see how investment mistakes can be made: An analyst for your broker's firm forecasts a 20% growth rate for company X. Your broker touts the stock as a "good, solid" company that will grow at 20% per year and urges you to buy 100 shares. But there is one problem your broker didn't factor in: even if his analyst is correct and the company does grow at 20%, the price of the stock will underperform the market and probably even decline if the forecast consensus had been for a 30% growth rate.

The Zacks study contained some convincing data concerning positive and negative surprises. Zacks found that "portfolios of companies whose consensus forecasts underestimated actual earnings growth [the positive surprise] outperformed the market on the average, whereas portfolios of companies whose consensus forecasts overestimated actual earnings growth [the negative surprise] underperformed the market."[51] The table below summarizes Zacks's findings.

CHANCES OF OUTPERFORMING S & P 500 INDEX

Consensus Forecast	Chance of beating S & P 500 Index
Underestimates earnings by 30% or more	99%
Within 10% of actual earnings	53%
Overestimates earnings by 30% or more	3%

Source: Financial Analysts Journal, March–April 1979.

In other words, Zacks found that when consensus forecasts were significantly overly optimistic—a common analyst error—there was only a 3% chance of a stock performing better than the market. In fact, most stocks are treated unmercifully after a negative surprise, not only underperforming the broad averages, but taking a severe price hit as well. While the study is ten years old, it has not been refuted, and no additional study has been done on the subject. "Analysts hate to be surprised, and they are vindictive as hell," one brokerage official told me. "I've seen good stocks just thrown away like they're about to go bankrupt."

Shareholders of Toys R Us can speak from experience about the effects of a negative surprise. In December 1984 the company announced a 20% increase in earnings, an increase that would easily qualify it for the "good, solid" company label of which brokers are so fond. Unfortunately, Wall Street had expected a 30% increase. In the weeks ahead, shareholders watched their stock being pounded as a result of overly optimistic forecasts over which they had no control. Within one day, the stock dived from $47 to $40. Eventually, the stock lost nearly 25% of its value.

Investors in high-technology stocks in 1983 and 1984 also experienced the bite of a negative surprise. Prices of computer and electronic stocks had shot up, containing the optimistic forecasts of analysts. Seduced by these forecasts, investors had stampeded to get aboard this apparently high-growth industry. When the eventual reality turned out to be below expectations, billions of investor dollars were lost as prices fell from 50 to 80%.

It is also quite possible for a company to experience extraordinary earnings growth and meet analyst expectations yet have its stock perform no better than the market averages. Zacks's data shows roughly an even chance of beating the market under these circumstances, *no matter how impressive the actual earnings gain.*

Only in situations where analysts underestimate the eventual earnings will stocks regularly outperform the market. But once again, there is a major problem: if analysts are negative about a company, they won't recommend it in the first place. "Analysts had a marked tendency to overestimate the growth rate of securities they believed would perform well and to underestimate the growth rate of securities they believed would perform poorly," concluded Elton, Gruber, and Gultekin.[52] The result: *investors are left at the station on stocks that rise, and are left holding the bag for stocks that fall.*

Psychoanalyst to the World?

In their fixation on compiling earnings forecasts, analysts also tend to ignore other major factors, such as market psychology. "Analysts tend to recommend stocks in a vacuum: this company's good, earnings will rise, therefore the stock will rise. But regardless of how well you grasp the fundamentals of a company . . . the market environment can make you a hero or a jerk," noted auto analyst Maryann Keller, to *Fortune*. [53] Analyst Harold K. concurs: "One of the problems analysts have is that they concentrate too much on earnings estimates . . . but it's the outside influences that will have just as great, if not greater impact on the stock, such as interest rates, and the price-earnings ratio of the market." Are these hard to predict? "Yes," admits Harold.

While the performance of individual stocks *relative to the overall market* is, as the Zacks study concludes, primarily a result of the way the eventual reality compares to the previously forecasted consensus, there is substantial evidence that overall corporate profits and the vertical gyrations of the stock market are not related at all. Harold said that in the 1950s the market averages were up over 200%, but corporate profits were up only 49%. In the 1970s, corporate profits more than doubled while the market barely broke even. Between 1966 and 1975, profits of the thirty Dow Jones Industrial companies rose 85%, but their collective stock price fell 43%. From 1978 to 1985 corporate profits declined while the market doubled. What's going on here? Nothing unusual, just market psychology at work. When the price-earnings ratio* of the market rises, the market will rise, regardless of earnings. When the price-earnings ratio of the market falls, stock prices will fall, even if earnings are rising. Above all, the price-earnings ratio is a function of investor psychology. Can analysts reasonably be expected to predict *that* too?

Occasionally, negative investor psychology will touch off a technical breakdown in a stock, leaving the analyst helpless and even unaware. Harold's comments capture the frustration analysts face during this time: "I had been right about a stock for two years on the earnings estimates and the stock went down 35%. While the stock is going down you are looking for reasons, you are trying to find out why. . . . There has to be a reason why the stock is dropping like that in a rising market. Are my earnings estimates wrong, is the company missing something? The management isn't telling you the whole truth. The stock is back up now and I can say beyond a shadow of a doubt that during the period it was declining there was virtually nothing fundamentally wrong. I couldn't believe it. I kept saying, 'I'm missing something.' Stocks don't drop 35% without a fundamental problem, but this one did." Why did it drop? "No reason," said Harold, but he suspects that a large foreign shareholder, concerned about a possible fall in the U.S. dollar, was gradually taking profits. As the large seller pushed the price down, he touched off the stop-loss orders* of other shareholders, causing yet more selling and pushing the price down even farther. Are analysts expected to predict the whims of individual shareholders halfway around the world?

Blind Man's Bluff

Just as in the case of predicting interest rates, or GNP, or inflation, or unemployment, or earnings, or market psychology, the answer is *no*. And there's no shame in that; some events simply can't be predicted. The shame only comes when an industry pretends that it can do what it clearly cannot. Brokerage firms collect billions of dollars each year from unwitting investors by nurturing the myth that they can somehow predict the future. The scores of academic studies contradicting that myth go largely unnoticed, and the marketing skill of the industry triumphs over facts and common sense. In the final analysis, however, the real value of brokerage research can be found in its replacement value—the *dime* tossed in the air to make predictions of approximately equal accuracy.

CHAPTER 4

Bait 'n' Switch

Nearly all professions do it: advertise a product or service that is intended mainly to bring customers in the door, after which they can be switched to other more profitable items.

Given the rudimentary nature of such manipulation, the only surprise should be that it took the brokerage industry so long to join the game. Since the early 1980s, however, the industry has hit on two marketing ploys designed to 1) bring customers in the door, 2) bring customers in the door with all their wealth, 3) get customers to reveal their complete financial holdings and assets, and 4) leave those assets under the control of a single salesman/broker. The mere prospect of accomplishing those four objectives with a single marketing scheme can be enough to send a commission-hungry salesman to broker heaven. What makes the whole ruse so effective is the seemingly benign and innocent nature of the "services" that double as a front in the brokerages' master marketing plan. Understanding the real value and ultimate cost of those "services" could help you avoid your broker's shrewdly disguised hook.

"One Stop Financial Shopping" and "Financial Planning" both have a ring of legitimacy and even common sense about them. Indeed, what investor would not want convenience and a financial plan to guarantee his or her financial nirvana? Yet it is precisely because of their universal appeal and implicit promise of financial security that these two marketing tricks have become the consummate bait of the brokerage industry. Whether fishing for the well-heeled investor or the occasional odd-lot trader, knowledge of and control over that investor's assets is the brokerage firm's goal. And once under a broker's control, those assets can be "managed" to produce a steady flow of commissions for the broker and his firm.

An Expensive Checking Account

Many investors have brokerage accounts at several firms; the spreading-out of potential commission dollars leaves brokers scratching their heads and dreaming for a larger slice of the pie, or better yet, the whole Lucullan feast. But how to induce customers to bring all their holdings to a single house? Enter the Managed Cash Account. Nearly all major brokerages market them, always under a derivative alias such as Cash Management Account, Active Assets Account, Financial Management Account, Resource Management Account, Vantage Account, Premium Account, or Total Asset Account. The Managed Cash Accounts (MCAs) all operate essentially the same way: For an annual fee (usually about $50), you'll receive a plethora of mostly trivial financial "services," many of which merely duplicate most of your existing accounts and services. These may include a checking account, a debit card, access to the brokerage firm's research recommendations, a single consolidated monthly statement, and the ability to borrow against the equity in your investment portfolio. Others of these highly touted services, such as the daily sweeping of interest and dividends into a money market fund* and toll-free access to service representatives to straighten out computer foul-ups, should be done anyway. To qualify for these invaluable benefits, you will have to bring in about $20,000 in securities and/or cash and maintain at least that amount in your account. You will thus be motivated to consolidate your holdings under one roof.

The Managed Cash Account itself is not an especially profitable endeavor for the firm, but what you might buy with the $20,000 or more in your account will be enormously profitable. Welcome to the brokerage firms' version of Bait 'n' Switch.

Before you shell out the $50 to open a Managed Cash Account, carefully consider several questions: Do you really need another checking account? Do you really need another credit card? Do you really want to borrow against your investment portfolio? Do you really need to buy travelers checks from your broker?

Even beyond these questions, there is the issue of the real cost of leaving $20,000 or more of your money under the management of a professional salesman. As the evidence in chapters one to three makes clear, the odds are high that your broker will underperform the broad market by an average of 3 to 10% each year, even before paying transaction costs. Given a $20,000 beginning portfolio and assuming your broker underperformed the market by only 3% per year (your broker earns 12% while the S & P 500 advances 15%), your managed cash account will be worth $134,405 *less* than the unmanaged S & P 500 index after twenty years; $134,405 is a lot to pay for a checking account.

The fact that managed cash accounts are actually successful in luring customers to consolidate their holdings under the watchful eye of a single salesman is evidence of how skillfully the brokerage industry is able to hide the issue of results behind the sugar-coated issues of its choice. Whether the bait is a batch of trifling financial services or the availability of computer-generated financial plans bound in Naugahyde, the results are usually the same: customers lining up at the door to *buy the image*.

Besides bringing in larger accounts, brokers like the managed cash account for another reason: prospecting on MCAs allows them to appear as helpful purveyors of countless innovative financial services instead of as commission-hungry hucksters. This dramatic change in image can truly work wonders: investors are inclined to recoil from sales pitches but salivate at trendy new "financial supermarket" offerings that promise to simplify their financial lives. Only after the MCA is established does the broker (who earns nothing by opening an MCA) take off his gloves and start pounding for commissions.

Baseball, Hotdogs, Apple Pie (and Financial Planning)

Bait 'n' Switch is also the essential doctrine behind the latest fad of the 1980s: financial planning. The phrase itself, of course, suggests that the world is divided into two groups: those who plan for their financial future and those who don't. Unless an individual cares to shoulder the requisite guilt associated with having no financial plan, there is only one solution: see a financial planner.

There certainly is no shortage of planners to see. Anyone who wants to call themselves a financial planner can do so, and by some estimates as many as 200,000 self-appointed planners are practicing their trade today. Some of them may even be qualified, but according to Marv Tuttle of the Institute of Certified Financial Planners, only 12,000 so-called planners have actually received the CFP (Certified Financial Planner) designation.[N] Most others are stockbrokers, insurance salesmen, accountants, and the guy next door who knows how to do your taxes.

Essentially, whatever it takes to motivate people to turn over their complete financial affairs—stocks, bonds, money market funds, life insurance, annuities, retirement plans—is what brokers will call themselves. Once in possession of all this data about a client, the broker will drag out the customary bromides about how the client's individual situation will be scrutinized by various "experts," fed into a computer, and in close consultation with the client, an individually tailored plan will emerge that will show the true path to financial independence.

There are many fallacies in this transparently manipulative marketing scheme. First of all, for the overwhelming majority of Americans, financial planning is a solution in search of a problem. Most people simply don't need it. As *Forbes* magazine observed: "Not since the Dark Ages, when monks peddled indulgences to the guilt ridden at Eastertide, has there been such demand for a product of such questionable value."[54] If your income is below $100,000 and your net worth is less than $250,000, it is hard to fathom how you could have any tax or estate problems that could not be handled by a competent

CPA or lawyer. And regardless of your investment needs, leaving money in the hands of a professional salesman is not the best way to achieve results. The goal of financial planning is to induce you to show all your assets, bring them together under one roof, then consent to a program that allows the planner to earn commission by plugging specific investments into the plan. Once a brokerage firm has prepared a financial plan for you, it stands to earn large commissions through its implementation. The ugly specter of *conflict of interest,* a phrase seemingly synonymous with the brokerage business, rears its head again. And even if the basic financial plan is sound, it will require successful investing to make it work. As noted in chapters one through three, there is little evidence to suggest that stockbrokers are as good at managing money as they are at attracting it.

Certainly there are some Americans who need and could benefit greatly from a qualified and unbiased financial plan. If you earn a large income, or have complicated tax or estate problems, you are a logical and legitimate candidate for financial planning. And when you really need a sound financial plan, it can make a world of difference to choose the right planner. Here's how:

1. **Avoid Salesmen.** Stockbrokers, insurance salesmen, or any person that stands to earn a commission off the execution of a financial plan has an inherent conflict of interest. Let them practice their sales skills on someone else.

2. **Hire a CFP.** The Certified Financial Planner designation is evidence of at least minimal competence in the field. It is not the equivalent of a Harvard MBA (many CFPs earn their designation by passing correspondence courses), but it is a good place to start.

3. **Hire a "Fee-only" CFP.** This is a crucial point. Planners compensated on the basis of a flat fee and not as a result of commissions generated by their recommendations have no conflict of interest. Using a fee-only CFP is the best way to insure unbiased competence. Finding such a

CFP may take some digging: only 18% of the 12,000 CFPs operating nationally work on a fee-only basis.

4. **Leave the Investing to Professional Money Managers.** Implementing the investment portion of a financial plan should be left to professional money managers who have a long record of consistent results and who have no conflict of interest (see chapter nine for ideas). Hire a fee-only CFP who prepares just the plan and leaves the implementation to proven, unbiased specialists.

There are several ways to locate CFPs; the easiest is simply to look in the yellow pages under Financial Planners. There will likely be a fairly long list; stand assured that any planner holding a CFP designation will advertise it prominently. The Institute of Certified Financial Planners and the International Association of Financial Planners will also provide referrals for local CFPs. Write or call these organizations:

Institute of Certified Financial Planners
3443 S Galena, Suite 190
Denver, Colorado 80231
(303) 751-7600

or

International Association of Financial Planners
5775 Peachtree-Dunwoody Road
Suite 120-C
Atlanta, Georgia 30342
(404) 252-9600

Once you have compiled a list of *Fee-Only-CFPs-Who-Leave-the-Implementation-to-Others,* the remainder of your selection process should be similar to choosing an attorney, doctor, or accountant: interview each candidate, ask for referrals, compare fees and services, and try to separate substance from salesmanship. If you truly need a financial plan, strictly adhering to these criteria will likely produce highly profitable results.

CHAPTER 5

Caution:
Amateur at Play

Results. Once upon a time, that was what investing was all about. Now the brokerage industry seems only too anxious to seize upon any marketing gimmick that will deflect public attention *away* from results. Behind the grim statistics of brokerage firm results are real people investing good money. When they lose that money they experience honest emotions and have true stories to tell. This chapter is their story, told in ways no statistics could capture.

Interestingly enough, there is a tremendous similarity in their stories. Many used identical phrases to describe their experiences: "They're just salesmen"; "I guess I expected too much"; "All they really want is to sell you something." Experience is truly the great teacher, and these investors have learned a costly lesson—not only have they lost money through stockbrokers, but this loss occurred during a period when the overall market was advancing dramatically, a period in which stock-picking by dartboard could have been a profitable enterprise. And their complaints go beyond mere incompetence: they told stories of fraud, lack of communication, endless hassles to get money that rightly belonged to them, a constant stream of sales pitches, and pushy salesmen hustling limited partnerships that seemed to benefit everyone but the investor. Perhaps most disturbingly, many investors were resigned to a future where they will keep their money in the bank, where at least they will be sure to earn 5¼%. And therein lies the final payment in the broker game: not only do investors frequently lose money when dealing with brokers; the experience can leave them so disillusioned that they forever shun the many successful and more professional investment alternatives (see chapters eight through ten). In the long run, the cost of this final payment on brokerage incompetence will be by far the most expensive.

If you have thus far been spared the high cost of brokerage under-performance, the anecdotes which follow[†], both in this chapter and the next, should allow you to learn and benefit from others' mistakes. If you have already been burned by a broker, these stories of pain and frustration ought to at least assure you that you are not alone.

Pure Incompetence

The broker game begins with the initial sales call, often heard crackling over long-distance telephone lines. Investor Richard T. tells what happens next: "I get calls from Florida, New York, Canada, California, Kansas City, Chicago, just everywhere. It's strange that these brokers have to reach across the country to make a living if all the deals they are touting are so good. They open up their pitches by saying, 'Hello, Richard, how are you today?' You know what's going to happen from then on; they all use the same lines to push their products. I think, 'Oh my God, here we go again.' " What is the typical sales pitch like? "They all start by saying that 'I can get you some immediate returns. You'll only have to put up $2,000 or $10,000 and you'll have a chance to get back $100,000 in six months.' I won't even talk to these people anymore," Richard said.

And with good reason: Richard lost thousands of dollars by listening to brokers before finally deciding to tune them out. "I remember

---

†The names of the customers involved in the following anecdotes have been changed to protect their privacy. In each case, however, documents certifying the accuracy of the stories have been secured by the author.

brokers telling me what to do, when to do it, and invariably it was wrong. When I was young and financially tender, I invested thousands with brokers and I lost—I lost almost half of it. It was traumatic; I was just starting out, so it really left an impression on my mind." Richard's lasting impression of stockbrokers? "Most brokers aren't even as knowledgeable as the average investor who has the money to invest and is interested in doing something. I now have a phobia against brokers." Fortunately, here is where Richard's story diverges from so many other victims of broker incompetence. Instead of retreating to the sanctuary of inferior bank returns, he began looking for professional alternatives to this amateur hour—and found them. He had heard from friends that there were many highly regarded professional portfolio managers available. "When I started looking into it a little further, I found that your private investment advisers didn't think too much of your typical stockbroker." Eventually, Richard hired a private money manager, and quickly learned what a difference *competence* can make. "This guy is just magic. In one stretch he made 34% in an eight-month period for our profit-sharing plan. I sign over all powers to him. I get statements each quarter. It's turned out well. He knows what he's doing; he's very good."

Besides competence, Richard noticed a difference in style between the investment professional and amateur: "One thing the professional managers don't do is sit in front of their quotrons* all day like the stockbrokers do. You get so damn nervous when you do that; everyone gets jumpy and nobody makes any right decisions." Richard's story had a happy ending; he found *investment* professionalism after a nearly fatal bout with *sales* professionalism.° It is an ending that most investors could also write for themselves (see chapter nine for more information on finding professional private money management).

Douglas W. wasn't so lucky; his experiences with brokers left him so shell-shocked that bank CDs are the only investment in which he can now feel comfortable. "I just can't even believe it," Doug said. "If nine out of ten stocks go up, the brokers will sure as hell put me in the one that goes down. It was ridiculous how much money I lost. I don't invest anymore; I just put my money in CDs and leave it. I've just been burned too many times." Does Doug ever get the urge to return to the scene of his lost battles? "Don't think I wouldn't still like to invest, because I think that investing in stocks is part of our heritage and part of the American way of doing business. But I've been dealt too many blows." Many of the blows Doug received were the result of investing in oil stocks on the basis of broker assurances that the price explosion in oil would last forever. When it didn't, Doug lost big; his broker, of course, kept the commissions earned from his sagacious advice.

The fact that so many brokers were pushing oil stocks at a time when the price of crude was peaking offers an interesting insight into the investment competence and sales psychology of brokers. As noted in chapter two, high sales quotas and low pay-out ratios put brokers under enormous pressure to sell. In order to maximize their sales, brokers usually sell what is hot, what is trendy, what appeals to investors' emotions. In the early 1980s, with the rapid rise in the price of oil hitting every American in the pocketbook, it was the most obvious and cheapest of all sales ploys to appeal to investors' natural desire to recoup through their investments what they were losing at the pump. Never mind the fact that nearly every investment professional will tell you that no trend lasts forever, that commodity price-fixing* will eventually collapse, that by the time the general public gets interested in an investment idea, it is usually too late. "Never mind investment wisdom, push what sells" is the broker's creed, a creed that assumes, of course, that the broker even *has* investment wisdom to disregard. Doug doubts it: "I got hooked in oil so bad. All the brokers were saying, 'Oil is going to go to $50 a barrel.' They were giving me this crock and I believed them—they talked me into it. Where is all this high-grade research they are supposed to have? Some of these brokers should not even be in the business. They just don't know what they're doing. They don't even check the background on some of these companies. I had a few of my stocks go bankrupt." How does Doug feel about his experiences with stockbrokers? "Every time I hear about investments I get sick. I look back and see what I could have made if I had just gone into the right stocks."[P]

The right stocks also had a way of avoiding James A.'s portfolio. "My broker picked a couple of winners, but he picked many more losers. When you average it all out, I'd have been better off putting my money in the money market. For every winner, he suggested four losers," Jim said. It does not help when investors see their stocks going down while the overall market is going up. "I'd always thought that in an up market you just couldn't lose, but that was before I met my broker. I just sold one of his ideas the other day. I bought it for $5 a share and sold it for 75 cents. Another of his recommendations went from $14 to $30, but he never told me to sell. Eventually, I sold it for $2," Jim said.⁹

Finding the "Hot" Button

While brokers may not know when to sell, they most assuredly know *how* to sell, a fact that did not escape the attention of investor Dennis N. Seduced into a limited partnership by a slick-talking salesman, he lost his entire $5,000 investment. "It was a selling job; the guy was good. He got us all hyped up. If a guy comes to you and says that you can make a lot of money in a short period of time and be able to write off the investment as well, that's a pretty good pitch," Dennis said. "They're just shrewd salesmen who know how to touch the greed button." Brokers know that selling on *greed* and *fear* puts food on their tables and money in their pockets. They also know that in addition to greed and fear, the desire to avoid taxes is still another investor "hot button" that can ring up commission dollars fast, which explains their enthusiasm for selling high-write-off tax shelters with often questionable economic value. "The salesman represented the partnership as a sure thing," Dennis said of his ill-fated investment. "Looking back, it was just a sales pitch."

Losing every penny of his investment taught Dennis another valuable lesson about brokers: "It's easy to work with someone else's money; if you lose it, you can just walk away. But people in other professions can't do that. It's only me. I'm the one that has to pay for it. I think that somehow a broker should have to pay for that, too." Dennis's experience with brokers was no better when buying stocks. "They always want you to sell what you own and buy something else, so they can make a double commission," he said. "I examined what's been going on in my portfolio and I haven't made anything. But the broker sure has. You get these brokers who want to trade all the time—buy and sell, buy and sell, buy and sell—that's fine for him. But the client never makes any money. I know that everybody has to make a buck. But I feel that if you're going to make a buck off of someone else's money, that person should make a buck too." And how does Dennis react to brokers' sales pitches now? "I don't listen to them anymore," he said.[R]

Brian T. found out how deadly the combination of sexy sales pitches and limited partnerships can be. In 1980 Brian bought an oil and gas limited partnership on the basis of a broker's arguments that oil was going to appreciate forever. Not only was the broker wrong about oil, he was pushing a limited partnership that would experience organizational and management difficulties as well. The results for Brian: his $5,000 investment in 1980 is now valued at less than $100. "Maybe I expected too much from these guys," Brian said. "I just assumed that they were in the know; after all, they make their living through investments so they should know what they're doing." Just as aggravating to Brian as the broker's lack of investment expertise was his lack of communication, especially after the investment turned bad. "They like to sell you something, but they never really help you. They don't take the time to stay in touch; maybe they just have too many accounts. And I don't think they keep any record of how well they're doing for their clients. They just sell you something and that's the end of the ballgame, unless, of course, they want to sell you something else. Then they get back to you." Judging from his results when using brokers, it was perhaps best that Brian's broker didn't get back to him. "I got hurt bad on one stock. The broker never warned me that the firm was going bankrupt. I guess you've got to find that out for yourself. So the market has not been very good to me. I guess I should probably just stay out of it unless I have my portfolio watched by a professional."s

Could You Help Me Pay My Mortgage?

David B. thought he *was* having his money watched by a professional when he walked into a broker's office five years ago in search of a safe, secure, investment. "I said I wanted to invest $10,000 in a safe, guaranteed, long-term investment," Dave remembered. "I said that if it was going to be risky, then I didn't want it. I said I'd take a couple points less yield to get something guaranteed. So what do I get?" Dave got an annuity underwritten by Baldwin-United Corporation, which eventually filed for bankruptcy, leaving investors high and dry. After years of litigation, most investors have received their principle investment back along with some interest, although far less than originally "guaranteed." "Maybe I was expecting too much, but if there was risk involved, the broker should have known it," Dave said, echoing that oft-stated refrain. Dave especially remembers the heavy-handed sales presentation: "The broker had a very heavy sell. He also talked me into the Petro-Lewis deal [which also went bad], to the point of becoming totally obnoxious. I can't see anybody selling anything that hard. I've spent a lot of time in sales, and when a guy says no I don't think it's right to call back two, three, four days in a row. He'd ramble on for twenty minutes; meanwhile, I'd sit here and do work while he was telling me that this investment was the greatest thing in the world and that he was putting his own money in it, he was putting his wife's money in it, that some widow that he made a lot of money for was putting her money in it, so it's the best deal in the world. This went on for three or four days in a row. He'd call me at home, at the office, anywhere. I've never seen anybody push anything so hard."

Dave had another experience that sheds considerable light upon broker motivations. He had been using a particular broker for several years; the man's sales presentations were seemingly honest and not overly pushy. Suddenly, it all changed. Why? "As soon as he bought a big new house, his whole outlook changed," Dave noticed. "I knew him when he was living a lot less expensively. Then he moved into something over his head—he admittedly buried himself in mortgage payments—and suddenly his whole philosophy on selling changed. He began pushing harder and trying to sell things with bigger commissions in it. I suppose he's got to look out for himself, and unfortunately, that's exactly what he was doing—looking out for himself and not the person he was investing for."

Dave's newly burdened-with-debt broker is unfortunately more the rule than the exception in a business that represents the perfect metaphor for the "you are what you own" philosophy. Indeed, it is a rare person that can spend ten to twelve hours each day, often six days a week, in the totally undisguised pursuit of money and not have it perversely affect his or her outlook and values. Many brokers, in fact, seemingly completely lose their sense of identity, preferring instead to measure their self-worth in *quantities*: the amount of commissions earned, the cost of the car they drive, the cost of the clothes they wear, the cost of the restaurants they are seen in, the cost of the homes in which they live. For too many brokers, meaning in life is derived largely from the ego satisfaction gained from exhibiting the trophies of their professional "success." Exhilaration comes not from earning superior investment returns for their clients, but from the pure excitement of the hunt for commission dollars; making a sale becomes an end in itself. Significantly, this empty and greedy materialism is openly encouraged by the brokerage industry. According to the *Wall Street Journal*, Merrill Lynch bought subscriptions to the *Robb Report* (a monthly glossy featuring articles on how the rich spend their money) for its brokers at two branch offices. One issue told Merrill brokers that big cars represent "a culmination of the ultimate materialistic expression of excess." "It's a great magazine," enthused one Merrill Lynch executive, while another urged that brokers "should also aspire themselves to be a part of the life-style."[55] Unfortunately, it is an aspiration that, when combined with high sales quotas, low pay-out ratios, and professional incompetence, results in the kind of stories chronicled here.

Dave also took notice of another annoying habit of many brokers: "I dislike it when a broker makes a suggestion to you which you reject, then you get a call maybe two months later saying, 'Hey, look what I could have made for you. This is what you lost by not going with me.' Yet, if you do take their advice and the investment turns south, you'll never hear from him again."

Not surprisingly, Dave is unimpressed with the state of the brokerage industry. "My present outlook on brokers is that I doubt that those guys are any better than anyone else on the street who would throw a dart and pick a stock that way. I just don't think that brokers have the best interest of their clients at heart. Doing what's right for their clients is not their ultimate goal. . . . If they have a conscience, I don't think they'd be a successful broker."[T]

Sell Your Winner, Buy My Loser

Losing money because of a broker's bad advice can be painful enough, but when a broker talks a client out of an investment that would have been profitable and into a disastrous one instead, it is a double kick to the wallet. Just ask Arthur K. The time was early 1983 and "I had a suggestion from a friend that I buy MCI stock," Art recalled. "When I called my broker and inquired about buying some MCI, he stated that he didn't track it and that he had another suggestion, which was a company called Oak Industries. The broker said that Oak was in the same business as MCI and was going for about the same price, $32 a share. So after about forty-five minutes of going back and forth, he finally convinced me to buy Oak Industries instead of MCI. Well, almost from the day I bought it, Oak started to go down. Meanwhile, MCI was going up and eventually split. But Oak just kept going down, down, down, until it hit a low of about $2. I was too busy making a living myself to keep track of the situation; I relied on my broker to keep me informed. Once, when the stock was at about $15, I called him up. I had wanted to buy some Hughes Tool stock, but he tried to talk me out of it and into another stock that he was pushing instead. At that point I told him, 'Wait a minute. Remember MCI and Oak Industries?' And he said, 'Oh, yeah. Well, I guess I slipped up on that.' Since then, of course, I haven't bought any more stock from him."[U]

Larry E. had a similar experience in 1984. "I had bought a few shares of Digital Switch, and had made quite a few bucks on it [the stock went from $5 a share to an eventual high well over $100]," Larry said, "but I could have made a lot more if I hadn't taken the advice of a broker who talked me out of buying more. Instead, he recommended a stock called Cornwall Petroleum. He got me to buy 500 shares. It has since had a reverse split* and it's worth nothing today. So instead of more Digital Switch, I own 25 shares of a stock worth nothing." Larry found this episode of broker incompetence to be all too frequent for his tastes. "That experience was typical of my dealings with the brokerage houses. Now when I get a call from a broker I just cover my ears."[V]

5¼% Never Looked So Good

Joseph V. probably wishes he had done just that before investing $100,000 of his and several partners' money in the stock market in 1983. "We talked to a broker and decided to go with him," Joe said. "But we didn't do very well, so we switched to another broker." Unfortunately for Joe and his partners, changing brokers didn't help: "We started with a $100,000 investment that eventually got as low as $69,000. Remember, this is happening during a time when the market was going up. We were told by the broker that our stocks were in strong industries like electronics and computers. For example, we had Verbatim. We rode that one from $13 to $7 a share. Most of our stocks were in 1,000-share increments, so it made it a little tough." All the while, of course, the broker remained optimistic that his selections were correct. They had to be, the broker said, since his very own research department said they were. "The broker said that his research department felt the stocks would come back and that there were predictions of much higher earnings, so things would get better," Joe said. And what is Joe's attitude toward the brokerage industry now? "We're a little scalded right now, and we say to ourselves, 'If we had just put the money in the bank at 5¼% we'd have been better off.' "[w]

Norm H. also found stockbrokers to be living advertisements for bank savings plans. "I've not had good experiences in the stock market. I don't believe I've gotten good advice in the past; I've taken the advice of brokers who've just called me cold," Norm said. "I'm to the point where I prefer to invest in a GNMA fund because every time I buy some hot stock from a broker I get burned. I've had many companies that were highly touted by local brokers. All of them did nothing." Specifically, Norm remembered a 1982 experience involving a broker-age recommendation. "My last experience was with a company called Farm House Foods. The broker told me what a great deal it was, he told me it had great management, it was a good company and that it was going to go from $7 a share to over $12 a share by the end of the year. Well, I had some money at the time so I said, 'Okay, I'll invest a little bit in there.' One year later the stock is down to $5. After I bought the stock the broker finally tells me that his firm is a market maker in the security. The next thing I know they are talking about going private and offering to take the investors out at $5 a share. All the while it was going down, the broker never called. The broker then switched to another firm; he finally called to ask me if I would switch my account over to him at his new firm. I told him no way. That's been my experience with brokers."[x]

Brokers, of course, are used to being fired by clients; most have been let go more often than Billy Martin, especially those servicing the account of one Donald F., who proudly claims to have pink-slipped over three dozen pitchmen in his years of playing the market. "I've been investing for fifteen years, and I've probably fired thirty or forty brokers because they weren't getting results. I'm using about eight brokers now, and at the end of the year I'm going to cross off another six," he promises. Don follows the advice of brokers because "I don't have the time to argue with them." And how has the brokers' advice turned out? "Poorly," he admits. "I haven't used mutual funds in the past, but I plan on doing that before too long," he says.[Y]

Too often, by the time a client has fired his broker, the damage has already been done. Raymond C. put $80,000 into a stock on a recommendation from a broker. "It was the first time I ever listened to a stockbroker and I went into the ash can for about $30,000," he said. "The broker said it was a fast-moving company that was really going to go. So I went ahead and bought $80,000 worth." He did it against his better judgment: "The money I've made listening to other people I could count on one hand. But the money I've made on my own has amounted to something. If I'm going to lose money, I'd rather have it be on my own opinion. I found out that I'm a very bad loser when I use someone else's opinion that doesn't work out," Ray said. Understandably, he has some strong opinions about brokers: "Stockbrokers are just hard-core salesmen, that's all they are. Sometimes they use some pretty bad tactics on you. They're always trying to push you into something. If they were such investment geniuses, they wouldn't need to sell me their ideas. They'd be wheeling and dealing for themselves."[Z]

Gary M., another oft-burned investor, complains, "There are so many brokers calling that I've turned off the phone. Some of them are even from out of town. I had one broker who kept calling me about Parker Pen. He had to be some kind of nut the way that turned out. If you had put money into that stock you would've lost your shirt," Gary said with the laugh of a man who still has his. "The broker said, 'Ya know, the company is going to be sold and the stock is going to go way up.' Well, the company was sold but the stock sure didn't go way up." Despite many bad experiences in the stock market, Gary is a survivor; he realizes that stocks can be an excellent investment, provided competent, professional management can be found. "It's really only in the institutions that you have the kind of professional investment expertise needed to really make money. The average person, with the type of analysts that work for the brokerage houses, can't really come out very well."[AA]

Can I Have My Money, Please?

As if losing a client's money isn't bad enough, brokerage houses occasionally make it difficult for clients to get at the money they have left. Carlton S. had invested his IRA* in a brokerage-sponsored mutual fund. He wanted to liquidate the account and rollover the funds to a more promising investment. Not so fast, said the brokerage firm. "It was like trying to rob a bank," Carlton said. "The broker gave me the runaround for about three weeks, saying I could roll it over to another of their in-house funds, but that I couldn't take the money out. I said, 'You're wrong about that,' and he said, 'Well, I'm sorry. It's our policy that you can't do this.' I had to call the branch manager, and he gave me the same kind of line. He said, 'Well, you're going to have to fill out a lot of forms,' and I said, 'Fine, I'll be right over.' Then he said, 'Ah, well, after we do that we'll have to send it to New York and you're still not going to get your money for another two weeks.' The manager was very abrupt and very abrasive. If this is the way they're treating their elderly clients, they are naturally going to go along with them because they don't know better." Carlton found the whole episode infuriating. "It was an experience I was so upset about that I was almost going to write the state securities examiner." And while the broker stonewalled his request, Carlton's investment opportunity passed. "The broker stalled it as long as he could, but I just kept coming after him. If I wasn't persistent, I would never have gotten my money out."[BB]

Barry S. also found the experience of having to beg for his monthly interest check more than he wanted to accept. Barry had purchased a number of government bonds, at least one of which would generate an interest check each month. "The problem was that I had government bonds that paid interest on the fifteenth of the month, but I wouldn't get the check from the brokerage firm until I would call them and ask for it," Barry said. "Sometimes the check would come around the end of the month, but most of the time I wouldn't get it at all. I would have to make a special phone call to get them to send it. They wanted to keep my money in their own account as long as possible so they could make interest off of my interest." Barry found that the firm routinely held onto his funds. "Out of the three or four years that I owned the bonds, there were only two or three times that I didn't have to call them and prod them into sending me my money," he said. "Sometimes it took several phone calls because the broker wasn't in and the person answering the phone said she'd check into it and never did. I would have to call again; all this just to get money that was due me anyway." Barry, who is retired and depends on the prompt payment of interest in order to pay his own bills, finally had to change his investment plans. "I eventually got so tired of calling that I just sold the bonds, which was too bad because they carried a good interest rate. I invested instead in a GNMA fund outside of a brokerage firm. They've been great, sending the monthly check exactly on the fifteenth of each month. I just didn't like the hassle of having to beg for my money each month."[cc]

When All Else Fails, Lie

One of the surest ways a broker can ring up commission dollars is to insinuate to a customer that he or she is in possession of inside information that indicates a certain stock will shoot up shortly. Ron E. received such a call from his broker. "The broker called and said he's got this hot tip from a friend of his that a stock is going to double," Ron said. "I'm kind of skeptical, of course, but he says that he has borderline inside information that the company is going to be bought out for $14 a share—it was selling for $7 at the time. He told me that he knows everything that's going on inside the company and I just couldn't miss. So, I went ahead and bought some. Well, it just sat there and none of the things that the broker said were going to happen are happening. Meanwhile, the broker is blaming it all on the chairman of the board of the company, whom he claims to know personally. Finally, the stock actually starts going down, and down some more, and all the while the broker is saying, 'I don't see how this stock can go below this price or that price because of this ratio or that ratio, and this news is going to be released soon.' It was all just one lie after another. By this time I was down $5,000 and I didn't want to sell and eat that kind of loss." Finally, Ron confronted the broker. "I said, 'What's going on here? Nothing you said would happen is actually coming true.' And he says, 'Well, one of the board of directors at the company is stubborn and he's not getting along with the lawyers representing the buying company. But I'm flying out to the company and I'm not coming back without a signed deal.' Well, he came back without a signed deal. When I questioned him about it he said, 'Well, I never said that.' That's when I knew I was in trouble. I had taken notes, so I had records of everything he said. Meanwhile, the stock had dropped to about $2.50." While being duped by his broker's lies, Ron had seen the value of his investment drop by about 64% during a period when the broad-market averages were nearly doubling. DD

Once in a while, some especially unfortunate investor will fall victim to a broker "triple play"—fraud, incompetence, and exploitation of the buddy system—allowing the investor a kind of round trip through the brokerage industry at its absolute worst. Gerald D. could hardly believe it happened to him: his broker was a personal friend for over thirty years. In early 1983, Gerald recalled, "I opened a money market account with my broker for about $230,000, but instead of putting the money into the money market fund, he bought stocks with it—on margin yet. By the time I figured out what he was doing, he had lost $140,000. Fortunately, the firm paid me back for my losses. I got suspicious when I got a margin call, but I couldn't read the statements. Heck, I know brokers who can't read the statements; my accountant couldn't read the statement. But when I called my broker about it he said, 'Don't worry about it. Just throw it away.' "

Gerald wasn't the broker's only victim; he was busily wracking up losses for just about everyone. "The broker was doing it to a lot of people. I was just one of five represented by my lawyer; about three or four others settled independently. And the broker didn't lose only his clients' money. I think he lost all his own money doing the same thing. He did it to strangers and to his closest friends." Gerald believes his broker was not motivated by any desire to defraud; he was a simple victim of his own incompetence. "He believed in what he was doing; he even did it in his own account. It's just that he wasn't very good at what he was doing." As a result of the unauthorized trades, over a ten-month period the broker made "$27,000 in commissions, and the brokerage firm made $70,000 in commissions. So, the brokerage people made about $100,000 on me, while I was losing $140,000," Gerald said. He blames the broker's firm for "not supervising him at all. That's why they eventually paid all the bills."

It is further testimony to the smooth charm and salesmanship of brokers that, despite his traumatic experience, Gerald still finds it hard to dislike the broker. "He's not a bad guy; to this day he's a very likable person. He has a very nice personality. He just believed that the stocks were going to go up and the market was going to go up. He really didn't do it to hurt people or for personal gain. He thought he was doing them a service. In his own mind, he was doing the right thing. I don't harbor any grudge against him. I just feel bad that he was so incompetent at what he was doing."[EE]

Not just incompetent. *Likable* and incompetent, a combination that aptly describes so many brokers in America today.

Too Many
Bad Apples

All industries have their share of unethical employees; within every profession there is a small percentage that will lie, steal, cheat, and defraud to advance their narrow self-interests. Though it is impossible to know if this criminal element is larger in the brokerage business, one thing is clear: few professions harbor the intrinsic ability to harm individuals as directly and profoundly through illegal acts as the brokerage industry.

What follows are just a few examples of broker frauds committed against you, the investing public. Whereas the anecdotes in chapter five (with the exception of the last case involving unauthorized trading) resulted from *legal* brokerage activity—mostly incompetence—the stories chronicled here reveal flagrant and frequently multiple violations of federal and/or state securities law. The names of the individual brokers have been omitted; the intent of this chapter is not to embarrass them or their firms, but instead to illustrate how absurdly high sales quotas, overcompetition, and incompetence can impact on you and your investments.

Civil and Criminal Prosecutions

The stories themselves are not pretty, but they are true. All information about the following civil and criminal cases filed against brokers is taken directly from court documents and rulings. Together, these cases graphically display the darkest side of an industry that has lost its soul, an industry that exists primarily to line its own pockets.

"Reckless and Wanton Disregard"

In early 1981, Mrs. Helen Aldrich transferred her brokerage account from Paine Webber to Thomson McKinnon; the account, worth over $400,000, consisted largely of tax-exempt municipal bonds and some stock, which together generated an annual income that constituted Mrs. Aldrich's principal means of support. At the time of the account transfer, Mrs. Aldrich told the broker assigned to her account that "she was interested in increasing the income from her portfolio in order to provide financial assistance to her elderly mother, but that she needed to maintain a large measure of safety in her investments," according to a ruling by the U.S. Second Circuit Court of Appeals.

According to Aldrich, the broker then had her sign a bank option-trading agreement form, which the broker later completed using inflated figures to represent Aldrich's annual income and "to falsely characterize her investment objective as short-term trading, rather than safety of principal," the court noted. Beginning in March 1981, the broker began an investment strategy of high-volume, high-risk trading in Aldrich's account; over 400 trades were made in the next ten months. During this time, $3,088,928.06 worth of securities were purchased and over $3,000,000 sold. The broker frequently violated Thomson McKinnon's own internal guidelines, at least once owning over 150 uncovered-option contracts in a single security. (An option is considered uncovered or "naked" if its owner has failed to put up sufficient collateral in the form of stock or cash to fulfill the option contract in the event its execution is demanded by the other party to the contract. If the market subsequently moves against the uncovered-option owner, the amount of loss is theoretically unlimited.)

The court noted that "While [the broker] flagrantly manipulated Aldrich's account, even earning commissions on trading that resulted in Aldrich again owning the identical stock or option that she just sold, Thomson McKinnon supervisors stood idly by." The court also remarked that the broker's immediate supervisors, "who are responsible for monitoring [the broker's] trading activity, indirectly profited from the churning of the account, as they were compensated by a salary plus bonus, with the bonus at least partially dependent upon commissions generated by the broker." Those commissions earned by the broker and Thomson McKinnon totaled $143,854, more than one-third the value of the entire account.

What results was Mrs. Aldrich receiving for her $143,854 in commissions? Let the court give the answer: "At the end of December [1981], apparently because a $60,000 margin call had provoked inquiry from the margin department, [the broker] advised his supervisor that the Aldrich account, worth over $400,000 less than ten months previous, was entirely exhausted." The holidays must have been especially joyful for Mrs. Aldrich: on Christmas Eve alone she lost $50,000.

Despite all this, Thomson McKinnon appealed a jury award of $175,000 in compensatory damages (less than one-half of the amount lost) and $3,000,000 in punitive damages. Thomson McKinnon argued that there was insufficient evidence to support an award of punitive damages. The appellate court disagreed: "The evidence amply supported a finding that Thomson McKinnon was reckless and wanton in its indifference to, and almost total disregard of, the gross manipulation and wasting of Aldrich's account." It called the handling of the account "inexcusable and outrageous" and noted that "Thomson McKinnon's wanton and reckless disregard of the trust placed in it by Aldrich was not only a wrong against her, but by what it portended for other investors, it was a wrong against the general public." The appellate court affirmed a lower-court decision in favor of Mrs. Aldrich, conditional upon Aldrich accepting a reduction in punitive damages from $3 million to $1.5 million, an amount it considered adequate to fairly "discourage repetition of Thomson McKinnon's grossly negligent conduct, or instances of such conduct by other brokerage firms."

"Victimized and Mistreated"

Pearl Kehr, a forty-four-year-old divorced mother of two children, opened a brokerage account at a branch office of Smith Barney, Harris Upham & Company, Inc. Mrs. Kehr immigrated from Korea at age twenty-nine and had only a grade-school understanding of the English language and no business or securities expertise. Her total net worth consisted of a $147,000 inheritance, which she intended to use to pay monthly living expenses and to provide for her children's education. Her own lack of education and job skills made employment nearly impossible; she had been without a job for six years prior to opening the account at Smith Barney.

In June 1978, Mrs. Kehr opened a cash account with a Smith Barney broker in the amount of $40,639. The broker knew Mrs. Kehr's total financial worth and limited earning power; he repeatedly urged Mrs. Kehr to trust him, and assured her that he would recommend only sound, conservative investments. At about the time she opened the Smith Barney account, Mrs. Kehr told the broker she would need to sell $5,000 worth of stock to make a down payment on a home for her family. Mrs. Kehr was raised in China and Korea and saw her family lose large sums of money in banks. Understandably, she was distrustful of them, frequently storing her cash under a mattress. She grew fond of hard assets such as real estate, and looked upon her new home as offering her security as well as comfort. The broker apparently saw Mrs. Kehr's need for $5,000 as an opportunity; knowing Mrs. Kehr's feelings about real estate and her extremely limited reading ability, the broker allegedly told Mrs. Kehr that she could make her account "more like real estate" if she would just sign a margin account agreement. Besides making her account "more like real estate," converting the account from cash to margin would generate $5,000 in "buying power," thus precluding the need to sell any stocks. Mrs. Kehr was told that using buying power in a margin account would help her invest just like "smart investors" do. Lacking the skills to read the form, and constantly reassured that in signing the agreement she would be making her account "more like real estate," Mrs. Kehr trusted her broker's advice and signed the form.

By October 1979, Mrs. Kehr noticed that despite substantial activity in her account, she did not seem to be making any money. She approached the branch manager of the Smith Barney office, who assured her that the account was in capable hands and that he would personally monitor all activity in the account. At about this time, the Smith Barney broker began buying options in Mrs. Kehr's account. Buying options, which are considered highly speculative and risky, involves a substantial probability that an investor will lose the entire amount of the investment, since approximately 90% of all options expire worthless. At first, the amounts of the option purchases were small, but on 29 January 1980, the broker allegedly pressured Mrs. Kehr into purchasing 100 call options on McDonnell Douglas stock, worth in excess of $100,000. The broker made this recommendation despite knowing that Mrs. Kehr could lose the entire $100,000, that Mrs. Kehr only had $50,000 in liquid assets, and in spite of the fact that only nine days earlier Smith Barney's research department had urged its brokers to avoid defense stocks in general and McDonnell Douglas in particular. The broker allegedly told Mrs. Kehr that since he expected McDonnell Douglas's stock to go up immediately, he could buy and sell the underlying options the same day, thus avoiding the need to pay for them. Although she didn't understand options, Mrs. Kehr trusted her broker and agreed to the purchase.

Within minutes of agreeing to the trade, Mrs. Kehr began feeling uneasy. She immediately called her broker and asked that the trade be canceled. The broker responded that the trade had already been executed and that the options could not be sold since her account was now restricted. These were apparently lies; evidence at the trial showed that only half the trade had been executed at the time of Mrs. Kehr's call, and that those options could have been immediately sold since the account was *not* restricted. Had the broker followed Mrs. Kehr's instructions, the trade could have been stopped at that point with little or no damage.

The broker, of course, was quite wrong about McDonnell Douglas stock; instead of going up, it began to decline sharply, taking the value of the underlying call option with it. The broker then suggested to Mrs. Kehr that she pay for the option by taking a second mortgage on her home, which she eventually did. The McDonnell Douglas options expired worthless, costing Mrs. Kehr the entire $100,000 she had invested. In addition to having a substantial percentage of her net worth wiped out in a matter of days, she was now paying interest and points to finance her new mortgage.

In a frantic attempt to escape responsibility for his actions, the broker took Mrs. Kehr to a dark restaurant, where he allegedly induced her to sign a document stating that the option purchase was actually her own idea. Mrs. Kehr's signature appears significantly under the dotted line, apparently because it was too dark in the restaurant to see the line—*or read the document.* The broker later admitted at a federal trial that the option speculating was, in fact, his own idea.

Smith Barney, the broker, and the branch manager, were found guilty by a federal court of engaging in fraudulent activity under the Securities Act of 1934 and ordered to pay Mrs. Kehr $107,143 in damages. Charges of breach of fiduciary duty brought under California state law were settled before trial, with the defendants agreeing to pay Mrs. Kehr an additional $204,000 in damages, for a total recovery of $311,143.

Despite the fact that, in the words of Mrs. Kehr's attorney Louis Raring, "An immigrant with limited understanding of our language and limited business sophistication is induced into the most aggressive speculative positions, and loses more in a matter of days than she has or has any ability to replace in a matter of decades," Smith Barney fought Mrs. Kehr nearly every step of the way. The giant broker, with assets of over $1.5 billion, had attempted to portray Mrs. Kehr as "sophisticated" and thus able to understand what she was doing and signing, in spite of the fact that in January 1980 Mrs. Kehr was studying from a reading primer that featured such words as "cat," "cap," "pad," "pat," and "pal." In appealing the federal court award of $107,000, Smith Barney did not take issue with the actual facts of the case, but instead contended that one of Mrs. Kehr's attorneys had engaged in misconduct because of various emotional statements at the trial. In rejecting Smith Barney's arguments, Circuit Court Judge Ely wrote: "It seems to me that when one has been so victimized and mistreated as was [Mrs. Kehr] in the present case, the wrongdoer deserves to be condemned in the harshest terms."

"An Outright Scheme to Defraud"

In January 1971, investor Samuel Mihara walked into the Santa Monica, California, office of Dean Witter & Company (now Dean Witter Reynolds) and opened a brokerage account of about $30,000. This money represented a considerable share of Mihara's net worth at the time. Mihara testified that because of his lack of financial background (he was a supervisory engineer for McDonnell Douglas Corporation) he was looking for someone with expertise on which he could depend for investment advice. He also testified that at the initial meeting with the broker, he expressed his fear of a possible layoff at McDonnell Douglas and his concern about the financial security and education of his two daughters. The $30,000 was to be invested according to the broker's recommendations, but subject to Mihara's approval.

The Dean Witter broker recommended that Mihara open a margin account and purchase shares of companies in the double-knit fabric industry. Some of the specific recommendations were: Venice Industries, Devon Apparel, Edmos, Fab Industries, D. H. Industries, and Leslie Fay. The results were disastrous: from January 1971, to May 1973, Mihara's $30,000 account generated losses totaling $46,464. For this "expertise," Mihara paid the broker over $12,000 in commissions.

The U.S. Ninth Circuit Court of Appeals, in affirming a lower-court finding of "churning," noted, "The history of Mihara's investment account with Dean Witter & Company reflects speculative investments, numerous purchases and sales, and substantial reliance on the recommendations of [the broker]." According to court documents, Mihara's account was turned over approximately fourteen times between January 1971, and July 1973. In 1971, 50% of the securities were held for 15 days or less and through June 1973, 81.6% were held for 180 days or less. In its decision, the court said, "The manner in which Mihara's account was handled reflects, at best, a reckless disregard for the client's investment concerns, and, at worst, an outright scheme to defraud plaintiff." The court upheld the district court award of $24,600 in actual damages (approximately half the entire loss experienced by Mihara) and $66,000 in punitive damages.

Check Kiting 101

In May 1985, E. F. Hutton & Company (now Shearson Lehman Hutton) pleaded guilty to 2,000 counts of mail and wire fraud. In what amounted to a check-kiting scheme, the Justice Department said, "Hutton obtained the interest-free use of millions of dollars by intentionally rigging checks in excess of funds it had on deposit in various banks." Hutton, which attempts to present itself to the public as a firm that can be counted on to successfully manage the life savings of investors, occasionally had overdrafts in excess of $250 million and agreed to pay a criminal fine of $2.75 million.

Churning a Charity

A federal court jury found Paine Webber, Jackson & Curtis Inc. and one of its brokers guilty of securities fraud and breach of fiduciary duty and awarded $28.2 million to its client, the DeRance Foundation, a Catholic charitable organization.

DeRance had, in 1983 and 1984, accused Paine Webber of losing $11.5 million of the foundation's money through churning and wildly speculative commodities transactions involving options and futures contracts. DeRance had also accused the broker and Paine Webber of misrepresenting the expertise and track record of the broker handling the account, of using misleading statements regarding the account's performance, and of deliberately misrepresenting the investment strategies the broker intended to follow. According to the complaint, the broker and Paine Webber earned commissions exceeding $3.8 million, with monthly commission charges often surpassing the value of the account.

The jury awarded DeRance $7.7 million in compensatory damages, and $20.5 million in punitive damages. It further ordered that Paine Webber and its broker recover nothing of the $3.2 million deficit in the DeRance account at the time it was finally liquidated. Paine Webber subsequently filed a counterclaim to recover the $3.2 million and to have the verdict overturned.

In rejecting both of Paine Webber's motions, Federal Judge John W. Reynolds noted that the Paine Webber broker "lied to [DeRance's] representatives before they hired him," and also "lied after he was hired" and "lied at trial." Reynolds wrote that Paine Webber "was aware of at least some of [the broker's] misrepresentations and breaches of contract and did next to nothing about them. In fact, Paine Webber compounded the problem by providing [DeRance] with misleading reports." Reynolds also ordered Paine Webber to pay DeRance an additional $3.2 million to cover lost interest during the period the account was being managed by Paine Webber.

In September 1987, Paine Webber appealed the case to the U.S. Seventh Circuit Court. As of the time of this printing, no ruling had been issued.

"It Doesn't Mean Anything"

On the morning of 22 November 1977, Dr. Arnold Silverberg, a veterinarian in Jacksonville, Florida, received a call from his Paine Webber broker, who informed him that a valve manufacturing company named Posi-Seal, Inc. was about to be acquired by another company for $12 per share. Silverberg immediately purchased 2,000 shares at an average price of $5⅜. Over the next four months the broker continued to call Silverberg to tell him that a merger between

Posi-Seal and Masoneilan Corp. was imminent. The broker claimed that this information came from two Masoneilan employees who bought Posi-Seal stock through him. Based upon these claims, Silverberg purchased an additional 31,500 shares of Posi-Seal stock by 22 March 1978. On 29 March 1978, Posi-Seal issued a news release stating that the company "has no knowledge of any reason for the recent price change in its stock." The broker told Silverberg to disregard the release since the merger negotiations were occurring without the knowledge of Posi-Seal's president. The broker's advice: buy more Posi-Seal stock, which Silverberg did, owning about 60,000 shares by mid-July 1978. At about that time, Silverberg attended a Posi-Seal shareholders' meeting; though he talked to no one at the meeting regarding a possible takeover of Posi-Seal, Silverberg returned from the meeting unimpressed with the company. The broker reassured Silverberg that the merger would take place regardless of Posi-Seal's financial position because of the value of a patented valve developed by Posi-Seal.

Based upon repeated assurances from his broker, Silverberg again purchased Posi-Seal stock; he noticed, however, that the confirmation slips were now being marked "unsolicited." Silverberg became concerned, but was told by the broker to "disregard it, it doesn't mean anything," according to court records. "In fact," noted the U.S. Court of Appeals, "Paine Webber had ordered its brokers not to solicit any more orders for Posi-Seal stock due to the substantial holdings of Paine Webber clients in the company."

In January 1979, the broker told Silverberg that a merger announcement was imminent and Silverberg increased his Posi-Seal holdings to a peak of 82,000 shares. On 11 May 1979, Posi-Seal did announce a tentative agreement for it to be acquired by Xomox Corporation; one month later, however, Posi-Seal issued a news release stating that the terms of the merger would be less favorable to Posi-Seal shareholders than initially announced. Posi-Seal's stock immediately dropped, resulting in Silverberg paying $47,000 to meet a margin call. Despite the drop in the price of the stock, the broker advised Silverberg not to sell.

On 5 November 1977, Posi-Seal announced that the prior agreement to be acquired by Xomox was being terminated. The price of Posi-Seal stock plummeted and when Silverberg was unable to meet margin calls, Paine Webber liquidated his account. In December 1979, Silverberg was informed that he owed Paine Webber $25,276; this amount represented the deficit in his margin account after Paine Webber had sold his Posi-Seal stock.

Silverberg filed suit against Paine Webber and the broker, alleging violation of federal securities law, the Florida Securities Act, and common-law fraud and negligence. A United States District Court found for Silverberg on all eight counts of his complaint and awarded $530,000 in compensatory and $75,000 in punitive damages. On 25 July 1983, the United States Eleventh Circuit Court of Appeals affirmed the lower-court ruling on all counts.

"A Scheme to Induce Borrowing"

In early 1974, Clyde and Joy Arrington asked a Merrill Lynch, Pierce, Fenner & Smith Inc. broker to purchase 20,000 shares of Western Airlines stock for them; the Arringtons had recently sold their small family business and retired. The proceeds from the sale—approximately $280,000—were originally invested in a certificate of deposit. The Merrill Lynch broker accepted the order and opened a cash account for the Arringtons.

Not long after opening the account, the broker told Clyde Arrington that Gulf Oil, Syntex, Monsanto, and Stone & Webster stock were good-quality securities and that "Merrill Lynch analysts in New York were predicting substantial near-term [three to six month] gains in these stocks," according to the U.S. Ninth Circuit Court of Appeals. In fact, the court found, "Merrill Lynch analysts had never made the predictions [the broker] had represented."

In April 1974, the broker tried to convince Arrington to open a margin account. Arrington resisted; he did not know what a margin account was and told the broker he did not want to borrow money. According to the court, "[The broker] explained that the interest charged on the margin account would be the prime rate on the day of the purchase plus 1%. Arrington asked what risk was involved. [The broker] responded that there was little risk, and repeated the nonexistent predictions of spectacular near-term gains." On the basis of these predictions, Arrington opened a margin account and purchased, over the succeeding three months, 2,000 shares of Gulf Oil, 1,500 shares of Syntex, 1,000 shares of Monsanto, and 1,000 shares of Stone & Webster. By 1 August 1974, Arrington had accumulated $252,664 in margin debt and was paying several thousand dollars per month in margin interest. As the value of the stocks began dropping, the margin calls started coming; by 3 September 1974, Arrington had received his third call for additional funds and was told that he "either had to put up money or sell some stock in a three-to-one ratio to maintain the account," according to court records. The value of Arrington's four stocks had dropped from an aggregate purchase price of $240,807 to only $190,500 by 26 August 1974.

In 1975, the Arringtons brought suit against Merrill Lynch and the broker, charging violation of federal securities law. After a bench trial, the broker and Merrill Lynch were found guilty of violating section 10(b) of the Securities Exchange Act of 1934, and the Arringtons were awarded $53,820 plus prejudgment interest from 26 August 1974. The defendants appealed the lower-court ruling, contending that no violation of securities law had occurred. The appellate court disagreed, finding that the Merrill Lynch broker "misrepresented to Arrington the risks of purchasing stocks on margin, the recommendations of Merrill Lynch analysts, and the increased risk of large margin accounts in the market decline he knew was occurring." These misrepresentations, said the court, "made up a scheme to induce Arrington to borrow money from Merrill Lynch to engage in commission-producing securities purchases through Merrill Lynch."

Ms. Raines's "Nephew"

A former broker for Merrill Lynch, Pierce, Fenner & Smith Inc. pleaded guilty to criminal charges that he illegally transferred $174,349 from the account of Ida Nell Raines to his own account.

According to the indictment, on 15 June 1981—four days before terminating his employment with Merrill Lynch—the broker transferred money from Ms. Raines's brokerage account to the Merrill Lynch Government Fund, without his client's knowledge or permission. In establishing the account, the broker forged Ms. Raines's signature on the application, which falsely listed her address as his own and established that all proceeds be sent to a fraudulent bank account without a signature guarantee. Two days after leaving Merrill Lynch the now-former broker posed as Ms. Raines's nephew in opening a joint account at a Memphis, Tennessee, bank. On 13 July 1981, and again on 17 July 1981, the former broker allegedly wired instructions to transfer a total of $174,349.16 to this account, and proceeded to use Ms. Raines's money for his own benefit.

The former broker pleaded guilty to mail and wire fraud and was sentenced to two years probation.

New York Stock Exchange Disciplinary Hearings

Stockbrokers can be held accountable for their actions in various forums besides the courtroom. The New York Stock Exchange carefully monitors the actions of all employees of member organizations. When a complaint regarding broker conduct is made, the matter is investigated and brought before an Exchange Hearing Panel for possible disciplinary action. In the first six months of 1986, over seventy brokers or their firms were disciplined by the exchange. What follows is a small sampling of these cases.

The information in these anecdotes comes directly from official exchange documents and are organized according to the aspect of securities law that was violated. These may include misappropriation of funds, misrepresentation (lying), falsification of documents, unauthorized trading, forgery, theft, churning, unsuitability, and breach of fiduciary duty.

All disciplinary actions in the cases noted are against individuals and not their employer firms and are subject to further review proceedings at the Securities and Exchange Commission. Brokers found guilty by the panel have the right of appeal.

Misappropriation

A former broker for Merrill Lynch was permanently barred from exchange membership by a New York Stock Exchange Hearing Panel for "engaging in conduct inconsistent with just and equitable principles of trade." According to the Exchange, the broker "on about fifty occasions, journaled [switched] positions from his family members' accounts to customers' accounts and profitable positions from customers' accounts to his family members' accounts." For example, on 28 March 1984, the broker purchased twenty-five call options at $3.75 for the account of a family member. Two weeks later, after the value of the options had declined, he "corrected" the trade by transferring the unprofitable purchase into a customer's account. On another occasion, three days after buying 2,000 shares of stock at $34 per share for a customer's account, the broker, after noticing that the stock price had risen to $35.75, again "corrected" the trade, resulting in the purchase being switched from the customer's account to the account of a family member. The broker subsequently sold the stock for a profit of $3,500 (excluding commissions). Merrill Lynch made restitution for the approximately fifty adjustments, repaying customers about $118,000. The broker consented to the Hearing Panel's findings without admitting or denying guilt.

Misappropriation, Misrepresentation

A former broker for E.F. Hutton & Company consented to a finding by a New York Stock Exchange Hearing Panel, without admitting or denying guilt, that he "obtained funds from customers based upon false representations, and misappropriated these funds." According to the panel, beginning in about 1980, the broker "falsely represented to customers of the firm, that if they gave him their funds, he would invest them in a safe, private investment that he was handling outside the firm. Based upon such representations, [the broker] obtained a total of $354,000 from ten customers of the firm." The broker did not invest the funds on behalf of his customers; instead, he allegedly used the money to finance his own securities trading. In the process, the broker lost nearly all the funds. The broker has since settled with two of the customers for about $40,000. Two other customers have forgiven the broker a debt of $35,000. The Hearing Panel imposed a penalty of censure and a permanent bar from membership with any NYSE organization.

Misappropriation, Theft

A former broker for Blunt Ellis & Loewi Inc. was found guilty by a NYSE Hearing Panel of misappropriating funds belonging to customers. The broker was accused of asking five customers of the firm to invest in a private diamond investment that was supposed to return more than 20% per year. In fact, there was no such investment, according to the panel. The broker then requested that the checks— totaling $34,500—be made payable to himself, which he then converted to his own use and benefit, without the knowledge or permission of the investors. On 10 February 1986, the Hearing Panel ordered that the broker be permanently barred from associating with any member organization.

In the case of the leaky mailbox, a former broker for Dean Witter Reynolds Inc. was found guilty by a NYSE Hearing Panel of misappropriating funds belonging to his customers. According to the panel, on 11 July 1984, a customer of the broker drew two checks, payable to the firm: one, for $2,000, was to be deposited in his brother's IRA account; the other, for $5,000 was to be credited to his mother's account. The broker telephoned the customer that the checks, which apparently were left in the broker's mailbox, had gotten wet and were unusable. The broker then went to the customer's house to get replacement checks, and asked that the payee lines on the checks be left blank, "because the transactions were in progress," according to exchange documents. The broker promised to fill in the blank payee lines later. The panel concluded that the broker did indeed fill in the lines—*with his own name.* He then negotiated the checks and converted the funds to his personal use and benefit. Dean Witter Reynolds has reimbursed the client for the $7,000 and the broker was permanently barred from associating with any New York Stock Exchange member organization.

A former broker for E. F. Hutton was found guilty by a NYSE Hearing Panel of misappropriating client funds. While working as a registered representative for Hutton, the broker allegedly received an order to purchase $2,000 of a mutual fund; the broker executed the order and asked the customer to make the check payable to him. The broker then cashed the check and converted the proceeds to his own use and benefit. Hutton reimbursed the customer for the $2,000 that was stolen. On 20 June 1986, the Hearing Panel permanently barred the broker from any association with New York Stock Exchange member firms.

Misappropriation, Forgery

A former Merrill Lynch broker was found guilty by a NYSE Hearing Panel of forging customers' names to letters of authorization regarding fund transfers and of misappropriating funds. While working as a broker at a Merrill Lynch branch office, the broker allegedly misappropriated $85,000; the firm has since fully reimbursed the customers whose funds were misused. On thirty-seven other occasions, from March 1983 through July 1985, the broker forged the signatures of nine of his clients, resulting in approximately $250,000 to be transferred out of the proper accounts and into the accounts of other customers. At first, the broker used the transfers to hide trading losses in some of his clients' accounts; later, transfers were made to reimburse customers whose accounts were raided earlier. The broker was permanently barred from associating with any New York Stock Exchange member organization.

Unauthorized Trading, Sharing in Losses

A former broker for Merrill Lynch consented to a finding by a NYSE Hearing Panel, without admitting or denying guilt, that he violated Exchange rule 408(b) by "exercising discretionary power in customers' accounts without written authorization and violated Exchange rule 352(c) by sharing in losses in a customer's account." According to exchange documents, the broker executed nine trades between 12 and 16 October 1981, in a customer's account without permission to do so. When these trades resulted in losses, the broker deposited $3,000 of his own funds into the customer's account to help cover some of the losses. Merrill Lynch settled with the customer for $61,800 and the broker contributed $44,500 to the settlement. One month later, however, the broker executed eleven additional unauthorized trades in another customer's account; these trades had a market value of approximately $175,000. The trades were canceled when the customer objected, and the firm subsequently reached a settlement with the customer, sustaining a loss of $4,500. The broker agreed to repay his firm for the full amount of the loss. The Hearing Panel censured the broker and barred him from associating with any member organization for six months.

Unauthorized Trading, Breach of Fiduciary Duty

A former broker for Paine Webber, Jackson & Curtis Inc. was found guilty by a NYSE Hearing Panel of violating Exchange rule 408(a) in that he "1) exercised discretionary power in customer accounts without prior written authorization; engaged in conduct inconsistent with just and equitable principles of trade in that he failed to enter orders given by customers." According to the panel, during January and February, 1984, the broker effected thirty-one trades involving gold and silver contracts in the accounts of three customers without their knowledge or consent. The broker also failed to enter seven gold and silver futures orders requested by five customers. The results of the broker's actions, said the panel, was a loss of $62,217.68 to these customers. The panel ordered that the broker be permanently barred from associating with any New York Stock Exchange member firm.

Misappropriation, Misrepresentation, Forgery

A former broker for Thomson McKinnon Securities, Inc., consented to a NYSE Hearing Panel finding, without admitting or denying guilt, that she "1) misrepresented to a firm customer the status of the customer's account, 2) signed a second customer's name, without his knowledge or authorization, to a letter authorizing [the broker firm] to issue a check drawn against that customer's account, payable to the first customer, and 3) misappropriated funds belonging to a firm customer." According to the panel, in August 1984, the broker told a client that the value of his account was over $30,000 when in fact the value was only $15,000. Shortly thereafter, the customer withdrew $15,000 (unknowingly emptying the account). Three months later, thinking that $15,000 still remained, the customer asked for the remainder of his funds. The broker temporarily solved this crisis by raiding another account, transferring $17,047 to the account of the first customer, who in turn withdrew and used the money. The firm has agreed to reimburse the raided client in full. The broker was barred by the Hearing Panel from ever associating with a New York Stock Exchange member organization.

A former broker for Thomson McKinnon Securities, Inc., consented to a NYSE Hearing Panel finding, without admitting or denying guilt, that he "1) falsely represented to a customer . . . that he had executed trades in the customer's account which the customer had requested, 2) signed a customer's name to a letter of authorization causing his firm to transfer funds from the customer's account without her knowledge or authorization, and 3) misappropriated funds belonging to customers of his firm." The trouble began, according to exchange documents, in mid-1985, when one of the broker's clients placed orders with the broker. Unfortunately, the client's account was restricted and no further business was permitted. (A customer's account can be restricted for a variety of reasons, including nonpayment of funds, insufficient margin, failure to deliver securities, and excessive or speculative activity which is deemed inappropriate given the client's financial condition.) Instead of telling the client that the account was closed to new business, the broker allegedly lied, telling the client that the trades had been executed. Some of the trades requested by the client would have been profitable and the client wanted his money. To prevent the client from realizing that the orders had never been entered, the broker raided the account of another firm customer for $27,000, without that customer's knowledge or permission. Later, when additional funds were needed, the broker tapped into still another customer's account, this time for $25,000, again without authorization. The firm has reimbursed both customers whose accounts were raided for the amount that was wrongfully transferred out of their accounts. The panel determined that the broker be permanently barred from association with any member firm.

Misrepresentation, Falsification of Documents, Forgery

A former broker for Merrill Lynch consented to a finding by a NYSE Hearing Panel, without admitting or denying guilt, that he: "1) made material misstatements to customers, 2) altered various entries on a monthly account statement, 3) wrote and signed a letter to a firm customer which falsely purported to have been written and signed by a member of his firm's legal department, and 4) caused a firm customer to pay unnecessary sales charges." In September 1984, the broker allegedly induced a client to sell a certificate of deposit by quoting an incorrect sale price, causing a loss of approximately $1,800. The broker also misrepresented that the mutual fund he was recommending as a replacement for the sold CD was no-load. In fact, according to the panel, the broker knew that this was a lie. To conceal the sales charge on the mutual fund, the broker altered a photocopy of the monthly statement. On at least four other occasions, the broker misrepresented mutual funds to prospective investors as no-load when in fact he knew otherwise. He also induced another client—a defined benefit plan—to sell a CD and invest in a mutual fund by again misquoting the sale price of the CD and representing the mutual fund as no-load. To make matters worse, the broker recommended that the proceeds from the CD be invested in three separate mutual funds; in fact, the broker knew the funds not only carried sales charges but by splitting the proceeds into three different funds, the customer would be forced to pay a higher sales charge by missing the cumulative breakpoints (reductions in the sales charge corresponding to increases in the amount invested). Merrill Lynch reimbursed all customers for the sales charges and the interest on the CDs, amounting to $19,478.50. The broker was censured by the Hearing Panel and barred from associating with any New York Stock Exchange member firm for three years.

Misappropriation, Forgery, Theft

A former broker for Smith Barney and for Paine Webber was found guilty by a NYSE Hearing Panel of "1) causing checks to be issued against customers' accounts without their knowledge or permission, 2) without the knowledge or authorization of customers, endorsed . . . their names on checks payable to the customers, and 3) misappropriated funds belonging to firm customers." According to the panel, from September 1983, through April 1984, the broker "caused twelve checks totaling $265,647, payable to three individual customers, to be drawn against their securities accounts without their knowledge or authorization." The broker then converted the funds to his own use and benefit. The Hearing Panel permanently barred the broker from associating with any New York Stock Exchange member organization.

A former broker for Dean Witter Reynolds was found guilty by a NYSE Hearing Panel of misappropriating funds belonging to a customer. The broker serviced a money market fund for the customer; the account was set up to allow for check writing privileges. According to exchange documents, the broker visited the client's home at least once a month, ostensibly to explain the account statements. While at the customer's home, and without her knowledge or permission, the broker removed several checks from the customer's money market checkbook. He subsequently wrote and cashed twelve checks, payable to himself, for a total of $72,000. The broker then deposited the checks and converted the funds for his own use and benefit. On 20 June 1986, the Hearing Panel ruled that the broker be permanently barred from associating with any New York Stock Exchange member firm.

Misrepresentation, Unauthorized Trading, Unsuitability, Falsification of Documents

A former broker for E. F. Hutton consented to a finding by a NYSE Hearing Panel, without admitting or denying guilt, that he "1) prepared an option account form which reflected materially false information about a customer, 2) effected unsuitable trading in the account of the customer, and 3) prepared and caused to be delivered to the customer a written summary of the equity in the customer's account which he knew to be false," according to the Hearing Panel. While working as a registered representative for Hutton, the broker suggested to a client that she trade options in her account, and proceeded to fill out the option agreement form using incorrect information. "[The broker's] material falsification of the option information form caused [the client's] account to appear not unsuitable for options trading," said the disciplinary summary. As an example, the broker is accused of listing the client's annual income as $25,000–$39,000, when in fact it was less than $5,000. The broker allegedly made these inaccuracies "knowingly and willfully." The broker then began making trades in the customer's account without written authorization; between

October 1980, and February 1983, the broker is accused of making 175 option transactions. The value of the customer's account fell from $80,547.25 at the beginning of October 1980, to a low of $372 in November 1982. In January 1983, the client asked to see a written summary of the equity in her account; the broker prepared a statement that "represented that her portfolio had a market value of $92,714— in fact, the market value at the time was $9,242." The panel found that the broker "knew that the document he prepared contained materially false information," and permanently barred the broker from associating with any New York Stock Exchange member organization.

Misappropriation, Misrepresentation, Unauthorized Trading, Forgery, Theft

A former broker for Gruntal & Company Inc. consented to a finding by a NYSE Hearing Panel, without admitting or denying guilt, that she "1) caused checks to be drawn against customers' accounts . . . without the knowledge or authorization of these customers, 2) signed the names of customers as endorsements on checks payable to their order, without their knowledge or consent, 3) misappropriated funds belonging to customers, and 4) improperly prevented the mailing of account statements to a customer." The broker was also accused of trading in a customer's account without that customer's prior written permission. On one occasion, a customer brought five municipal bonds, with a face value of $25,000, to the broker, with instructions to deposit them in the customer's account. Instead, according to exchange documents, the broker put the bonds in her own account, sold them, and used the proceeds for her own benefit. The customer never received any information about the account because the broker allegedly intercepted all correspondence. On another occasion, the broker caused a check for $2,700 to be drawn against the account of another customer; the broker then forged the customer's signature, added her own endorsement, and converted the proceeds to her own use and benefit. On still another occasion, the broker bought 300 shares of stock, worth approximately $2,900, in a client's account without that client's knowledge. On 18 May 1984, the broker also caused a check to be drawn in the amount of $2,000 against the account of that same customer; the broker then forged the customer's signature and converted the proceeds to her own use and benefit. The Hearing Panel permanently barred the broker from associating with any New York Stock Exchange member organization.

Unauthorized Trading, Theft, Misappropriation, Falsification of Documents, Misrepresentation

A former broker for Prudential-Bache Securities was found guilty by a New York Stock Exchange Hearing Panel of exercising discretionary authority in a customer's account without prior written permission, and of engaging in conduct inconsistent with fair and just principles of trade. The panel found that the broker "1) sold bonds which did not belong to him and wrongfully retained the proceeds of that sale, 2) misappropriated funds belonging to a customer, 3) prepared and delivered to this customer confirmation of trades which had not occurred, and 4) made a material misstatement to this customer; engaged in fraud or fraudulent acts in that, with the intent to deceive customers, he obtained bonds from those customers, sold the bonds, wrongfully retained the proceeds of the sale, and prepared and delivered to the customers false confirmations to conceal his conversion of the bonds." According to the Hearing Panel, in July 1982, the broker asked his father and stepmother to lend him ten revenue bonds for his use in opening his own account at the firm. The broker promised his father that he would return the bonds within thirty days; instead, he sold the bonds without the knowledge or permission of his parents and retained the proceeds of the sale—$10,646.11—for his own use and benefit. After the thirty-day loan period had expired, the broker's father asked that the bonds be sold and the proceeds used to purchase other bonds. The broker told his father that the requested trades had been executed; to cover his tracks, the broker then prepared confirmations that falsely showed the sale of the original bonds and subsequent purchase of other bonds. The Hearing Panel permanently barred the broker from associating with any member firm.

Falsification of Documents, Unsuitability, Churning, Misappropriation, Theft

A former broker for Bache Halsey Stuart Shields (now Prudential-Bache Securities) consented to a finding by a NYSE Hearing Panel, without admitting or denying guilt, that he "1) violated the principles of Exchange Rule 405(1) by providing inaccurate information concerning a customer on an option client information form, 2) caused unsuitable trading in the account of a customer, 3) churned or excessively traded a customer's account in view of her financial objectives and securities experience, 4) effected trades in a customer's account for his own benefit, 5) utilized the equity in the account of a customer of his member organization for his own purposes, and 6) misappropriated the funds of a customer." The broker was accused of effecting 176 trades in the account of a client without receiving written permission; an analysis of account activity revealed an annual portfolio turnover rate of 9.74. The activity, much of it speculative in nature, generated commissions of $69,278, which represented 33.9% of the original value of the account. The broker's unauthorized trading caused a loss of $34,935 to the customer; in December 1983, the firm paid the customer $54,000 to settle a claim arising from the broker's actions. The Hearing Panel ordered that the broker be permanently barred from associating with any New York Stock Exchange member firm.

Securities and Exchange Commission Actions

As the government agency charged with the general oversight of the securities industry, the Securities and Exchange Commission regularly conducts investigations into alleged broker fraud and is empowered to temporarily or permanently suspend a broker's license. Following are four examples of SEC actions against brokers:

Stock Manipulation

A former broker for Bache Halsey Stuart Shields Inc. consented to a Securities and Exchange Commission ruling, without admitting or denying guilt, that she manipulated the stock of Intercontinental Diamond Corporation in 1980. The agency accused the broker of generating buying interest in the stock by falsely touting it to investors and by prearranging trades to make the market for the stock appear hotter than it really was. The SEC suspended the broker from working for any brokerage firm for sixty days.

Playing the Float

E. F. Hutton & Company was censured by the Securities and Exchange Commission for keeping nearly $200,000 in interest from its customers' accounts that should have been sent to mutual funds purchased by the clients. From 29 December 1981, until 15 April, 1983, Hutton "played the float" for up to five days and earned $191,000 in interest that rightly belonged to its customers.

Falsification of Documents, Unsuitability, Unauthorized Trading

A former broker for Smith Barney was censured by the SEC for allegedly falsifying the applications of several customers, including several retired investors, to allow for high-risk, uncovered-option trading. According to the SEC, the broker then began making trades without the knowledge or permission of the clients. "Certain customers had no knowledge of [some] transactions in their accounts until they received telegrams informing them of their losses," the SEC charged. By June 1982, nine of the broker's customers had incurred losses totaling $780,000. The broker consented to the SEC findings without admitting or denying guilt. "I acted in the best interest of my customers," the broker told the *Wall Street Journal*.[56]

Misrepresentation, Falsification of Documents, Failure to Supervise

An administrative law judge for the SEC ruled that a Merrill Lynch broker made false and misleading statements to customers regarding a 1979 tender offer for Harnischfeger Corporation stock. The SEC complaint alleges that the broker induced customers to buy Harnischfeger stock by lying about the prospects for a takeover. At the time, Mannesmann AG of West Germany was attempting to acquire Harnischfeger; the broker apparently neglected to inform clients that the Federal Trade Commission was trying to block the Harnischfeger acquisition in federal court. The SEC official also ruled that the Merrill Lynch broker falsified order tickets for customer purchases of Harnischfeger stock. Merrill Lynch consented to a SEC finding that it failed to adequately supervise its broker, without admitting or denying guilt. The broker has the option of appealing the charges.

Insider Trading

No discussion of fraud and corruption in the brokerage business could be complete without at least some mention of the insider-trading scandals that first came to public attention in early 1986. Investor Ivan Boesky, accused by federal prosecutors of earning more than $50 million from illegal insider trading, paid a $100 million civil penalty and was sentenced to three years in prison. As part of his plea bargain, Boesky was reportedly "singing" to authorities about others involved in his scheme, and the general consensus among Wall Streeters was that Boesky and others already nabbed represent just the tip of a very large iceberg.

While Boesky himself was not employed by any Wall Street broker, his scheme began to unravel when the SEC closed in on the illegal trading activities of several prominent brokerage-house investment bankers. Investment banking, especially that area dealing with mergers and acquisitions, is a natural breeding ground for illegal tips since the nature of the work requires information not yet available to the general public. But the reasons for Wall Street's worst scandal since the 1920s go far beyond the ready availability of top-secret information. Indeed, the scandal's roots touch the very heart of a sick and perverted business.

It is only poetic justice that the brokerage industry's involvement in the insider-trading scandal would come courtesy of its investment banking divisions, since these sectors are perhaps the perfect metaphor for the brokerage industry as a whole: drunk with greed, practicing the most materialistic and inhumane of values, and serving no useful purpose aside from aiding wealthy and greedy men and women to become still wealthier.

It is a widely shared belief among those not standing to profit from investment banking deals that the multibillion-dollar merger and acquisition business contributes little to overall gains in productivity, efficiency, or job formation. Far from creating new and useful businesses, most deals merely shuffle existing assets, often at the expense of jobs and careers, and for the exclusive benefit of an already wealthy corporate raider, a brokerage firm, and the investment bankers it employs. While jobs are lost and careers destroyed, the brokerage firms involved can earn sums as high as $10 million per deal.

Attracted by starting salaries of close to $100,000, business majors and MBAs from America's most prestigious schools are flocking to investment banking in numbers formerly reserved for law and advertising. According to the Harvard School of Business, more than 25% of its MBAs graduating in 1986 will choose investment banking. Why? In the words of *Newsweek* magazine, "The naked pursuit of money has gripped the imagination of today's best and brightest the way the dream of ending war and discrimination inspired an earlier generation. The motive: money, pure and simple."[57] The MBAs know that within five years they could well be earning in excess of $1,000,000 per year; in 1986, the superstars of the mergers and acquisitions business earned close to $3 million in salary and bonuses. Typical of the moral bankruptcy of the industry is the fact that few of these fortune hunters seem to care what good actually results from their work; satisfying their greed is their main concern. "I don't need to make billions of dollars," one investment banker told *Newsweek*. "I only need to make millions."[58]

In the process of earning those millions they will work seventy to eighty hour weeks, leaving little time for family, friends, physical fitness, or personal growth and reflection. Success will be measured not by whether a better world results from their work, but by the final figure on their W-2 form.

It should not be entirely surprising then that some members of the brokerage industry would not be satisfied with their six- and seven-figure incomes, and would use their positions to gain still more profit through illegal trading and the outright selling of secret information. As this book goes to press, more than a dozen insider-trading cases involving brokerage-industry personnel had already been disposed of. Following are brief summaries of five of these cases; the names of the guilty are provided, since each case had already received extensive publicity and the identities of the accused are already part of the public record.

"See How Rich I Am"

Dennis Levine, a former managing director and mergers and acquisitions specialist at Drexel Burnham Lambert Inc. was charged by the SEC with using confidential information to earn profits in excess of $11 million. For a six-year period beginning about 1980, Levine used his position at the vortex of the high-roller corporate takeover game to profit by trading on inside information in his own account and by selling inside information to others, including Ivan Boesky. On 5 June 1986, Levine pleaded guilty to four felony charges, including one count of perjury and two counts of income-tax evasion. As part of his plea bargain, Levine agreed to tell the SEC and federal prosecutors what he knew about illegal insider trading on Wall Street and to pay back the $11.6 million he earned through his illegal activities. He was sentenced to four concurrent two-year prison terms and fined $362,000.

It is an interesting and revealing curiosity of the Levine affair that as the SEC began to close in on him—a fact of which Levine was almost certainly aware—his illegal activities became even more brazen, as if calling out to be caught. Levine's curious behavior speaks volumes about the value system of many brokers and investment bankers: In an industry in which the size of one's bank account becomes the sole measure of personal worth, illegally earned profits, which, by necessity are not registered on the public scoreboard, contribute nothing to ego gratification until the activity is detected and the booty tallied. Only then can the public, and more importantly, one's fellow securities-industry workers, truly appreciate what an exceptionally bright and wealthy person the perpetrator is. In the case of Dennis Levine, now we know.

Surviving on $2 Million a Year

Kidder Peabody investment banker and managing director Martin A. Siegel was charged by the SEC with trading takeover secrets to Ivan Boesky in exchange for $700,000. Beginning in 1982, Siegel allegedly provided information to Boesky regarding the takeover activities of six Kidder Peabody clients: Carnation Co., Natomas, Inc., Bendix Corp., Getty Oil, Midlands Energy, and Pargas, Inc. From this information, Boesky earned profits of about $33 million. Siegel pleaded guilty to two felony counts and is awaiting sentencing. Information provided by Siegel to government investigators led to the indictment of three additional brokerage officials.

An Extra $3 Million

Robert M. Wilkis, a mergers and acquisitions specialist for the broker-age firm of Lazard Frères & Company was charged by the SEC with padding his six-figure salary with about $3 million in profits resulting from illegal trading on inside information. Wilkis allegedly used various aliases and secret bank accounts in the Cayman Islands, Liberia, and the Bahamas in an effort to conceal his identity. According to the SEC, Wilkis conducted about fifty illegal trades over a six-year period beginning in 1979; in one trade alone, in 1984, he bought

20,000 shares of Carter Hawley Hale Stores stock after learning that a client of Lazard Frères was planning a takeover bid. When the tender offer was eventually made, Hawley stock shot up, resulting in a $95,000 profit. Charged with securities fraud, mail fraud, tax evasion, and unreported income, Wilkis signed a consent decree, without admitting or denying guilt, in which he agreed to pay back $3.3 million in illegal profits and fines. He was sentenced to one year in prison.

"Putting" It to the Public

The SEC charged the giant Wall Street firm of First Boston & Company with earning $132,138 through illegal trading in Cigna Corporation stock and options. According to the SEC complaint, investment bankers at First Boston were consulted in early 1986 by executives of Cigna regarding its plans to add about $1 billion to its casualty-loss reserves, a development with negative short-term implications for Cigna's stock. SEC rules require that once in possession of such inside information, a brokerage firm cannot trade in that company's securities. The equity trading desk at First Boston, however, allegedly used the information to dump 21,000 shares onto the public market and to buy "put" options on the stock (which appreciate in value as the stock declines). When the price of Cigna's stock did in fact fall about five points in one day, First Boston had made its profit and bought back the shares it had sold earlier. First Boston called its actions "inadvertent but serious" and agreed to settle the complaint by paying a $246,276 penalty. It did so, however, without admitting or denying guilt.

Their Word Was Not Their Bond

The giant Wall Street firm of Drexel Burnham Lambert, which earned billions of dollars for its role in the megabuck corporate takeover game of the 1980s, agreed to plead guilty in December 1988 to six federal felony counts of mail, wire, and securities fraud in exchange for the government's dropping of possible racketeering charges against the firm. Under the terms of the plea bargain, which was contingent upon Drexel reaching a settlement with the Securities and Exchange Commission on charges of insider trading, stock manipulation and fraud, Drexel would pay the largest fine ever handed down for securities fraud—$650 million—and agree to cooperate fully with the government's continuing investigation into possible criminal wrongdoing on the part of Drexel Burnham Lambert employees. Drexel earned a profit of more than $600 million in 1986 alone, largely through its aggressive underwriting of high-yield, high-risk "junk bonds,*" which are used by its corporate raider clients to finance takeovers of American corporations.

"Parking" Its Ethics

In June 1987, Kidder Peabody & Company consented to an SEC decree, without admitting or denying guilt, that it return $13.7 million in profits earned through illegal insider trading and pay an $11.6 million penalty. In return, federal prosecutors agreed to drop criminal charges against the firm. According to the SEC, Kidder Peabody not only benefited from illegal tips supplied by its then managing director, Martin Siegel, but also aided arbitrageur Ivan Boesky's illegal-trading schemes by deliberately concealing his identity as the owner of certain large stock positions—a practice known as "parking*"—apparently in return for his substantial investment business.

Avoiding the Mess and Getting Even

Professional salesmen masquerading as investment professionals. Relying on research that is too inaccurate to be useful. Laboring under a morass of conflicts of interest and holding enough power to deeply harm. That's the American brokerage industry.

Fortunately, there are alternatives to playing the broker game: no-load mutual funds, private professional money management, and advisory newsletters each can offer you competent and valuable investment advice without the conflicts of interest that permeate the broker business. And if you have already been harmed by some type of broker fraud, legal relief is available.

CHAPTER 7

Getting Your Due

You are an investor and you feel you have been burned by a stockbroker. What legal recourse do you have? Is there any way to get your money back? What is this arbitration procedure you've heard about? Would it do any good to complain to the SEC? What would a complaint cost, and what are your chances of winning? What documents should you retain? What are the respective advantages and disadvantages of arbitration and lawsuits? Can you undertake any legal action without hiring an attorney? When would a class-action suit be useful?

These and other questions are of more than academic concern to thousands of investors who find themselves caught in the middle of a battle between brokerage houses that impose outrageous sales pressures on their brokers and the brokers' natural inclination to do whatever is necessary to remain employed. These pressures, exacerbated by the rapid growth in the number of brokers scavenging the public's investment dollar, create an atmosphere in which brokers frequently feel the need to break the law in order to keep their jobs.

Fortunately, there are several possible legal remedies available to you if you've suffered at the hands of your broker; this chapter will attempt to explain the key features of each and serve to alert you to some of the legal options at your disposal. The information is not intended as a substitute for legal counsel, however, as each case is unique and should be analyzed on its own merits.

What to Look Out For

First of all, it must be noted that the largest single category of broker fraud—that of a professional salesman masquerading as an investment professional—is not illegal. It is not unlawful to be incompetent, and most of the cases in which investors lose money arise simply as a result of brokers trying to perform tasks for which they are not qualified. If you follow a broker's bad advice and lose money as a result, there is usually no legal recourse available. There are, however, several categories of events leading to investor losses that go beyond mere incompetence and are often sufficient grounds in themselves for legal action. The following are brief descriptions of several areas of possible contention.

UNSUITABILITY. Nearly all investments sold by stockbrokers require that the buyer be "suitable," i.e., have the sufficient financial net worth, annual income, experience, and knowledge necessary to understand and shoulder the risks inherent in the investment. Additionally, the investment must be consistent with the client's stated investment objective of growth, income, tax relief, etc. Some investments, such as limited partnerships, have black-and-white requirements with respect to net worth and annual income; others, such as stocks and bonds, are more judgment calls requiring a degree of common sense and interpretation. For example, a seventy-five-year-old widow struggling to make ends meet on a monthly social security check would have an obvious need for a safe, liquid, relatively high-yielding income-producing investment. For such a client, even a high-quality growth stock such as IBM may be considered unsuitable because of its low current yield (dividend), although terms such as "high" and "low" are relative and sure grounds for controversy. But whether the suitability standards are explicitly spelled out or somewhat vague, they apply equally to all investments; it is not surprising that unsuitability is the leading cause of legal actions taken against stockbrokers.

CHURNING. Churning is the practice of generating frequent and pointless trading activity in a client's account for the sole purpose of creating brokerage commissions. It can occur regardless of whether or not the client has granted the broker "discretion" (the power to trade without the client's prior knowledge or approval), though it is considerably easier to prove in discretionary accounts, if only because the abuse is often more blatant. Churning can also occur in instances where the broker secures the client's permission before making each pointless trade; after all, the ability to repeatedly dupe an investor does not insulate the supersalesman from the law. (See *Mihara v. Dean Witter*, chapter six.) While there is no universally accepted numerical definition for what constitutes churning, if the total value of the buy and sell transactions in your account exceeds four times the account's original value in a given year, chances are good that you've been churned.

FAILURE TO MENTION ALL PERTINENT FACTS. Even though stockbrokers have a legal right to be incompetent, they do not have the right to withhold information that could be considered material to an investor's ability to make an informed decision. For example, a broker pushing U.S. Government bonds as "government guaranteed" but failing to warn of the inherent resale price fluctuations would certainly be guilty of withholding pertinent information, as is a broker who hustles XYZ Corp. stock without mentioning that the company's balance sheet is 95% debt. A broker could also be liable for failing to mention a significant negative event that may be pending and of which the broker is aware, such as an antitrust action, or the imminent introduction of a competing product, or perhaps an IRS ruling regarding back taxes. If the information is important, the broker must tell a prospective buyer of it before accepting any business.

HINTS OF INSIDE INFORMATION. It is illegal for anyone, including brokers or their clients, to invest on the basis of information not also available to the general public. Such use of inside information creates an unfair advantage and is prohibited. But precisely because that advantage can be so profitable, references to inside information, whether firsthand, secondhand, or total fiction, can be an extremely effective method for a broker to generate activity in a client's account. Significantly, however, recent court decisions have come down solidly in favor of investors who have lost money on the basis of "hot tips" from brokers, even though the attempt to capitalize on the tip was itself illegal.

EXCESSIVE MARKUPS ON MARKET-MAKER SECURITIES*. Brokerage firms often sell securities from their own inventories, i.e., stocks or bonds in which they are "making a market." Since most of the securities are over-the-counter and trade on the basis of nebulous bid and ask prices, a firm can often hide commissions, which in fact can be double, triple, or even quadruple the rate payable on listed stocks. The investor receives only a "net" price on the confirmation and can only guess at the actual size of the commission paid.

MISREPRESENTATION. This category goes beyond mere incompetence or lying through omission. Often a broker will simply overtly lie, using a figure or story he knows to be wrong to buttress a sales presentation. The misrepresentation need not be spectacular to be significant; a broker pushing an oil company's stock on the basis of its supposed 100 million barrels of reserves could be found liable if the actual level of reserves turned out to be only 50 million barrels. Similarly, a broker promoting a stock on the basis of earnings projections that he knows to be overly optimistic can be held accountable for resulting investor losses. Simply put, brokers have the obligation to tell the whole truth. When they do not, they are liable.

FOOTDRAGGING ON ACCOUNT TRANSFERS. Let's say that you are unhappy with the performance of your brokerage Individual Retirement Account (IRA). You ask for a full liquidation in order to transfer the account's asserts to another money manager. The brokerage is not pleased to receive such a request and reacts by delaying, stonewalling, and generally doing nothing. In the meantime, the investment into which you had intended to switch takes off, resulting in missed profits and a subsequent higher purchase price. Is the brokerage firm liable for the lost profit? Each case is different, but under New York Stock Exchange Rule 412, adopted in 1971, accounts must be transferred within ten days. The Securities and Exchange Commission has reported that footdragging on account transfers (especially IRAs) is a rapidly growing source of investor complaints.

POOR EXECUTIONS. While in the final deliberative process before buying a stock or bond, a prospective investor will frequently ask for the latest price quote; if satisfied, the client will request that the security be purchased "at the market," and await the confirmation of the exact price. Occasionally, that price may be a light-year removed from the price the broker had quoted only moments before the trade was executed. What happened? Several possibilities exist: the market may have spurted just prior to the execution; the quote may have been on the "bid" side and the purchase transacted on the higher "ask" side; the broker may have lied to induce the buying decision; or perhaps the firm's floor trader may have done a poor job of executing the trade. Whatever the reason, poor executions are a common cause of broker litigations.

BACKOFFICE FOUL-UPS. There are times when mistakes will be made that are the result of human error by a firm's backoffice personnel: a typesetter may punch in the wrong number or date; a secretary may lose a check; a certificate may be lost. Any number of essentially clerical errors may occur. They are almost always unintentional and should be easily solved without legal action.

Arbitration

If you feel that you have a legitimate case against a broker or brokerage firm, you must then decide what specific form of action to take in your attempt to obtain relief. There are essentially two choices:

arbitration or lawsuit. Each has distinct advantages and disadvantages. The choice of most investors is arbitration, largely because it is usually cheaper, faster, and more private than taking a brokerage firm to court. Arbitration would likely be the choice of even more investors if the process were more widely publicized and understood; because the entire procedure is designed to move in complete privacy, many investors have no idea that the arbitration option even exists.

Arbitration functions much like a small-claims court, though it follows carefully spelled-out rules. Investors filing for arbitration must submit a deposit to the sponsoring organization of from $15 for disputes of $1,000 or less, to $750 for claims exceeding $100,000. (A complete list of sponsoring organizations can be found on pages 129–30.) The director of arbitration then appoints a panel of one, three, or five arbitrators, depending on the size of the claim. Unless otherwise instructed by the claimant, the majority of the arbitrators will be from outside the securities industry. A hearing date is then set, usually in a large city near the claimant's residence, and the claimant and respondent (the party against whom a claim is made) are allowed to subpoena documents and witnesses. Claimants are not required to be represented by legal counsel, though whether or not they choose to use an attorney, the broker's firm almost certainly will.

The hearing itself flows much like a court case; opening statements are made, witnesses testify, cross-examination is allowed, rebuttal evidence is presented, and summations are made. The arbitrators make no immediate award; both parties can expect to be notified of the decision by mail, usually within six weeks. The total elapsed time from the date of initial filing to the final judgment averages nine months, though Simplified Arbitration cases—those involving $5,000 or less and handled without a hearing—are usually resolved in about four months. The ruling of the arbitrators is final; in choosing arbitration the claimant waives the right of appeal and also surrenders the ability to pursue the same charges in court. Additionally, until very recently punitive damages were virtually never awarded in the arbitration format.

The arbitration process is sponsored by the various stock exchanges and generally receives mixed reviews for impartiality and fairness. Nearly everyone agrees, however, that despite its continuing flaws, the system has been improved in recent years. In response to the widely held public perception of industry bias in the 1970s, the Securities and Exchange Commission, the government agency charged with the overall supervision of the securities industry, formed the Securities Industry Conference on Arbitration, which included representatives of all stock exchanges and the National Association of Securities Dealers. The result of that conference was a unified code of arbitration, assuring investors that the arbitration process will be the same regardless of where it is pursued, as well as significant improvements aimed at giving the small investor a better chance against the large brokerage houses.

Dan Brecher, a noted New York City attorney specializing in securities law and author of many highly useful articles and a book on the subject, has noticed the improvement. "There has been a change. Arbitration now has allowances for some of the things that I was critical of in the past," Brecher said, "such as pre-hearing discovery so that you could find out what was going to be brought out at the hearing." The rule changes have apparently been implemented as well. "I've been serving recently on some arbitration panels just to see if they're really going forward with the kind of changes that had been put into the rules, and they have," noted Brecher.[FF]

The apparent increase in fairness is reflected in the better than 50% pro-claimant decision rate since 1980. The table below measures the growth of arbitration cases since 1980 involving the public and includes only cases brought to a final decision.

Year	Public Cases Decided	Claimant Wins	% of Claimant Wins
1980	410	205	50%
1981	532	264	49%
1982	558	293	52%
1983	622	331	53%
1984	736	336	49%
1985	961	530	55%
1986	432	210	49%
1987	378	200	53%
Totals	4,629	2,369	51%

Source: New York Stock Exchange

It is important to note that the 51% rate of awards to claimants does not necessarily mean that the claimant received the full amount in dispute, only that the claimant received *something*. Many of the claimant "winners," in fact, receive little more than a small fraction of their original claim. Nonetheless, it is clear that the arbitration process is a viable option for investors seeking a low-cost, relatively fast way to recoup losses suffered as a result of some types of broker fraud.

If you are considering taking a dispute to arbitration, there are a few simple procedures you should follow. In order, they are:

1. **Phone Call to Broker.** In some cases disputes can be handled by simply communicating the problem to the broker. There is no need to proceed further if the matter can be resolved with a phone call.

2. **Letter to Branch Manager.** Assuming your broker does not provide the relief you are seeking, the next step is to notify the branch office manager, in writing, of the problem. A phone call will not be sufficient; brokerage management will not take any problem seriously that is not in writing. Send a copy of the letter to the Director of Compliance of the brokerage firm in question. Usually, the Compliance Department is located in the home office of the brokerage firm.

3. **Write for Arbitration Forms.** If the dispute is serious, or if the brokerage is intent on fighting your request, it will begin stonewall operations at this point. If there is not a substantive response from the firm after a reasonable period of time, say, four weeks, write for the forms necessary to begin the arbitration procedure. Listed below are the ten stock exchanges or securities organizations sponsoring arbitration; as noted earlier, the procedure is standardized and there is no advantage in choosing one sponsor over another. The only requirement is that the firm involved in the dispute be a member of the exchange or organization

chosen by the investor to sponsor the arbitration. To receive the appropriate forms, write to the Director of Arbitration at:

American Stock Exchange, Inc.
86 Trinity Place
New York, New York 10016
(212) 306-1000

Boston Stock Exchange
One Boston Place
Boston, Massachusetts 02108
(617) 723-9500

Chicago Board Option Exchange, Inc.
LaSalle at Van Buren
Chicago, Illinois 60605
(312) 786-5600

Cincinnati Stock Exchange, Inc.
205 Dixie Terminal Building
Cincinnati, Ohio 45202
(513) 621-1410

Midwest Stock Exchange, Inc.
120 South LaSalle Street
Chicago, Illinois 60603
(312) 368-2222

Municipal Securities Rulemaking Board
1150 Connecticut Avenue, N.W.
Suite 507
Washington, D.C. 20036
(202) 223-9347

National Association of Securities Dealers, Inc.
Two World Trade Center
98th Floor
New York, New York 10048
(212) 839-6251

New York Stock Exchange, Inc.
11 Wall Street
New York, New York 10006
(212) 656-3000

Pacific Stock Exchange, Inc.
618 South Spring Street
Los Angeles, California 90014
(213) 614-8400

Philadelphia Stock Exchange, Inc.
1900 Market Street
Philadelphia, Pennsylvania 19103
(215) 496-5000

4. **File Claim Letter and Submission Agreement.** The Submission Agreement will be included with the information sent by the exchange. Complete and return three copies of the agreement, which must be notarized. By signing the Submission Agreement, you will be agreeing to submit the dispute to arbitration (although the process can still be stopped at any time before the hearing), and to abide by all of the decisions of the arbitrators. You are also required to file three copies of a Claim Letter, simply a typewritten or printed letter stating all relevant facts about the case, including names and dates and the amount of monetary or other relief sought. Copies of supporting documents, such as confirmations, bank and brokerage statements, new account forms, and date logs should also be attached. The letter must also mention if you will be represented by counsel, and if so, provide the name and address of your attorney. Lastly, the letter should state where you would like the case to be heard and why.

5. **Deposit Fee.** This deposit must accompany the Submission and

Claim Letter. The size of the deposit will depend upon the size of the dispute.

Amount in Dispute	Deposit
$1,000 or less	$ 15
$1,001 to $2,500	$ 25
$2,501 to $5,000	$100
$5,001 to $10,000	$200
$10,001 to $20,000	$300
$20,001 to $100,000	$500
$100,001 and above	$750

Source: Securities Industry Unified Code of Arbitration

Claimants should be aware that this amount is only a deposit; all but $25 will be returned if the dispute is resolved before the first hearing. Arbitrators also have the right to return the full amount of the deposit after a hearing is held. Clearly, the claimant's chances of receiving the full deposit back will depend upon the strength of the case. If a customer's case is deemed frivolous by the arbitration panel, the chances of receiving even a portion of the deposit back are poor. But if the case seems close (as most disputes are), with each side scoring points, claimants can fairly assume that they will receive at least a portion of their deposit back. Each arbitration panel is different, however, and there are no hard-and-fast rules governing the return of claimant deposits.

Once the Claim Letter, Submission Agreement, and fee deposit have been received by the exchange, the opposing party will be notified and given twenty business days to respond. The exchange in turn will forward that response to the claimant, who then has ten business days to reply to any counterclaim.

After the bout of paperpushing is complete, both parties will settle down to the business of preparing their respective cases during the approximately eight months that will pass before the hearing. Finally, about two to four weeks before the arbitration is to occur, the exchange will notify both parties of the time, date, and location of the hearing.

The arbitration process has been designed with simplicity in mind;

in any legal proceeding, however, even the seemingly simple can get somewhat complicated, and questions arise. Here are a few of the more commonly expressed questions regarding arbitration:

WHAT ARE THE ADVANTAGES OF ARBITRATION? Arbitration is designed to provide a fast, low-cost method of pursuing justice. It certainly is fast: the average case is disposed of in nine months, compared to several years for lawsuits. Partly because of its relative speed, it is likely that legal fees will be far less than those for lawsuits. Arbitration also affords investors the possibility of some types of recovery no longer available in court, particularly in cases involving regulatory violations by a broker.

WHAT ARE THE DISADVANTAGES OF ARBITRATION? The decision of the arbitration panel is final; appeals are permissible only on an extremely limited basis. Investors choosing arbitration also waive their right to simultaneously pursue the identical charges in court. But the largest potential disadvantage of arbitration concerns the pesky issue of industry bias. Is the system stacked in favor of the large brokers, and can an investor get a better deal from arbitrators or from a jury? Dennis Bell, a Chicago attorney specializing in securities law, has worked for the SEC and sat on arbitration panels as well as argued arbitrations and lawsuits. Bell believes that there *is* some industry bias in the arbitration process, although that bias may be slight. "Investors choosing arbitration give up the opportunity to have cases heard by a totally independent person," Bell said. "That's not to say that arbitrators aren't fair, but probably more often than not, there is an industry bias, although there are situations when that industry bias may actually be helpful to the customer, as in cases when the brokerage firm involved is basically just a boiler-room operation," Bell noted.[GG] Example: Many of the so-called non-industry arbitrators are actually attorneys who have in the past, and may again in the future, work for legitimate brokerage firms. Their sympathies, therefore, will generally not be with the small-time, fly-by-night brokerage operator or the average brokerage customer. Finally, it is possible that arbitration panels, made up as they are of highly informed, educated professionals, are more likely to view certain instances of broker fraud as resulting merely from an investor's own ignorance and naiveté—"Anyone who is that stupid deserves what they got." Juries, however, tend to be more sympathetic to victims of outrageous scams and are more likely to make common-sense moral judgments while taking the side of swindled customers.

WHAT IS THE LAW AND WHAT IS THE REALITY CONCERNING PUNITIVE DAMAGES IN ARBITRATION AWARDS? Until very recently, punitive damages were never awarded by arbitration panels, which for years had followed a ruling by a New York State court that prohibited the recovery of punitive damages in arbitration. In the past two years, however, several cases have established the right of arbitration panels to award punitives, based on interpretation of the Federal Arbitration Act. Many state courts, with the notable exception of New York, have followed the lead of the federal courts in ruling that punitive damages can be awarded. It is an area of law that is still evolving, but already there have been significant awards: In April 1986, a three-member arbitration panel in Florida ordered Paine Webber, Jackson & Curtis, Inc., to pay $19,000 in compensatory and $100,000 in punitive damages to a former client for violations of securities law. Two months later, arbitrators awarded $150,000 in punitive damages to a couple who were allegedly victimized by a Dean Witter Reynolds, Inc., broker. In that particular case, the arbitrators wrote that they were "shocked to determine that the [brokerage] industry as a whole ignores the clear mandate of supervision of accounts and account executives in safeguarding the investing public and particularly unsophisticated investors." Bob Dyer, the Orlando, Florida, attorney who won both of these landmark cases, said that arbitration panels now "have plenty of authority" to award punitive damages whenever they feel it is appropriate. Whether the awarding of punitives in arbitration ever becomes routine, however, is highly questionable.

CAN YOU FORCE YOUR BROKER/DEALER TO SUBMIT TO ARBITRATION? Yes. Brokers and their firms are required to abide by the Uniform Code of Arbitration as long as they are a member of the exchange through which the arbitration is being pursued.

IS THERE A TIME LIMIT ON BEGINNING ARBITRATION? Yes. A controversy is not eligible for arbitration if six or more years have elapsed from the date of the disputed event (shorter statutes of limitations may take precedence in some states).

WHAT IS SIMPLIFIED ARBITRATION? Simplified arbitration works exactly as the standard arbitration process with one exception: instead of the case being presented at a hearing in front of three to five arbitrators, the dispute is handled by one arbitrator *without* a hearing. This is only an option, and it is available only for cases involving disputes of $5,000 or less. Simplified arbitration cases are usually resolved in about four months.

WHAT CONTROL DOES THE CLAIMANT HAVE OVER THE CHOICE OF ARBITRATORS? As stated previously, unless otherwise requested by the claimant, the majority of the arbitrators will be from nonindustry professions. In addition, the claimant has the right to veto one arbitrator without cause, and more than one by demonstrating cause.

SOMETIMES A CASE SEEMS TO BOIL DOWN TO ONE PERSON'S WORD AGAINST ANOTHER'S. IN THESE CASES, WHO WINS? To legal professionals, very few cases can ever be distilled to such a basic issue; there is almost always evidence of some kind that can tip the scales in one party's favor. Said Edward Morris, director of arbitration for the New York Stock Exchange: "In those situations, arbitrators will look at collateral documents in the case, plausibility based upon the past investing history of the individual. There are a number of factors that people who are experienced as arbitrators take into consideration when making a decision where it's one person's words against another's."[HH]

WHAT ARE THE CHANCES THAT WITNESSES WILL LIE AT AN ARBITRATION HEARING? All testimony is given under oath. This includes cross-examination and questioning from the panel of arbitrators. Therefore, the chances of a witness lying are the same as in a court of law.

SHOULD THE CLAIMANT HAVE AN ATTORNEY? Ideally, yes. Securities law can be complicated, and the broker certainly will be represented by an attorney specializing in that field. Practically, however, it should depend upon the size of the dispute and the strength of the case. If a case seems weak and/or the amount in question is small, it might seem a good idea to be your own Perry Mason. An additional consideration is the method of compensation to the attorney; some lawyers charge by the hour ($100 per hour is a common figure), while others work only on a contingency basis (usually 30% of the award). An attorney's willingness to accept a dispute on a contingency basis should be considered a reliable indicator of the strength of the case. In any event, there is usually no charge for an initial consultation, and most lawyers will be honest in assessing the risk/reward factors of your case.

IF YOU LOSE YOUR CASE, CAN THE BROKERAGE FIRM ATTEMPT TO RECOVER ATTORNEYS' FEES? In the bullying process that will make up the broker's initial rebuttal, you will probably be threatened for attorneys' fees unless the case is dropped immediately. Such bluster should go unheeded. "I can't think of a single instance where a brokerage house was awarded attorneys' fees against a customer," said the New York Stock Exchange's Morris. "There have been some very unusual situations where there have been awards of attorneys' fees, but it's always been to an investor, or to someone in the business from someone in the business." Attorney Bell notes, "There are some contracts that brokerage houses make clients sign that say, 'If we get into litigation or arbitration and you lose, you pay our legal fees.' Those are not generally enforceable in arbitration and I doubt that even in situations where they may be enforceable that many arbitrators would give it much stock, except in very egregious situations."

Should You Sue? Can You Sue?

Perhaps the most important question of all regarding arbitration is when to forego it entirely in favor of a lawsuit. In some cases, there will be no decision to be made: The June 1987 Supreme Court decision of *Shearson/American Express v. McMahon* established the right of brokerage firms to include an *enforceable* arbitration clause in any customer account form. By signing such a form, customers agree to arbitrate any dispute arising from activities within that particular brokerage account and waive their right of access to the courts. Nearly all brokerage firms include such an arbitration clause in their margin and option account forms, but a substantial percentage of firms (with the notable exception of Shearson Lehman) do not require a signed account form, and therefore a court waiver, for their basic cash account, the account under which most retail brokerage activity occurs. However, if you have signed an account form containing an arbitration clause, the law is now clear: arbitration is the *only* avenue available for seeking redress to alleged broker frauds that may have occurred within that account.

Assuming, however, that no signed arbitration agreement exists, the arbitration versus lawsuit question remains as tricky as ever. In making such a decision, the two principal weaknesses of arbitration—uncertainty regarding punitive damages and possible industry bias—must be weighed against the two major disadvantages of a lawsuit: enormously high costs and protracted hearings.

Despite the recent awarding of punitive damages in the Florida cases noted earlier, such awards are still generally rare, and the availability of such damages in arbitration should be viewed as being far from certain. In contrast, as the cases of broker fraud chronicled in chapter six make clear, courts are hardly bashful in awarding substantial punitives when faced with sufficiently odious broker conduct. Further, many attorneys believe that the court system is better designed to protect a plaintiff's interest than is the industry-sponsored arbitration process. "I'm a great believer in the court system," said attorney Bell. "I've served as an arbitrator; I argue many arbitrations and I would recommend to my clients that they go to arbitration in certain matters. However, I would feel more comfortable in court if it could be cost justified. The courts are designed to get out all the facts, whereas arbitration is designed for expediency."

The question of cost is a crucial one; litigation can be an enormously expensive proposition, especially if your broker decides to fight, which most do. Arbitration will in almost all circumstances be much cheaper, and faster.

Obviously then, strong cases involving large sums of money and which attempt to recover substantial punitive damages are the types of disputes best pursued in court, assuming, of course that you have not waived your right to a court hearing by signing an arbitration clause. And if you do decide to go to court, be prepared for some very nasty tactics from your broker. "Brokerage firms have now taken the tack of hiring negligence lawyers and using some very annoying tactics in making customers pay for suing," said attorney Brecher. "They take you through the mud, they take you through the rule book, they delay things. They spend more money defending the case than they would if they wanted to settle it. If you reach a jury, you do pretty well, but they really make it tough." It is a discomforting thought that the very same commission dollars you've paid to buy an inappropriate investment are used to pay lawyers to hassle your every move when you attempt to get them back.

One path around the high cost of private suing is to bring a class-action suit against a broker or his firm. This procedure is most applicable when an identical investment is sold to many investors, as in the case of the Baldwin-United annuity disaster. Class-action suits cost nothing to initiate since they are almost always handled on a contingency basis, but relief must be shared equally with all investors joining in the class action.

Protecting Your Interests

The surest way to protect yourself from securities fraud is simple enough: do not deal with stockbrokers. Handing over your hard-earned money to a professional salesman laboring under intense conflicts of interest and with scarce qualifications to manage money is asking for trouble. But for those investors who just cannot seem to break the habit (or who are not aware of the profitable alternatives to brokers listed in chapters eight through ten), there are some precautions that, if taken, can serve to reduce your chances of becoming a victim of broker fraud. **Always . . .**

1. **Read all sections of a new account form.** Pay particular attention to the net worth and annual income figures, as well as the section pertaining to investment objective. Never sign an application that is not totally filled in: the broker could easily insert false numbers later that could undermine your efforts to prove unsuitability. After signing the new account form, ask for a copy on the spot—and don't leave until you get it.

2. **Retain discretion over your own account.** Giving a stockbroker the right to trade your account without your prior permission would be like giving the neighborhood wino your liquor store credit card. (Refer to chapter six for the case histories of some all-too-typical churning examples.)

3. **Report any problems with your account immediately.** Juries and arbitration panels might look with some suspicion upon claims made only after an investment turns sour. If a broker breaks the law, it should be reported at once; do not wait in the hope that the market will correct the mess. The longer you delay in making a claim, the more it will appear to be a simple case of trying to make your broker a scapegoat for an unwise investment.

4. **Retain all documents relevant to each investment.**

These normally would include the new account form, monthly brokerage statements, confirmation slips, all broker correspondence, prospectuses, and if available, a log containing the pertinent details of the broker's sales pitches. In keeping such a log, record all information and phrases thrown out by the broker that seem important and date each entry; it is even legal to tape record a broker's presentation, as long as the broker is aware of the recording. In fact, making your broker aware that you are recording each sales presentation can virtually assure that the presentation itself will not contain fraud.

5. **Refuse to sign any account form that contains an arbitration clause.** Despite the fact that, in most cases, arbitration would be the preferred route under which to seek satisfaction of broker frauds, waiving your right to a court hearing in advance undermines your leverage in seeking out-of-court settlements and obviously blocks your ability to pursue the court process in those cases in which a lawsuit can be cost justified. If you want to do business with a certain broker or firm, first try scratching out the arbitration language on the account form; if your broker wants your business badly enough, there is a good chance he or she will not argue. Besides, in contesting the arbitration clause, you will be putting your broker on notice that you are aware of the potential for fraud and that you will be watching carefully.

6. **Make all checks payable to the brokerage firm, not to an individual broker.** There will never be any instance in which your broker should be paid directly for any transaction that he executes for you. All purchases made through your broker's firm will be settled by making payments directly to the firm, or in some instances, to a particular mutual fund or limited partnership. If a broker ever asks that a check be made payable to himself, refuse the request and report the activity to the broker's manager and the state securities examiner.

An Obligation to Try

The system of justice under which investors seek to recover from broker foul play is far from perfect; *Shearson v. McMahon* was a stunning reversal of a legal trend that had been running steadily in favor of the investor versus the behemoth industry. Additionally, the question of a possible pro-broker bias in the arbitration process is a legitimate concern. An American Bar Association task force is studying the problem, and it seems inevitable that political pressure will eventually change the composition of arbitration panels. But while the system is far from perfect, neither is it fatally flawed; each year hundreds of investors gain at least some measure of relief from broker duplicity and countless others are spared trouble by its very presence. And regardless of the difficulty involved, investors have a moral obligation to seek justice. Failure to report fraud only encourages more fraud; when you suffer losses that are the result of broker subterfuge, you owe it to yourself and to your fellow victims to make sure those lies are not the final word.

SECTION TWO

Introduction

It seems only natural to wonder, in spite of a mountain of evidence pointing to brokerage house underperformance, incompetence, and outright fraud, why anyone would still choose to rely on stockbrokers for their investment advice, especially in light of the many safer and more profitable alternatives.

Unquestionably the largest single reason relates to the fact that little effort has ever been made to compile, document, and tie together the plethora of evidence against brokerage firms. Certainly, from time to time a story will appear in the popular financial press, reporting still another example of poor brokerage results, or yet another case of broker fraud, but these stories are too diverse and academic to be meaningful for most investors, who already feel that they pay far too little attention to the market to make decisions for themselves anyway. And can these same investors be expected to peruse law libraries in order to understand the latest in broker frauds, or to read the many informative but arcane trade journals such as *Financial Management Digest*, *Management Science*, and *Accounting Review*, publications that usually contain the most meaningful evidence against brokers?

Still another factor, mentioned briefly in chapter one, relates to the powerful marketing effort employed by the brokerage industry, which expertly shifts attention away from comparative results and frauds and on to emotional buzz phrases such as financial security, family, and financial planning. Unfortunately, name recognition—and little else—remains the prime consideration of many investors when choosing an investment "professional" to manage their money. The large brokerage firms, each of whom spends tens of millions of dollars each year establishing name recognition, are of course going to win the marketing battle over, say, a no-load mutual fund, which does comparatively little advertising, or a private money manager who does no advertising. Those tens of millions of ad dollars, ironically, once belonged to investors, whose commission dollars went to buy research that, on the average, underperformed the market by 3% to 8% each year and are now being used to bait other unwitting investors into the same trap.

But marketing muscle and a lack of readily available coherent evidence against brokers does not explain, by itself, the phenomenon of seventeen million Americans paying $50 billion each year for advice that is essentially worthless. A significant amount of brokerage business derives from the widespread public feeling that the financial markets have become so complex and the number of financial products so numerous that only a trained investment "professional" can possibly sort out all the available options. Obviously, most of those seventeen million investors identified by the New York Stock Exchange (share-ownership study referred to in chapter one) spend their days employed in fields outside the financial-services industry; they have all they can handle to keep up with changes and demands from their own jobs without trying to become investment advisers as well. The amazing proliferation of financial products in the 1980s has created a kind of mind-numbing paralysis among many investors, a feeling that the stakes are too high and the amount of time required to adequately understand the markets too immense to possibly do it themselves. As the next three chapters will make clear, such a feeling is an expensive and entirely avoidable mistake.

Yes, the day-to-day gyrations of the financial markets are surely too complex for anyone, even true investment professionals, to understand. But earning superior investment results has nothing to do with predicting or even understanding the daily ups and downs of the stock or bond markets. Instead, it is the result of knowing how to hire truly qualified, unbiased investment professionals to manage your money, and then applying a coherent long-term plan to those investments.

The concept of hiring a qualified money manager, either through a no-load mutual fund, private investment adviser, or advisory newsletter is a task that virtually anyone, even a total investment neophyte, is qualified to do. The information provided in each of the next three chapters is sufficient to make a totally informed investment decision regardless of an individual's previous investment knowledge.

Chapters one through seven of this book attempted to overcome an important impediment to "Do it yourself" investing by providing clear and convincing evidence that allowing salesmen brokers to manage your money is both expensive and dangerous. Chapters eight through ten are designed to provide the information and the motivation necessary for investors of all backgrounds to successfully take control of their own investments through qualified, unbiased investment professionals.

The age-old axiom, "If you want it done right, do it yourself," is nowhere more correct and meaningful than when it comes to your own investments. The information that follows will show you how.

CHAPTER 8

No-Load and Low-Load Mutual Funds: Ten Proven Winners

The often horrifying results experienced by many investors when using stockbrokers become even more difficult to accept in light of the many phenomenally successful, and less expensive investment alternatives.

Over the past ten years (1979–1988) an investment in any of the ten mutual funds listed below—none of which are handled by brokers—would have bettered the S & P 500 index while returning at least 456%.

1. Fidelity Magellan   + 1,029%
2. Weingarten Equity   + 615%
3. Stein Roe Special   + 563%
4. Windsor   + 560%
5. Twentieth Century Growth   + 577%
6. Nicholas   + 505%
7. Twentieth Century Select   + 503%
8. Evergreen   + 503%
9. Acorn   + 460%
10. Fidelity Equity-Income   + 456%

Those ten funds represent an average gain of 573%, a return that could have been attained by any investor and without the services of a single stockbroker. In dollar terms, at 573%, a $10,000 investment would have grown to $67,300 (before taxes) over those ten years. Compare *that* to the sorry record of the brokerage industry.

While stockbrokers also sell mutual funds, they once again are working under an inherent conflict of interest which works to the disadvantage of their customers. For example, since brokers are paid only by selling commission products, they obviously cannot sell those mutual funds which contain little or no sales fees (the no-load or low-load funds*). There is no evidence to suggest that load funds, on average, perform any better than no-load funds, and in the case of broker-sponsored funds, they usually perform far worse. Brokers, therefore, are making investment recommendations for their customers without having access to the top-performing funds, and end up pushing inferior funds with high front-end sales fees as well. Most growth mutual funds sold through brokers contain a sales fee of 8.5%, which means that an investor putting $10,000 into such a fund has paid an $850 commission for an investment that in all likelihood is no better, and probably grossly inferior, to what he or she could have purchased without any sales charge.

Besides being unable to handle most of the top mutual funds, brokers often try to sell "house" funds, i.e., funds sponsored by the brokerage firm for which they are working, since they usually receive a higher pay-out on such sales. Sadly, the performance of broker-sponsored funds is often even worse than load funds in general (see chapter one). Finally, many brokers try to avoid selling any mutual funds since, in the long run, the one-time 8.5% commission will fall far short of that which can be earned by trading in individual stocks at 3% to 5% per transaction. The bottom line: once again the brokerage customer gets the wrong product for the wrong reasons.

The fact that many investors are willing to pay an 8.5% commission for a product that is inferior to one they could have purchased for free is further evidence of the type of public confusion and intimidation outlined in the introduction to this section. ("My broker says this fund is good, therefore it must be good. After all, he is the investment professional, not me.") It should be noted, however, that if an investor, for whatever reason, absolutely insists on using a broker for his or her purchases, a non-broker–sponsored load fund would still be preferable to relying on brokerage recommendations to buy individual stocks. (The Templeton Growth Fund, a full-load that can be purchased through most brokers, would be an excellent choice.)

The Case for Mutual Funds

There are several solid reasons why no-load and low-load mutual funds can help you to earn superior returns. Here are just a few:

PROFESSIONAL MANAGEMENT. Unlike stockbrokers, whose qualifications to manage money are usually nonexistent, mutual funds are managed by individuals with business and investment expertise. These managers devote nearly every minute of their working days to seeking out hidden investment values and studying the financial markets; they are professional money managers, not professional salespeople. They will be judged by the investment results they produce, not by the commissions they generate.

ACCOUNTABILITY. Not all professional money managers generate extraordinary returns; however, all mutual funds are required to file an audited record of the investment results obtained by the fund each year. Some financial newspapers report the track records of mutual funds as often as each quarter. There is simply nowhere to hide bad performance; professional money managers not achieving excellent results will soon find themselves replaced. Mutual fund investors thus have the advantage of choosing their manager according to the most basic and fair of criteria: results. While your fund manager's past performance is no guarantee of future results, it is certainly a far better indicator than either slick TV commercials or polished salesmanship.

DIVERSIFICATION. The oft-quoted axiom, "Anyone with less than $100,000 to invest should use a mutual fund," has its roots in a basic principle of successful investing: diversification. If your portfolio is holding less than twenty issues, it is not properly diversified; a disproportionate share of your assets is in one or more companies. When negative developments strike one of these companies, the impact can be devastating to the overall performance of the portfolio. Even the most successful of mutual fund managers have their share of losers; however, the poor choices are usually more than offset by the many above-average holdings in the fund. It is not unusual for a mutual fund to own as many as 100 to 200 different issues; the Fidelity Magellan Fund holds over 1,000 different securities. Greater diversification simply means greater stability and safety.

LOW COSTS. The mutual funds reviewed in this chapter are either no-load or low-load, meaning they charge no sales fee or a very small one (4.75% or less). Compare that to the cost of doing business with your stockbroker, where *each trade* incurs a commission of from 2% to 5%. Since your broker is paid only by generating activity in your account, it can be expected that you'll pay 100% or more in commissions over a ten-year period. And what do you get in return for your 100% in commissions? You get the underperformance and horror stories described earlier.

Mutual funds are also highly efficient, enjoying trading benefits not available to small investors. Prior to 1975, all commissions were regulated and equal: if you bought 100 shares of a stock, you would pay the same percentage commission as the mutual fund buying 10,000 shares. But the "May Day" decision of 1975 by the Securities and Exchange Commission changed all that; in place of regulated uniform commissions came unregulated "negotiated" commissions. Since the 100-share buyer has considerably less negotiating clout than the 10,000-share buyer, the effect of the decision was to increase the cost of buying and selling stocks for the small investor and decrease dramatically the transaction costs for the large institutions. Many mutual funds, pension funds, banks, and insurance companies pay as little as 8 cents per share to trade a stock; a 10,000-share purchase of

General Motors at $80 per share would cost the mutual fund only $800, or 0.1%. Your purchase of GM through a full-service broker would cost about 2%, or twenty times more. Lower transaction costs mean higher returns on your investments.

LIQUIDITY. While individual stocks and bonds are also quite liquid (funds are yours in seven days), mutual funds offer even greater liquidity. Many funds offer check writing privileges against an investor's share balance, and liquidations can usually be made over the phone, with the proceeds in the mail the very next day. Partial distributions, often a messy task with individual stocks and bonds, are easy with mutual funds, and special services, such as the regular withdrawal of a fixed monthly amount (a valuable service for retired investors) can easily be established.

REINVESTMENT PRIVILEGE. Let's say you own 100 shares of XYZ Corporation. Now XYZ pays its regular quarterly dividend of 15 cents per share and you receive your check for $15. What do you do with it? You can't reinvest it in XYZ Corp. You could put it in a bank savings account at 5¼%, or in your checking account at 0%, but most likely such a small sum will end up being spent, which, of course, is not the best way to make your investment grow.

All mutual funds offer you the opportunity to reinvest your dividends and capital gain distributions in additional shares of the fund. This reinvestment privilege allows a successful investment to become even more successful through compounding.

Aunt Tillie's Revenge

Despite the obvious success of so many mutual funds and the compelling reasons for using them, many stockbrokers, and even some investors, go to great lengths to deny the obvious. Here are a few of the more frequently offered excuses for avoiding mutual funds:

THE "AUNT TILLIE" SYNDROME. This rationale is offered most often by investors, and goes something like this: "My Aunt

Tillie's great-grandfather's niece once had a friend whose uncle's cousin once lost money in a mutual fund. Therefore, all mutual funds always lose money." It is quite difficult to argue with first-grade logic, even though Aunt Tillie's distant acquaintance probably did once lose money in a mutual fund. There are millions of mutual fund owners, however, who would gladly tell Aunt Tillie's friend that he's been listening to the wrong people.

MUTUAL FUNDS ARE BORING. This is an argument often advanced by stockbrokers, and to some extent they are right. There are no individual stories to tell, no individual companies to watch, no announcements of new products (or pending Chapter 11's), and watching a mutual fund can be a little like watching grass grow. But it would take a supersalesperson indeed to convince any straight-thinking investor that making money is boring.

YOU CAN'T HIT A HOME RUN WITH A MUTUAL FUND. Once again, this argument is advanced mostly by stockbrokers, and once again, they are quite right. Because of the high degree of diversification in each mutual fund, earning 75 to 100% in any twelve month period is nearly impossible. Speculators looking for the quick score would be wise to look elsewhere. What is quite possible, however, is to consistently hit singles and doubles in mutual funds; it is unfortunate that so many investors, in their desire to hit home runs, choose to rely on the advice of a stockbroker who more often than not strikes out.

Stocks vs Bank CD's: Which Is Best?

The frequent strikeouts usually leave an unpleasant and unforgettable impression upon investors (see chapter five), who often react to their painful experiences by withdrawing from the investment scene altogether, choosing instead to buy bank CD's* or Treasury Bills*. One look at a chart of the stock market's performance since 1900 (a period that includes the 1929 and 1987 crashes and the Great Depression) shows how unnecessary the strikeouts are, and what an awful price investors are paying for their abstinence.

As the chart clearly shows, the underlying trend of the stock market has been up for the past fifty-four years, although this fact must come as a considerable surprise to the many investors who have experienced only frustration in trying to capitalize on that trend. And as the following chart points out, $1 invested in common stocks on 1 January, 1926 would have grown to $198.74 by 1983, compared with only $6.32 for Treasury Bills (the equivalent of bank CD's) and $7.29 for long-term bonds. Clearly, common stocks are the best-performing investment available, and the fact that stocks have performed thirty-one times better than Treasury Bills over the last sixty years serves only to underscore another hidden cost of the broker game: not only do investors frequently lose money when dealing with stockbrokers; perhaps the greatest loss of all is that the experience so often drives them

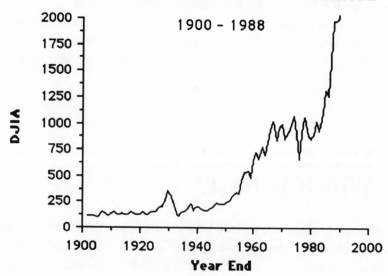

DOW JONES INDUSTRIAL AVERAGE
1900 - 1988

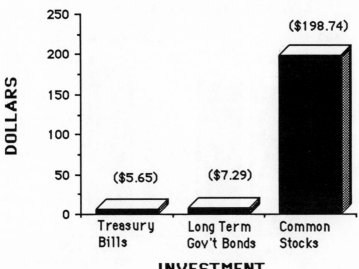

$1.00 INVESTED 1926 - 1983 BECAME:

DOLLARS vs INVESTMENT

Treasury Bills ($5.65) — Long Term Gov't Bonds ($7.29) — Common Stocks ($198.74)

Source: Ibbotson, Roger G., and Rex A. Sinquefeld, *Stocks, Bonds, Bills, and Inflation* (SBBI), 1982, updated in *Stocks, Bonds, Bills and Inflation 1984 Yearbook™*, Ibbotson Associates, Inc., Chicago. All rights reserved.

to the sidelines and into investments that are so grossly inferior, such as money market funds*, bank CD's*, Treasury Bills*, and long-term government* and corporate* bonds.

In order to turn that $1 into $198, you would only have had to achieve average results (the figures, after all, reflect the Dow Jones Industrial Average, a widely quoted market index). Historically, however, mutual funds have achieved considerably *above* average results; from 31 December 1972 to 31 December 1987, a period which saw the Dow Jones Industrial Average advance 300% and the S & P gain 311%, the average mutual fund outperformed both indexes, climbing 344%. If you can achieve excellent returns by simply matching the market averages, and if the average mutual fund performs *better* than the market averages, it follows that investing in a diversified portfolio of mutual funds offers you your best opportunity to earn excellent returns.

But you need not settle for only average mutual funds. Because

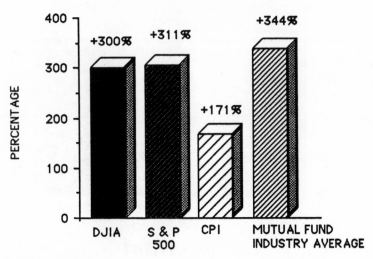

15 YEAR TOTAL RETURN
JAN. 1, 1973 -- DEC. 31, 1987

Source: Lipper Analytical Services, Inc.

mutual fund track records are so easily accessible, you can pick from the cream of the crop, funds that have doubled, tripled, or in some cases quadrupled the market averages over a long period of time.

Understanding the Basics

The following section contains information on the top ten–performing mutual funds over the 1978–1987 period. Only no-load or low-load funds are listed; sector funds, or those that are currently closed to the public, are omitted. I have chosen the ten-year time period for obvious reasons: Any mutual fund can get "hot" for a brief period, and many can achieve excellent returns while they are small. But to earn extraordinary results over a ten-year period—a period covering several highly diverse market cycles, including a severe recession and stock market crash—requires true investment savvy and expertise. The longer the period over which a fund has achieved excellent results, the better the indicator that those results will continue.

Before listing my "Ten Proven Winners" it might be helpful to briefly define some of the different terms and charts used and to explain the significance of each fund.

PERFORMANCE CHART. This chart shows graphically how quickly your money can grow when it is managed by a highly skilled professional. Each bar represents the amount of pre-tax money you would have had at the end of the corresponding year, assuming you began with $10,000 on 1 January 1978, and had reinvested all dividend and capital gain distributions.

ADDRESS AND PHONE NUMBER. Your investment cannot be accepted into a mutual fund until you have received a current prospectus, which describes in dreary detail how the fund operates, its objectives, fees, etc. The prospectus is essentially a document written by lawyers for lawyers since its basic objective is to absolve the fund of any liability in the event of future problems. It is therefore highly legalistic and negative in tone. The average prospectus can make even the most basic and simple investment sound about as promising as nuclear war. (It has been argued that the surest way to quit smoking would be to read a prospectus on the subject.) For better or worse, prospective mutual fund investors should order and carefully read a current prospectus before investing. Therefore, the address and telephone number of each fund is provided.

TEN-YEAR AVERAGE ANNUAL TOTAL RETURN. This figure is the average annual percentage return of the fund, before taxes and assuming reinvestment of dividends and capital gains, over the ten-year period of 1978–1987.

TEN-YEAR AVERAGE ANNUAL DIFFERENTIAL TO THE S & P 500. The yardstick by which the success or failure of any equity investment should be judged is its performance relative to the S & P 500. The longer the period over which that relative performance is measured, the more meaningful the comparison. This category lists the average total return differential between each fund and the S & P 500 index for each of the years 1978–1987.

LEAD MANAGER, CONSECUTIVE YEARS WITH FUND. The single most important factor in a mutual fund's ability to outperform the S & P 500 is the expertise of the manager. Before investing in any mutual fund, it is important to know if the manager who compiled a given track record is still making the day-to-day investment decisions for the fund.

SALES FEE. This is the amount of money the fund charges the investor to buy its shares. On a $10,000 investment, a 3% sales fee, for example, would mean that $9,700 is invested for the customer, while $300 is retained by the fund. By means of comparison, most "load" funds charge a front-end fee of 8½%; in this section, I have listed only no-load or low-load funds.

REDEMPTION FEE. The amount of money a fund retains from the sales proceeds due the investor is known as the redemption fee. None of the funds in this section charge a basic redemption fee, although two funds charge a small fee on shares held for less than ninety days. Redemption fees have become a covert means for brokerage firms to sell mutual funds as no-load; the brokerage firm advertises its mutual fund as having no front-end sales fee, but if you sell your shares within a six-year period you will be slapped with a fee of from 1 to 6%. Further, this type of fee structure often carries with it a hidden "distribution" fee of up to 1.25% each year, which the fund uses to pay the broker, regardless of how long the investor holds the shares. Replacing a front-end fee with a back-end fee is the brokerage industry's answer to competition from no-load funds. Unfortunately, it represents the triumph of marketing expertise over common sense.

ASSETS. The amount of money invested through the fund is listed. The sizes of mutual funds vary widely; some new funds, or funds with undistinguished track records, may be as small as $10 to $50 million.

In fact, more mutual funds fall into the $100 million or less asset category than any other. The sizes of the ten funds detailed in this section range from the $187 million of the Stein Roe Special Fund to the $8.5 billion of the Fidelity Magellan Fund. There is no evidence to suggest that there is any relationship between a fund's size and its performance relative to the S & P, and therefore *results*, not size, should remain the best determinate of a fund's worth. These ten funds have continued to achieve excellent results even as they have grown larger.

TELEPHONE SWITCH. This privilege allows investors to transfer money from a stock fund to a money market fund with only a phone call. If a simple "buy and hold" strategy is being followed, this feature is not necessarily important; many investors, however, want the instant flexibility to switch their money into a money market fund whenever they perceive a negative trend developing in the stock market. The telephone switch privilege can usually be established by simply checking a box on the fund application.

EXPENSE RATIO. The amount of expenses incurred by the fund, expressed as a percentage of the total assets under management, is known as the expense ratio. For example, a $200 million fund with expenses of $2 million would have an expense ratio of 1%. This category includes investment management fees, legal fees, custodial fees, transfer agent fees, and brokerage commissions. Most mutual funds, especially those investing heavily in common stocks, will have expense ratios of 1 to 1.5%. Funds which utilize more short-term trading strategies tend to have higher expense ratios since trading stocks is not free, even for large institutions. The ten funds listed in this section had an average annual expense ratio of 1.04% for the ten-year period 1978–1987. The investment returns reported for each of the funds are *after* expenses.

PORTFOLIO TURNOVER RATE. The rate at which mutual funds trade their holdings is expressed as a percentage of the total portfolio. Example: a fund which turned over each holding in its portfolio once in a twelve-month period would have a portfolio turnover rate of 100%. The average annual portfolio turnover rate of the ten funds listed here was 97% for 1978–1987 period, though the range varied widely from the 30% of the Acorn fund to the 181% average turnover rate of the Fidelity Magellan fund. A higher portfolio turnover rate is simply the result of a different investment philosophy: some funds play for short-term gains and immediately sell; other funds buy long-term value and hold. It is important to know which strategy your fund follows, but in the end, it is results that count.

RETIREMENT PLANS. Nearly all mutual funds offer some variety of retirement plans. Most offer the full range, including IRAs*, Keoghs*, 403b's*, 401k's* and profit sharing*. If you are interested, you should ask for specific retirement plan information when ordering the prospectus.

MINIMUM INITIAL INVESTMENT. The minimum dollar amount required by a fund to open an account is indicated. Nearly all mutual funds impose some initial minimums, usually ranging from $500 to $5,000.

SUBSEQUENT MINIMUM INVESTMENT. Some funds require a minimum amount for subsequent deposits to an existing account. This amount is usually less than the initial minimum and ranges from nothing to $2,000. Nearly all mutual funds will allow you to make subsequent investments through regular monthly automatic checking account deductions. The form necessary to set up an automatic systematic withdrawal plan can be found in the prospectus.

INVESTMENT OBJECTIVE. Most investment objectives fall into one of three categories: growth, income, or some combination of the two. Many funds use the term "capital appreciation"* as a substitute for growth.

INVESTMENT APPROACH. A fund's investment approach is the means by which it intends to achieve its stated objective. Mutual funds that seek capital appreciation can nevertheless employ vastly different policies to achieve that end. In this section, specific investment philosophies, strategies, or tendencies each fund employs in its attempt to fulfill its investment objective are described. For example: some funds prefer to invest in small, emerging growth companies; others like larger capitalization stocks. Some funds buy stocks and hold them for the long term, while others buy for intermediate-term trading profits. Many funds will switch heavily to cash positions during periods of market weakness; others will stay fully invested and ride out the storm. Additionally, there are certain investment policies that can affect the risk level of a fund: Does a fund buy stocks on margin? Buy put* and call options*? Concentrate its investments in one industry? In short, there are about as many investment strategies as there are investment managers; investing is, after all, an art, not a science. But when judging a mutual fund, the primary criterion should still be results, especially the *consistency* of those results. The individual strategies employed by each fund are merely the means to that desired end.

MANAGEMENT. This section will list the investment advisory firm managing the day-to-day investment decisions of the fund. The fee structure is also listed, although you should remember that the fees charged by a fund's investment adviser already show up in the fund's overall expense ratio. Of more importance is the length of time the adviser has been with the fund; as with the manager, a successful track record is only meaningful if the adviser who compiled it still works for the fund. When buying a mutual fund, however, do not expect that there will be any personal contact between yourself and your fund's adviser. Mutual funds do send quarterly reports to shareholders and hold an annual shareholders meeting, but in-person or telephone contact between a shareholder and a fund's investment adviser is not encouraged, since most mutual funds have thousands of shareholders.

Having properly dispensed with the definitions, a disclaimer is in order: the performance records of each of the funds listed in this section are not meant to be a guarantee of future performance; in the investment business there are no guarantees. (Can bankers guarantee that the fixed-rate CDs they sell will not lose purchasing power to inflation?) Further, no assurances can be given as to the total accuracy of the information provided, although it has been obtained from sources believed to be reliable, including the official prospectus of each of the funds.

Making Your Money Grow

The following are ten compelling alternatives to the broker game:

Fidelity Magellan Fund

Up 1,029%
$10,000 became $112,980

Address:	82 Devonshire Street
	Boston, MA 02109
Phone:	(800) 544-6666
Ten-Year Average Annual Return:	+28.9%
Ten-Year Average Annual Diff. to	
S & P:	+12.9%
Lead Manager, Cons. Years with	
Fund:	Peter Lynch, twelve
Sales Fee:	3%
Redemption Fee:	None
Assets:	$8.5 billion
Telephone Switch:	Yes
Expense Ratio:	1.22%
Portfolio Turnover Rate:	181%
Retirement Plans:	IRA, Keogh, Profit Sharing,
	403b, 401k

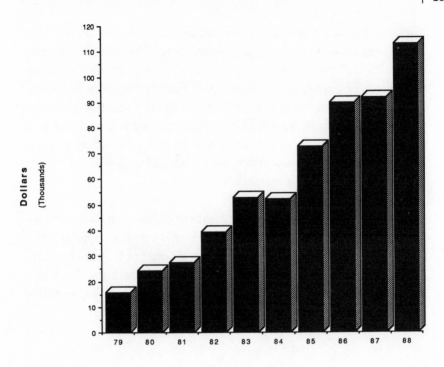

Minimum Initial Investment: $1,000
Minimum Subsequent
  Investments: $250

INVESTMENT OBJECTIVE. Capital appreciation.

HISTORY. The fund was originally offered to the public in June 1965.

INVESTMENT APPROACH. The fund seeks capital appreciation through an aggressive approach to stock selection. The Fidelity Magellan Fund has no philosophical predisposition; it invests in any company it believes will appreciate in value in excess of the market averages, no matter how big or small, what industry it belongs to, or whether it is a foreign or domestic company. The fund also makes extensive use of intermediate-term trading, as evidenced by the large 181% average annual portfolio turnover rate. The fund's size, currently $8.5 billion, allows it to achieve a level of diversification unattainable by virtually any other fund; Fidelity Magellan frequently holds over 1,000 securities in its portfolio. This diversification serves to mitigate, to some degree, the volatility normally associated with such an aggressive investment approach. In fact, *Forbes* magazine, in its 1987 mutual fund issue, rated the Fidelity Magellan Fund "A" for its performance in down markets.[59]

MANAGEMENT. Fidelity Management & Research Company has served as the fund's investment adviser since inception. In fiscal 1987, the adviser received compensation in the amount of 0.76% of average net assets under management. When the fund outperforms the S & P 500 index, the investment adviser receives an incentive fee; when the performance falls below the S & P, the basic fee is reduced.

Twentieth Century Growth
Up 539%
$10,000 became $63,938

Address:	P.O. Box 419200
	Kansas City, MO 64141
Phone:	(800) 345-2021
Ten-Year Average Annual Return:	+24.0%
Ten-Year Average Annual Diff. to S & P:	+8.0%
Lead Manager, Cons. Years with Fund:	James Stowers, seventeen
Sales Fee:	None
Redemption Fee:	None
Assets:	$1.3 billion
Telephone Switch:	Yes
Expense Ratio:	1.17%

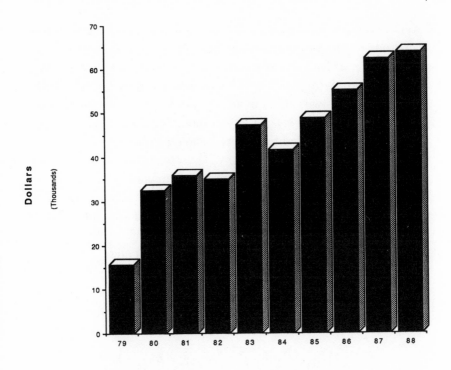

Year End

Portfolio Turnover Rate:	113%
Retirement Plans:	IRA, Keogh, 403b, 401k
Minimum Initial Investment:	None
Minimum Subsequent Investments:	None

INVESTMENT OBJECTIVE. Growth.

HISTORY. The fund began operations on 31 October 1958.

INVESTMENT APPROACH. The fund seeks capital appreciation through investment in a diversified portfolio of common stocks. Twentieth Century Growth attempts to retain maximum flexibility in its choices of investments, although, because of its size, it tends to invest in larger-capitalization companies. The fund further intends to invest only in those companies that have a record of continuous operations for at least three years and whose securities enjoy a fair degree of marketability. Unlike many mutual funds, which often turn heavily to cash during periods of anticipated market weakness, Twentieth Century Growth attempts to remain fully invested in its stock positions during all market cycles. Additionally, buy and sell decisions are made by the fund without regard to holding period.

MANAGEMENT. Investors Research Corporation has been the fund's investment manager since inception in 1958. Investors Research Corp. receives compensation from the fund in the amount of 2% of the first $10 million of average daily net assets, 1.5% on the next $20 million, and 1% on the remainder. During the year ended 31 October 1987, the manager's fee amounted to 1.00% of the fund's average daily net assets.

Weingarten Equity Fund

Up 615%
$10,000 became $71,558

Address:	11 Greenway Plaza
	Suite 1919
	Houston, TX 77046
Phone:	(800) 231-0803
Ten-Year Average Annual Return:	+23.9%
Ten-Year Average Annual Diff. to S & P:	+7.9%
Lead Manager, Cons. Years with Fund:	Harry Hutzler, twenty
Sales Fee:	4.75%
Redemption Fee:	None
Assets:	$286 million
Telephone Switch:	Yes
Expense Ratio:	1.18%

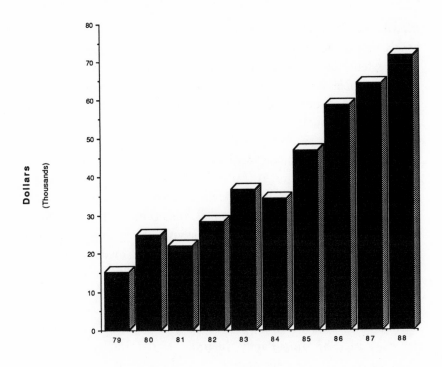

Year End

Portfolio Turnover Rate: 112%
Retirement Plans: IRA, Keogh
Minimum Initial Investment: $1,000
Minimum Subsequent
  Investments: $100

INVESTMENT OBJECTIVE. Capital appreciation.

HISTORY. The fund began operations in 1967 as the Compufund. The fund's name was changed in 1969 when the Weingarten Management Corporation became the fund's investment adviser.

INVESTMENT APPROACH. Weingarten follows a statistically based, long-term approach to stock selection, preferring to buy companies that have shown at least a 15% annual growth rate in earnings over the previous ten years. Stocks are held as long as they meet the fund's 15% growth rate criterion, and sold when they slip below. To a lesser extent, the fund will also buy stocks for the short term based upon statistical evidence of a dramatic cyclical upturn in earnings. Weingarten does not consider the predictions of securities analysts to be evidence of such a turn; instead, the fund waits until positive earnings surprises are in fact reality before buying. The fund intends to invest primarily in large-capitalization companies.

MANAGEMENT. In 1986 the fund entered into an Investment Advisory Agreement with AIM Capital Management, Inc., of Houston, Texas, to serve as its investment adviser, replacing Weingarten Management Corporation, which had managed the investments of the fund since 1969. The new agreement calls for the adviser to be compensated at the rate of 0.50% of the first $30 million of the fund's assets and 0.37% on assets in excess of $30 million. By contrast, the Weingarten Management Corp. received fees amounting to 1.4% of net assets in 1985. Importantly, however, Harry Hutzler, the fund's principal portfolio manager since 1969, will continue in that position under the new agreement.

Twentieth Century Select

Up 667%
$10,000 became $77,707

Address:	P.O. Box 419200
	Kansas City, MO 64141
Phone:	(800) 345-2021
Ten-Year Average Annual Return:	+22.0%
Ten-Year Average Annual Diff. to	
S & P:	+6.0%
Lead Manager, Cons. Years with	
Fund:	James Stowers, seventeen
Sales Fee:	None

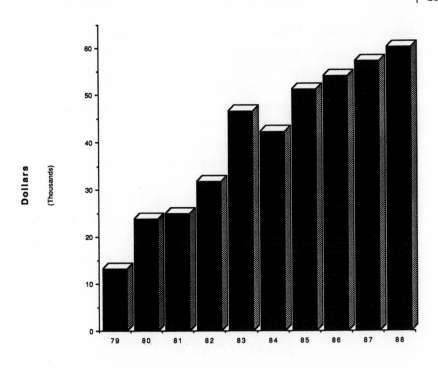

Redemption Fee: None
Assets: $2.4 billion
Telephone Switch: Yes
Expense Ratio: 1.17%
Portfolio Turnover Rate: 113%
Retirement Plans: IRA, Keogh, 401k, 403b
Minimum Initial Investment: None
Minimum Subsequent
  Investments: None

INVESTMENT OBJECTIVE. Growth, with current income a secondary consideration.

HISTORY. Began operations on 31 October 1958.

INVESTMENT APPROACH. Twentieth Century Select follows the same investment philosophy as its sister fund, Twentieth Century Growth, with one minor addition: the fund will invest only in the securities of companies that pay dividends or interest. The income, however, is usually small and in any event is secondary to the fund's primary objective of growth. The fund will tend to invest in larger-capitalization companies, trade without consideration to holding period, and attempt to remain fully invested in common stocks throughout all market cycles.

MANAGEMENT. Investors Research Corporation has managed Twentieth Century Select since its inception. Terms of compensation to the adviser are identical to those of the Twentieth Century Growth fund.

Evergreen Fund
Up 503%
$10,000 became $60,311

Address:	550 Mamaroneck Avenue
	Harrison, NY 10528
Phone:	(800) 635-0064
Ten-Year Average Annual Return:	+21.0%
Ten-Year Average Annual Diff. to	
S & P:	+5.0%
Lead Manager, Cons. Years with	
Fund:	Steven Lieber, eighteen
Sales Fee:	None
Redemption Fee:	None
Assets:	$691 million
Telephone Switch:	Yes
Expense Ratio:	1.23%
Portfolio Turnover Rate:	74%
Retirement Plans:	IRA, Keogh, SEP*

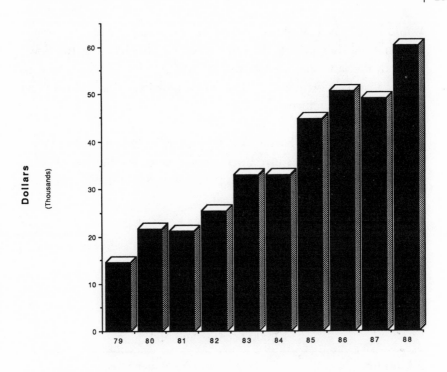

Year End

Minimum Initial Investment: $2,000
Minimum Subsequent
   Investments: None

INVESTMENT OBJECTIVE. Capital appreciation.

HISTORY. Began operations in 1971.

INVESTMENT APPROACH. The fund seeks capital appreciation
primarily through common stock investments in three major areas:
special situations, little-known companies, and small-capitalization
companies. The fund defines a special situation as one in which a
recent or anticipated change in management, product, or services
creates the potential for price appreciation. Because the focus of the
fund's investments is toward smaller companies, the fund's shares

would have to be considered somewhat more volatile than the average mutual fund. Remarkably, however, Evergreen has had only two down years in the last ten (-1.6% in 1981 and -3.0% in 1987), and in 1977, a year in which the Dow Jones Industrial Average declined 12.8%, the fund returned 25.4%.

MANAGEMENT. Saxon Woods Asset Management Corporation has served as the fund's investment adviser since the fund was organized in 1971. The adviser is paid a fee equal to 1% of the average daily net assets of the fund during the year.

Nicholas Fund

Up 505%
$10,000 became $60,504

Address:	700 N. Water Street
	Milwaukee, WI 53202
Phone:	(414) 272-6163
Ten-Year Average Annual Return:	+18.5%
Ten-Year Average Annual Diff. to S & P:	+2.5%
Lead Manager, Cons. Years with Fund:	Albert Nicholas, nineteen
Sales Fee:	None
Redemption Fee:	None
Assets:	$1.0 billion
Telephone Switch:	No
Expense Ratio:	0.96%
Portfolio Turnover Rate:	34%
Retirement Plans:	IRA, Keogh
Minimum Initial Investment:	$500
Minimum Subsequent Investments:	$100

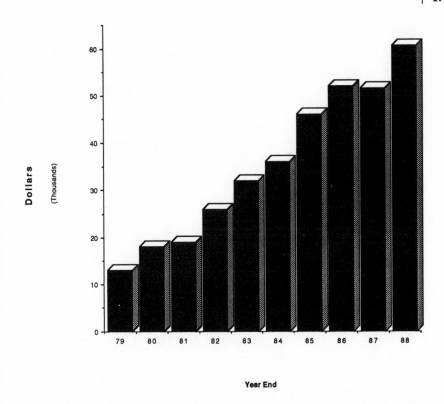

Year End

INVESTMENT OBJECTIVE. Capital appreciation, with income a secondary consideration.

HISTORY. The fund began operations in July 1969, as the Nicholas Strong Fund. Its name was changed in 1974 after Richard S. Strong, a co-founder and manager, left the fund.

INVESTMENT APPROACH. The Nicholas Fund follows a long-term, value-oriented approach to stock selection, and specializes in small- to medium-sized companies, i.e., those with annual sales of between $100 and $500 million. The fund has strictly adhered to its guidelines on value, normally avoiding stocks with price-earnings ratios in excess of one-half their growth rates. The fund has demonstrated the discipline necessary to maintain that policy, occasionally holding cash positions as high as 50% (even in up markets) rather than violate its own definition of value. The emphasis on long-term value has resulted in an A + rating from *Forbes* for its performance in down markets.[60] The long-term value approach is also evidenced by its extremely low average annual portfolio turnover rate of only 34%.

MANAGEMENT. The Nicholas Company, Inc., has served as the fund's investment adviser since the initial public offering in 1969. The adviser receives compensation from the fund in the amount of 0.75% annually on the first $50 million of assets and 0.65% on the remainder. During the fiscal year ended 31 March 1987, the fund paid the adviser 0.55% in fees.

Stein Roe Special Fund

Up 563%
$10,000 became $66,333

Address:	P.O. Box 1143
	Chicago, IL 60690
Phone:	(800) 338-2550
Ten-Year Average Annual Return:	+22.5%
Ten-Year Average Annual Diff. to S & P:	+6.5%
Lead Manager, Cons. Years with Fund:	Al Kugel, twenty-one
Sales Fee:	None
Redemption Fee:	None
Assets:	$187 million
Telephone Switch:	Yes
Expense Ratio:	0.95%
Portfolio Turnover Rate:	78%
Retirement Plans:	IRA, Keogh, SEP
Minimum Initial Investment:	$1,000

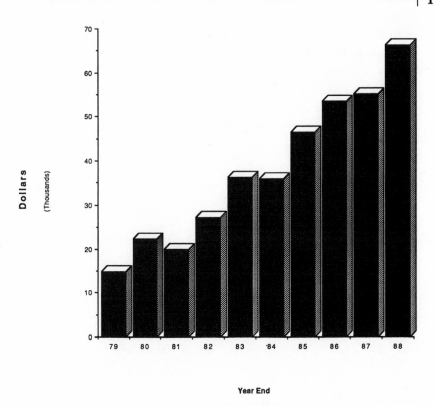

Year End

Minimum Subsequent
Investments: $100

INVESTMENT OBJECTIVE. Capital appreciation.

HISTORY. The fund began operations on 22 May 1968.

INVESTMENT APPROACH. To achieve its goal of maximum capital appreciation, the fund invests primarily in common stocks and securities convertible into common stocks. The fund intends to switch heavily to cash during periods of perceived approaching market weakness. The Stein Roe Special Fund, as its name suggests, invests largely in special situations—companies that it believes will benefit from expected management changes, new technology, products, or services, or in expected changes in demand patterns. The fund will also invest in the securities of relatively small companies, as well as new issues.

MANAGEMENT. Stein Roe & Farnham, Inc., has served as the fund's investment adviser since the fund began operations in 1968. The adviser is compensated in the amount of 0.75% annually of all assets under management.

Acorn Fund

Up 460%
$10,000 became $56,086

Address:	Two North LaSalle Street
	Suite 500
	Chicago, IL 60602-3790
Phone:	(312) 621-0630
Ten-Year Average Annual Return:	+19.9%
Ten-Year Average Annual Diff. to S & P:	+3.9%
Lead Manager, Cons. Years with Fund:	Ralph Wanger, seventeen
Sales Fee:	None
Redemption Fee:	None (2% on shares held less than 60 days)
Assets:	$417 million
Telephone Switch:	Yes
Expense Ratio:	0.88%
Portfolio Turnover Rate:	30%
Retirement Plans:	IRA, Keogh, SEP
Minimum Initial Investment:	$4,000
Minimum Subsequent Investments:	$1,000

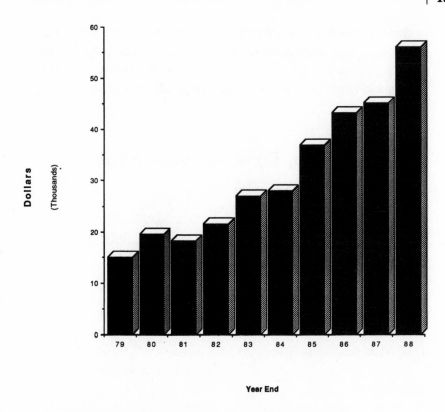

Year End

INVESTMENT OBJECTIVE. Capital appreciation.

HISTORY. Acorn began operation in 1970.

INVESTMENT APPROACH. The fund attempts to identify industries that it believes will benefit from superior relative strength trends
over the long term. This long-term outlook is reflected in the fund's
low 30% average annual portfolio turnover rate for the 1978–1987
period. Once industries have been identified that are believed to be
enjoying above-average long-term relative strength, the fund then looks
to invest in smaller-capitalization companies within those industries.
The fund's emphasis on smaller companies should, in theory, make
its performance more volatile than the overall market; however, during
the 1978–1987 period the fund had only one down year, and has been
named to the *Forbes* Honor Roll four consecutive years.[61]

MANAGEMENT APPROACH. Harris Associates, Inc., and its predecessor organization has served as investment adviser to the Acorn Fund since its inception. Compensation to the investment adviser during 1986 amounted to 0.64% of average daily net assets.

Fidelity Equity-Income Fund

Up 456%

$10,000 became $55,699

Address:	82 Devonshire Street
	Boston, MA 02109
Phone:	(800) 544-6666
Ten-Year Average Annual Return:	+19.2%
Ten-Year Average Annual Diff. to S & P:	+3.2%
Lead Manager, Cons. Years with Fund:	Bruce Johnstone, six
Sales Fee:	2%
Redemption Fee:	None
Assets:	$3.8 billion
Telephone Switch:	Yes
Expense Ratio:	0.82%
Portfolio Turnover Rate:	121%
Retirement Plans:	IRA, Keogh, 403b, 401k
Minimum Initial Investment:	$1,000
Minimum Subsequent Investments:	$250

INVESTMENT OBJECTIVE. Current income, with growth a secondary consideration.

HISTORY. The fund was originally offered as the Everest Income Fund in 1966. In 1975, the fund merged with the Fidelity Convertible & Senior Securities Fund.

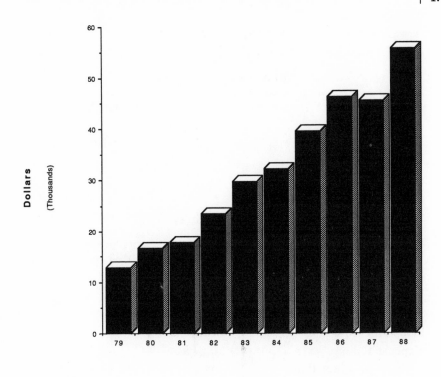

Dollars (Thousands)

Year End

INVESTMENT APPROACH. The Fidelity-Equity Income Fund seeks to produce above-average current income by investing in income-producing equity securities, such as common and preferred stocks, and in securities convertible into common stocks. The fund looks for yields that exceed the composite yield on the securities comprising the S & P 500 index. Because of its emphasis on above-average income, the fund is likely to be less volatile than most pure equity funds. The fund's track record confirms this greater stability: during the 1978–1987 period, the Fidelity Equity-Income Fund had only one down year, returning − 1.6% in 1987.

MANAGEMENT. Fidelity Managment & Research Company has served as investment adviser since the fund's merger with Fidelity in 1975. During fiscal 1987, the fund paid FMR a fee equal to 0.65% of its average daily net assets.

Windsor Fund

Up 560%
$10,000 became $66,030

Address:	Vanguard Financial Center
	P.O. Box 2800
	Valley Forge, PA 19496-9901
Phone:	(800) 662-7447
Ten-Year Average Annual Return:	+21.2%
Ten-Year Average Annual Diff. to	
S & P:	+5.2%
Lead Manager, Cons. Years with	
Fund:	John Neff, twenty-five
Sales Fee:	None
Redemption Fee:	None
Assets:	$5.1 billion
Telephone Switch:	Yes
Expense Ratio:	0.61%
Portfolio Turnover Rate:	44%
Retirement Plans:	IRA, Profit Sharing, Pension
Minimum Initial Investment:	$10,000
Minimum Subsequent	
Investments:	$100

INVESTMENT OBJECTIVE. Long-term growth, with income a secondary consideration.

HISTORY. The fund began operations on 23 October 1958. It was closed to new accounts during 1986 and 1987 and reopened 3 January 1988.

INVESTMENT APPROACH. Portfolio manager John Neff remains a near-legend in the investment community, and relies on a contrarian approach to investing. In tangible terms, Neff looks to purchase stocks with low price-earnings ratios, meaningful current

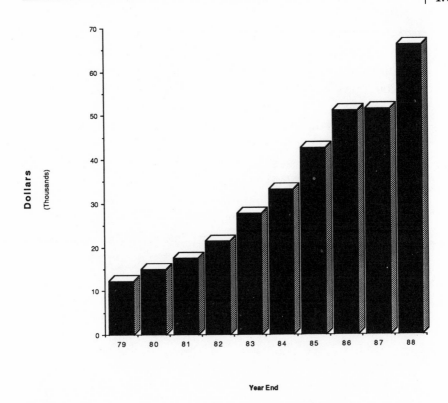

yields, and high book values relative to per-share stock price. Like most contrarians,* Neff's portfolios usually have an extremely low turnover rate, which also serves to minimize the fund's expense ratio, which averaged only 0.61% over the 1978–1987 period.

MANAGEMENT. The fund is managed by the Wellington Management Company, which earned an advisory fee of 0.19% of assets under management for the fiscal year ending 31 October 1987. That amount included a 0.17% base fee and a 0.02% bonus earned by management for its investment performance relative to the S & P 500.

While all the funds listed above have demonstrated an ability to outperform the broad-market averages over a long period of time, and while that performance can be taken as a strong indication of competence, the future ability of each of these funds to outperform the market is far from assured. Even for the world's top money managers, beating the market over the long term is a Herculean task. If you are uncomfortable with *any* possibility of underperforming the market (and you should be), there is only one solution: *buy the market*. Sound expensive? It is not. For only $1,000, it is yours.

As mentioned in chapter one, the Vanguard family of no-load mutual funds has introduced the first "index" fund, i.e., a fund which precisely allocates its assets to a broadly based, widely followed index, in this case the S & P 500. The fund invests only in companies comprising the S & P, and in proportions which exactly duplicate the index. If you had invested $10,000 into the S & P 500 on 1 January 1979, your investment would have grown to $42,993 ten years later, a gain of 329%, *without taking the slightest risk of underperformance.*

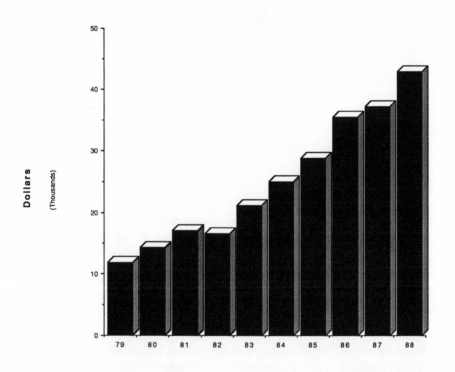

Year End

Again, if the idea of never underperforming the market sounds interesting, write or call for a prospectus at:

> The Vanguard Group
> Vanguard Financial Center
> Valley Forge, Pennsylvania 19496-9901
> (800) 662-7447

Putting It All Together

Great, you're thinking. These funds all sound nice, but what do I do with them? How can I turn this information into a coherent investment plan?

Here is a strategy that might make some sense for you, a strategy that you could begin with as little as $2,000.

Given X number of dollars to invest, put half of it into the S & P index fund, and divide the remaining half among as many of the other ten funds listed as possible, given the minimum investment requirement of each fund. Then set up your account to automatically reinvest all dividend and capital gain distributions, and try to add a modest amount to one of your funds, on a rotating basis, each month. As larger sums of money become available each succeeding year, again put half of the new money into the S & P fund and divide the other half equally between whichever of the ten funds you do not as yet own. Within just a few years, your portfolio should be made up of 50% of the S & P fund, and 5% each of the ten proven winners.

The benefits to you in following this approach are many: by investing 50% of your funds in the S & P 500, you will be anchoring at least half of your portfolio to a large segment of the market itself, guaranteeing that at least half of your money will never underperform the market. The other half will be diversified among ten of the most successful and brilliant money managers in the world; this half has an extremely high probability of meeting or exceeding the market averages.

You will be adding to your account each month, compounding your dividends and capital gains, paying no brokerage fees, doing no guessing, hearing no sales pitches, taking no chances of falling victim to broker fraud, and enduring no amateur-hour advice.

Your investments will be growing steadily according to a logical, sober, diversified investment strategy. Long-term trends will work to your advantage; history will be your broker.

No one can control, or predict, what returns the stock market will generate over the coming years. And since you can't control the market, your only job as an investor is to maximize the probabilities of your meeting or exceeding those returns—whatever they may be— over the long run. The investment plan I have just outlined can take you to that end.

If It's Income You Want . . .

Despite the fact that, over the long term, stocks will almost certainly outperform income-oriented investments, for a variety of reasons, stocks are not an appropriate investment vehicle for everyone.

If you are not comfortable with volatility, the seemingly inexplicable and mercurial nature of the stock market might give you nail-biting days and sleepless nights. Or, you might not be currently in a financial position to absorb the potential near-term risks of an investment in stocks. Perhaps you have already made enough money to live comfortably the remainder of your life; in that case, what you might have to gain in the stock market is not worth what you have to lose. Also, for you, the long-term advantages of a growth fund may be less essential than your need for current income to help offset living expenses.

For these reasons, mutual funds that invest for the purpose of achieving high *current* income (as opposed to long-term growth) have become increasingly popular in recent years, with over $128 billion flowing into such funds in 1986 alone.

Income-oriented mutual funds attempt to achieve their stated objective by investing in a diversified segment of the bond market, i.e., that market which trades the debt securities of various corporations, municipalities, and governments. These securities carry fixed rates of interest and their resale value will fluctuate inversely to the course of interest rates. To illustrate, an IBM bond with, say, a 10% fixed rate and a twenty-year maturity is quite valuable if current rates on comparable bonds are around 8% and less valuable if the rate on newly issued paper of similar quality and maturity is 12%. Its price in the resale bond market will float to reflect these relative changes in value.

While it is generally true that the bond market is less volatile and risky than the stock market (if only because the high current yields help to offset periodic resale price declines), the bond market has taken a number of severe price hits over the past two decades, most notably in 1979–1980 when long-term interest rates soared to 15% or higher, pushing the resale price of some existing bonds as low as thirty cents on the dollar. While that type of bond market collapse is rare (and was followed by a historic rally), the possibility of at least a temporary capital decline is a fact of investing life that should be fully considered before putting any money into an income-producing mutual fund.

Bond mutual funds fall into three basic types: government securities funds, corporate bond funds, and tax-exempt municipal bond funds. Following are brief explanations of each category.

U.S. Government Securities Funds

These funds have become enormously popular in recent years; in 1985, U.S. Government securities fund purchases represented over one-third of all mutual fund sales.

Government securities funds, which are not to be confused with money market funds investing only in U.S. Government securities, invest exclusively in direct or indirect debt obligations of the U.S. Government, such as treasury bills, bonds, notes, and Ginnie Maes (GNMAs). Because the securities in these types of funds are backed by the full faith and credit of the U.S. Government, you can be assured that you will not lose any of your principal or interest due to default.

However, the phrase "government guaranteed," which brokers frequently use to sell these funds, is a lie because it is not the whole story. While you can feel safe from any possibility of losses resulting from default, there is no guarantee that the resale price will be the same or higher than your original purchase price. As noted earlier, the resale price of any fixed-income security will move inversely to the course of interest rates. Therefore, if interest rates have risen during the time you held the investment, chances are good that the resale price of the fund will have declined. Conversely, if interest rates fall, your resale price will have climbed.

Despite these price fluctuations, U.S. Government securities funds offer two important benefits to investors: a high yield, usually 3 to 4% higher than bank CD's or money market funds, and the flexibility to switch (often with only a phone call) into a money market fund, thereby avoiding risk to principal during periods of rising interest rates. If you are in need of additional monthly income and have no foreseeable need to sell, government securities funds are ideal and should be strongly considered.

Listed below are five of the top-performing U.S. Government funds over the 1982–1987 period, ranked according to each fund's average annual total return for the period. All are no-load funds.

AVERAGE ANNUAL

Fund	Total Return
Vanguard GNMA Portfolio (800) 662-7447	+14.4%
Value Line U.S. Government (800) 223-0818	+13.6%
Fidelity Government Securities (800) 544-6666	+12.2%
Mutual Omaha America (800) 228-9596	+11.0%
Twentieth Century U.S. Government (800) 345-2021	+11.0%

Corporate Bond Funds

Like the U.S. Government securities fund, the corporate bond* fund seeks to produce high monthly income as its basic investment objective. However, these funds invest primarily or exclusively in securities of corporations; the correspondingly higher degree of risk is reflected in somewhat higher yields, which generally range from 1 to 3% above U.S. Government fund yields, depending upon the quality of the corporate securities being held. Despite the theoretical possibility of bankruptcy and default among one or more holdings in a corporate bond fund, the securities purchased are carefully selected and monitored by professional money managers, which, along with the high level of diversification inherent in any mutual fund, largely mitigates the risk of default significantly affecting the fund. The question of resale price fluctuation remains, however, and as in the case of U.S. Government securities funds, implies that the investment is only appropriate for those with no immediate liquidity requirements.

Following are five leading no-load corporate bond funds, ranked according to their average annual total return for the 1982–1987 period.

AVERAGE ANNUAL

Fund	Total Return
Fidelity High Income	+19.2%
(800) 544-6666	
Axe Houghton Income	+17.0%
(800) 431-1030	
Vanguard High Yield	+16.2%
(800) 662-7447	
Nicholas Income	+15.0%
(414) 272-6133	
Babson Bond Trust	+14.6%
(800) 821-5591	

Municipal (Tax-Free) Bond Funds

There are two types of municipal or tax-free bond funds: unit trusts, which pay a more or less fixed rate of interest for the life of the trust (which may range from two to thirty years), and mutual funds, whose investment managers actively trade the fund's portfolio, thus creating a fluctuating yield with no specific maturity date. In both cases, the income from the funds is exempt from federal—and in some cases state and local—taxes, which can be a significant advantage for investors in the top tax bracket. Reflecting this tax break, yields on municipal bond funds are lower than for taxable funds, and if you are in the 28% tax bracket or lower (about $43,000 maximum income for a single return and $71,900 for a joint return), in most cases you will be better served in a fully taxable corporate or government bond fund. Like the corporate and government funds, the resale price of tax-exempt municipal funds will move inversely to interest rates.

Following are five top-performing no-load tax-exempt mutual funds, ranked according to annual average total return for the ten-year period 1978–1987.

AVERAGE ANNUAL

Fund	Total Return
Stein Roe Managed Municipals (800) 621-0320	+12.5%
T. Rowe Price Tax-Free Income (800) 638-5660	+11.2%
Scudder Managed Municipal Bonds (800) 225-2470	+ 9.9%
Dreyfus Tax-Exempt Bonds (800) 645-6561	+ 8.9%
Fidelity Municipal Bonds (800) 544-6666	+ 7.5%

Three Basic Rules

Whether you are investing for growth or income, whether you will be following the specific investment approach outlined earlier or one of your own, before putting money into any mutual fund, you should consider and follow a few basic rules of good investing. If you follow these principles and choose specific funds based upon a long-term track record of consistency and superior results, the odds are very strong that you will equal or exceed the returns generated by the broad-market averages.

Three points to remember:

1. **Never make an investment that cannot be held for at least three years, and preferably longer.** The financial markets go both ways, and if you catch the wrong part of a market cycle, it is quite possible that twelve to eighteen months later the value of your original investment will have declined, even if it has outperformed the market. The possible forced liquidation of a mutual fund to meet liquidity requirements is by far the single most risky development that could impact the success or failure of your investment, even more so than a recession, bear market, or any other political or economic event. A study by Ibbotson & Associates found that if you had bought the S & P 500 index at any point in the last sixty-one years and held it for five years, you would have shown a positive return 86% of the time.[62] Big losses, and even many small losses, could be almost entirely avoided by being careful to never invest money that might be needed for any other purpose within a three-year period. In those instances where money must be kept liquid, bank CD's, money market funds, and treasury securities are the only appropriate investments available; the low historic rates of return for each are simply a price that an investor must pay for liquidity.

2. **Never try to guess short-term market swings; invest for the long-term.** The switching privilege offered by most mutual funds creates the potential for making switches based upon short-term guesses rather than long-term trends. Keep in mind that no stockbroker, brokerage firm, investment guru, or mutual fund manager has ever demonstrated an ability to consistently predict the short-term course of any market. Short-term predictions are nothing more than guesses. Do not guess, invest! There is no evidence to suggest that any type of market timing strategy will work over the long haul; a simple buy-and-hold approach is the best way for you to earn superior returns over the long term. Remember: if anyone could accurately predict the short-term course of the stock or bond market, he or she certainly would have no need to tell anyone else about it.

3. **Never marry just one fund—Diversify.** No matter how successful a mutual fund may have been in the past, it is always prudent to diversify into several other funds as well. Diversification, even among previously highly successful money managers, decreases risk and increases the chances that you will exploit the underlying market trend.

And that is all there is to it: *Invest only for the long-term using only long-term money spread over several consistently successful mutual funds.* All that is needed now is for you to put that strategy into action.

CHAPTER 9

Private
Money Managers

Mutual funds are not the only way to achieve professional money management; if you have a significant five- or six-figure investment portfolio or are responsible for a pension or profit-sharing plan* of equal size, you can hire a private professional money manager by choosing directly from the over 8,000 belonging to independent portfolio management companies. Many banks also offer private portfolio management in the form of trust departments; unfortunately, with few exceptions, bank trusts are notorious under-achievers. Low salaries and an overly stodgy investment approaches combine to make trust departments an only marginally better bet than using a stockbroker or dartboard. This chapter will discuss the benefits and difficulties in hiring a private money manager, as well as provide information on where you can find them, how to evaluate them, and how much a good manager will cost. Five of the top portfolio managers, each of whom has consistently outperformed the broad-market averages, are also profiled.

Not Everyone Can Play

Certainly the major difficulty in obtaining professional portfolio management is the high minimum investment required to open an account. Most private managers will not accept accounts below $100,000, and it is not unusual for minimums to reach $250,000, $500,000, or even $1,000,000. The size of these minimums obviously tends to exclude nearly all but the wealthiest individual investors, but are set low enough to attract many pension and profit-sharing plans. (Included in the subsequent profiles are managers with relatively small minimums of $50,000 and $80,000.) Managers cite two reasons for the stratospheric minimums: cost and service. The expense of setting up, managing, and maintaining a $10,000 account is every bit as high as running a $1,000,000 account; the economics of private money management is such that "small" accounts are simply not profitable. Additionally, private managers make themselves available to any client who wishes a conference. Clearly, if the number of clients grows overly large, managers could easily find themselves doing more hand-holding than money managing.

Another obstacle to hiring a competent private money manager is the lack of a readily available central rating system. Unlike mutual funds, whose track records are reported monthly in many parts of the financial press, results obtained by private money managers are usually not reported, thus the process of comparing track records requires painstaking correspondence and careful evaluation. In examining the track records of money managers, it is also wise to keep in mind that the results are the *average* for all portfolios managed; any one client may have earned more or less than the average. (Managers are not required to disclose the results obtained by any specific account to anyone but the client.) For most private managers, this distinction is not major since there is usually very little difference in the overall portfolios of any of his or her clients. A manager with 100, 200, or 500 clients clearly cannot take the time (nor would it be useful) to design portfolios for each. So while the reporting of an average may be off somewhat for any given client, it can generally be assumed to be an accurate barometer of the manager's ability.

Disputes have also arisen as to the method of calculation used in arriving at a final performance record. With no attempt to mislead or misinform, it is possible for managers to use alternate forms of calculation and thus arrive at somewhat different final numbers, even given the exact same performance. With an eye toward unifying the performance calculation methods, the Investment Counsel Association of America, which has over 100 member firms, has recently published a *Standards of Measurement and Use for Investment Performance Data*. This highly detailed, forty-page booklet sets explicit guidelines for calculating performance records, which must be followed by each of its member firms. While the bulk of private managers are not bound by the document, its creation is an acknowledgement of a serious (and totally unnecessary) credibility problem that must be addressed. The eventual benefactor of greater uniformity in performance calculation methods will not only be the investing public, but the private managers themselves, who surely suffer from the generally inaccurate perception that their track records are not all they claim to be.

Many Benefits

But even if the selection process can be arduous, choosing an excellent private manager can be well worth the trouble, and can offer some benefits that mutual funds cannot. Because private portfolio managers are smaller (generally ranging from $10 to $200 million under management), they can be more flexible and move faster. For example, many mutual funds would have great difficulty liquidating a sizable percentage of their holdings and raising cash if market conditions seemed to warrant a defensive position. A private manager handling, say, $50 million, would have little trouble achieving 70 to 80% cash in a relatively short period of time and without depressing the prices of the very same stocks he or she is trying to get out of. Besides flexibility and speed, private managers will talk personally with any client whenever that client has questions or concerns. Mutual fund managers, rarely, if ever, communicate directly with any shareholder. In the end, however, the primary advantage to you in hiring a private manager is the same as for buying a mutual fund: you are hiring a well-trained, proven professional to manage your money, one who not only has the proper qualifications and track record, but whose basic interests run exactly parallel to your interests—the production of superior investment *results*. The private manager will not be judged on the basis of how many trades are made, or on total commissions generated, or on sales skills, or upon any ability to successfully infiltrate wealthy social cliques. The private money manager will be held accountable only by the client, and for only one thing: results. This direct and clearly focused accountability virtually assures that only those managers achieving excellent results for their clients— i.e., consistently beating the S & P 500 index—will survive over the long term.

Five Survivors

What follows are profiles and in-depth interviews with five widely respected and highly successful private money managers. (These conversations, along with those found in chapter ten, were conducted during varying periods in 1987 and 1988.) While all the managers have demonstrated an ability to consistently better the market averages over a long period of time, each has achieved their success through occasionally dissimilar methods. When choosing a private portfolio manager, be careful to understand the basic investment philosophy and approach of the person you hire. That approach should be compatible with your own philosophies and comfort level. It should be noted that few managers who have consistently taken large risks or tried to outguess the market over the short term survive for long periods of time. In fact, despite a few subtle differences, there seem to be several common threads linking many of the truly successful money managers: most, but not all, tend to be fundamentalists*, most are contrarians, and most are long-term oriented, have an innate sense of value, are doggedly consistent in the application of their investment philosophy, and, interestingly enough, tend to reside in small or distant locales, far removed from the repetitive drone of the investment establishment. You will probably note many of these underlying similarities in the interviews that follow, both in this chapter and the next. And whether you are actively seeking a private money manager or not, you are certain to profit from the wisdom, professionalism, and true investment aptitude of these fine accomplished managers.

G.J.G. Inc.

Address:	1801 Avenue of the Stars Suite 306 Los Angeles, California 90067
Phone:	(213) 551-1453
President:	Gary J. Goodman
Year Established:	1979
Assets Under Management:	$20 million
Minimum Investment:	$50,000
Fees:	2% on the first $50,000, plus 1% thereafter
Average Annual Return Since Inception:	+20.7%
Average Annual Diff. to S & P Since Inception:	+4.5%

The following is an interview with Gary J. Goodman, president and chief portfolio manager of G.J.G. Inc.

TDS: *How do you define value?*
GJG: There is a real intrinsic value to every stock. Unfortunately, it can be very hard to pin down. If there was an omniscient person and he knew all the cash flows from a given company, and he knew the right interest rate to discount those cash flows back,

then by properly discounting the cash flows in the future you would have the true value of the company. Obviously, nobody knows that, so one tries to do certain things to get around it. One way is a dividend discount model* that approximates those factors. Another way is to buy companies, or factories, or raw land, or inventory, or cash. So I tend to be an asset buyer. I buy a lot of assets at prices below what I view to be their replacement costs. Hopefully, those assets are also generating a lot of earnings and/or cash flow.

TDS: *What critera are you looking for in terms of earnings growth* and price-earnings ratios?*

GJG: I like to buy stocks that are selling under ten-times earnings*. I like to buy below book value*. I use different strategies; sometimes I'll use Benjamin Graham's net/net book strategy* and buy a company below that number. Occasionally, very rarely, I'll be able to buy a company below cash value*, which is a very good deal. I've been able to do that a few times in my career, but it doesn't happen often.

TDS: *Do you prefer to buy small- or large-capitalization companies?*

GJG: Historically I have dealt with small-capitalization companies. About one-third of my companies are on the New York Stock Exchange, and about one-third are on the American Stock Exchange, and the remaining third are over-the-counter.

TDS: *Why the preference for smaller companies?*

GJG: I think there is a small stock effect. Small stocks are more efficient and historically have outperformed large stocks. It's not quite clear why they do that, but there are several possibilities. It might be that when a company becomes large it becomes inefficient, or becomes a big bureaucracy. It's very difficult for even an IBM to continue to grow rapidly. Large companies simply have some problems that small companies don't have. Small companies tend to be more efficient and are able to grow faster. Also, there are forty, fifty, or even one hundred analysts looking at IBM. I have visited a number of companies where they tell me that I'm the only analyst that has ever come out to visit them. So, obviously, you're not going to find anything undiscovered at IBM, but you have a good chance of doing that with a smaller company.

TDS: *And if no analyst has discovered the company, it's likely that no institution owns it yet?*

GJG: That's correct, and institutions won't even buy below a certain capitalization.

TDS: *How closely do you watch the overall market?*

GJG: There have been times when I've been 100% invested in cash, and I'm 30% cash right now. I get into cash in various ways. A bull market may take all my stocks to their goals and I sell, or sometimes I just sell purely to raise cash. I will raise cash at times if I see enough red flags out there.[II]

North American Capital Management

Address:	P.O. Box 6728
	Shawnee Mission, Kansas 66206
Phone:	(913) 381-8401
President:	Robert J. McElwain
Year Established:	1981
Assets Under Management:	$11.5 million
Minimum Investment:	$80,000
Fees:	2% on first $100,000, declining
	to 1% at $500,000
Average Annual Return Since	
Inception:	+18.5%
Average Annual Diff. to S & P	
Since Inception:	+4.6%

The following is an interview with Robert J. McElwain, presdient and chief portfolio manager of North American Capital Management.

TDS: *Your stock-selection process is known as "top-down." Could you explain?*

RJM: When you are talking about top-down, you are talking about viewing the overall condition of the market first and then looking at industries to see which are strongest. Thirdly, you look at individual companies within those industries.

TDS: *You are primarily a technician*. Do you use fundamental analysis* at all in your stock-selection process?*

RJM: Yes. Once we have gotten down to the stocks that we really like, we go back and recheck our decisions by looking at the fundamentals. The reason we use technical analysis* is that more times than not, stocks will begin to strenghthen and move up well before the fundamentals are known. And if you're trying to get in close to the bottom and get out close to the top, you can't always afford to wait until the fundamentals are available.

TDS: *Do you access the market on a long-term, intermediate-term, or short-term basis?*

RJM: We do it on all three. We look at the very long-term, meaning three to five years. Then we come down to the one- to two-year time frame. Finally, we look at the one- to six-month frame. We're constantly checking all three areas to make sure that the trends we have seen previously are still intact. My guess is that with the change in the tax laws we will probably be a little more aggressive and maybe a bit more short-term oriented in our stock selection. We tend to buy stocks and hold them for nine to eighteen months anyway; that's our general time frame.

TDS: *Do you have a preference for large or small companies, and what are your requirements regarding price-earnings ratios?*

RJM: Basically, PE's don't mean much to us because our approach is technical, but we only look at what amounts to Fortune 1000 companies—the large capitalization, established companies, 99% of which are on the New York Stock Exchange. So we don't go too far away from the blue chip arena.

TDS: *Do you maintain different portfolios for each of your clients, or are all the portfolios basically invested in the same securities?*

RJM: They tend to be very similar in that if we're buying oils then we'll buy oils for almost all the portfolios. We have essentially two account categories with respect to management approach.

They're either growth accounts or we have a small number of accounts which designate growth plus current income. These are mostly retired people who want their dividend checks paid out to them as they accrue to the account. Even so, I would say there is not much difference between the two categories.

TDS: *Most technicians tend to view predictions, especially those involving the overall economy, with a great deal of skepticism. What is your impression of the forecasting accuracy of economists?*

RJM: I don't really have much faith in most economists. They have a lousy record for predicting recessions and predicting recoveries and calling interest rates. There are probably a few of them that are good and a lot of them that aren't. When you look at the estimates from economists and compare them to the technical indicators within the market and see which industries are doing what, you just know that some of these predictions have absolutely no way of coming true.

TDS: *You're singing the technician's theme song, that the market is infinitely wiser than the analysts.*

RJM: Absolutely. It almost sounds religious, but the stock market is all knowing, because it is the consensus of all opinion. It takes into account everyone who has a nickel to invest. The big problem is being able to read the technicals correctly. As with any analyst, whether he is fundamental or technical, everyone gets a chance to call their numbers wrong, and every technician has been wrong. But I think the technician works with a set of numbers that are a bit more reliable than the numbers a fundamentalist uses.

TDS: *The purpose of my book is to explain to investors that trying to beat the broad-market averages through a stockbroker is pure folly, and that they would be much better served by employing some form of professional management. You've been on both sides, first as a broker and now as a professional portfolio manager. Do you agree?*

RJM: Absolutely. There is an incredible conflict of interest for a stockbroker who is managing money. I was a broker for twenty years and I never was a big producer. I never got the gold stars, simply because I couldn't do some of the things that were necessary to be a big hitter. I was more interested in beating the market and making profts for clients, which is really a direct conflict with what the brokerage firm wants you to do. They want production every day. They want X-number of dollars in the till on a regular basis. In order to do that you have to make investment decisions that are not necessarily to the benefit of the client."

Compu-Val Investments, Inc.

Address:	1701 Shallcross Avenue Wilmington, Delaware 19806-2321
Phone:	(302) 652-6767
President:	Dr. James Kalil, Sr.
Year Established:	1974
Assets Under Management:	$170 million
Minimum Investment:	$250,000
Fees:	$225 plus 1%
Average Annual Return Since Inception:	+24.8%
Average Annual Diff. to S & P Since Inception:	+11.8%

The following is an interview with Dr. James Kalil, president of Compu-Val Investments, Inc.

TDS: *Most money managers will claim that they try to buy value. How do you define value?*

JK: We define value specifically in terms of assets. A stock has to be selling at or below book value or adjusted book value*. This is the focus point of what we call value. It has to be at or below book value on the theory that book value represents a kind of bottom side for the stock. On a theoretical basis, if the company were liquidated, you would get book value for it. On an actual basis, of course, it might depend on a lot of factors. Then we look at a lot of other criteria. The company has to be sound, and by sound, we mean a couple of things. We look at the debt structure; we don't like to invest in companies that have more than 50% long-term debt*. We also look at the credit rating to be sure that they are financially strong in case they would need to borrow money. You never know when that is going to happen so you've got to build that in. The result is that we've never had a single company go bankrupt on us, because of looking so carefully at the financial strength. We also look at management in a number of ways. One way is to actually talk to management, but that is only marginally helpful because they are all optimistic and they are always going to conquer all the problems that face them. A better way is to look at their past record and see how they've done under more normal circumstances. They're obviously selling at a bargain because their current earnings are in trouble. If their earnings* weren't in trouble, they wouldn't be selling at this bargain.

TDS: *What criteria are you looking for in terms of earnings growth, price-earnings ratios, return on shareholders' equity*, etc.?*

JK: We try to go for about a 100% projected increase in earnings over a one- to three-year period, and therefore project a 100% increase in the price of the stock. We try to project the long-term earnings; it is very difficult to project quarter-to-quarter earnings so we don't put much emphasis on that. Short-term projections have, in my opinion, almost a random character to them. Even management has great difficulty with short-term projections.

TDS: *How long do you usually hold a stock?*

JK: Our average holding period is about two years.

TDS: *Do you try to time the market?*

JK: No, we don't time the market [market timing]*. We're not market players, we concentrate more on the stocks and ignore the stock market. Our theory is that as long as we can find companies that are undervalued, you can buy them. Of course, if we ever reach the stage where there are no more bargains, we stop buying. And as the market goes up, we do have more trouble; we have to look harder.

TDS: *Since your stocks are selling at or below book value, their earnings are obviously down. You are looking for a turn in their earnings in . . . ?*

JK: Within one to three years. We're not necessarily expecting any immediate improvement. We buy based upon expected long-term improvement. Stock prices, generally, are based on short-term changes. For that reason we don't pay much attention to the short-term gyrations of the stock. We look more for the long term.

TDS: *Do you buy mostly large or small companies?*

JK: One of our requirements is that they be liquid*. That puts us mostly in medium-sized companies. We do buy some pretty large ones, but if you averaged out our portfolios you'd find the average stock to be about medium capitalization. About 85% of our stocks are on the New York Stock Exchange. That's due mostly to the liquidity requirements.

TDS: *What is the most common mistake the average investor makes in managing his or her own investments?*

JK: The most common mistake is due to emotion. He tends to do the opposite of what really should be done. At the bottom of markets, the average investor wants to get out, and I think this is one time when a professional money manager can really earn his money, in trying to convince the client that selling at market bottoms is not the right thing to do. Market drops are temporary, just like market rises are temporary. There's no such thing as a trend that lasts forever; it just doesn't happen. Market trends will always reverse themselves. Unfortunately, the tendency of human nature is always to assume that whatever trend is going at the time will continue forever. That's just part of human nature. So the average investor tends to get in when things are booming and get out at the bottom. If you're constantly doing that, you're bound to lose money. The basic problem is not intellect, but emotion. Most of the clients have sufficient intellect; they just get all tied up in their stomachs when they have to make investment decisions.

TDS: *Is is possible to remain unemotional when your own money is on the line?*

JK: It's very difficult. The biggest contribution that a professional manager can make is to take the emotion out of the decision-making process.

TDS: *Does the fact that most of the television and radio coverage of the financial markets is superficial and appeals to emotion rather than reason to make it even more difficult for the average investor to keep his head?*

JK: Absolutely. You get a constant stream of quotes and media advice. You can't turn on the radio or TV without hearing stock price quotes. It bombards you from every angle. I won't even allow a quotron in my office.

TDS: *Because it encourages a myopic view of the market?*

JK: Yes, it does encourage a myopic view. I've even moved away from downtown to get away from all the quotrons.

TDS: *That is interesting. It seems that a common thread linking many of the truly successful money managers is their tendency to reside in locales far removed from the investment establishment.*

JK: That's absolutely correct. It goes back to what I said about emotion and why the average investor does so poorly. The farther away I get from Wall Street, the more I can think in fundamental terms. I find it easier to get a sense of perspective to my actions. A New York University professor once made a study of the most successful money managers and found that they had two common traits: they didn't trade the market and they were consistent in their philosophy. They never deviated from the basic approach; they had an element of consistency. Those consistencies were not necessarily the same from money manager to money manager, but each stuck with whatever style was best for him. The money managers who are really in it for the long term don't trade the market, because if you do, you're eventually going to end up with egg on your face. Anyone trying to trade the market is trying to do the impossible. There are just too many imponderables, too many factors.^{KK}

Fenimore Asset Management

Address:	118 N. Grand Street
	P.O. Box 310
	Cobleskill, New York 12043
Phone:	(518) 234-4393
President:	Thomas O. Putnam
Year Established:	1976
Assets Under Management:	$57 million
Minimum Investment:	$100,000
Fees:	1% ($1,500 minimum)
Average Annual Return Since	
Inception:	+15.6%
Average Annual Diff. to S & P	
Since Inception:	+1.4%

The following is an interview with Thomas O. Putnam, president and chief portfolio manager of Fenimore Asset Management, Inc.

TDS: *Every portfolio manager tries to buy value. But value is clearly in the eye of the beholder. How do you define value?*

TOP: Basically, we're looking for what we consider to be a discrepancy between the true business worth of a corporation and what the marketplace is saying it is worth. We are evaluating the company almost as if we were going to buy the entire corporation, taking a look at its real economic value and seeing what underlying strength the company has to propel it to grow internally. We are hoping that if the company has that kind of economic potential, then the markets will eventually recognize it and move its stock price higher. We don't want to pay a premium for that kind of advantage, but instead buy it at what we consider bargain-basement prices. The one thing that is apparent in our approach is that we believe you are only going to find value when other people are selling. So, we may be a bit early on the investment, but that doesn't disturb us because we are long-term investors. Our average holding period is between two and four years, so we are not in for a six- or twelve-month trade. It would be nice if the fundamentals came that quickly and the marketplace then took note of those fundamentals in that short of time, but that generally doesn't happen.

TDS: *Do you apply specific criteria in terms of price-earnings ratios, earnings growth, etc., to your stock-selection process?*

TOP: In general, yes. We do look for some specifics. We probably will not buy a company that is selling for more than twelve-times earnings. We are looking for companies that have low debt structures, basically around a maximum of 40% debt to equity*. We only want companies with good balance sheets, and we want them to return about 15% or better on capital. Beyond that, we look at other fundamentals such as profit margins and book value. But of all the fundamentals that we look at, the analysis of the quality of the management team is probably the number one requirement for any good investment. We know that occasionally we are going to be incorrect about the timing of some of our economic assumptions, but if we are right about the quality of the management team with respect to their ability to define and meet their own objectives, at least the investment has the opportunity to work out. And we not only talk very closely with management, but we also talk to their customers, suppliers, and competitors to get a handle on management's ability to achieve their objectives.

TDS: *Do you prefer to buy small or large companies?*

TOP: We'll look at a company of almost any size, but what we eventually buy depends a lot on the environment we are in. Today, we are buying smaller-capitalization companies, but we will look at companies from $30 million capitalization on up to billions of dollars. Normally, however, large-capitalization companies are highly visible in the marketplace and we don't like a lot of institutional ownership because it tends to drive up the price of a stock very rapidly, and they therefore get out of our valuation ranges. So, most of the time it is the small- to medium-sized companies that fit our niche.

TDS: *Are your stocks generally uncovered by brokerage analysts?*

TOP: One of the things that is very attractive to us once we start analyzing a company is if very few people are following it, or if the company has very little institutional ownership. If we can accumulate a position slowly, then have the stock begin to get some recognition, that's going to be a more comfortable situation for us because our downside risk is very minimal under those conditions. But if we were to buy a company that already had large institutional ownership and some negative news is subsequently announced, we would be at considerable risk. So, we would prefer to have lesser-recognized stocks in our portfolio.

TDS: *How do you feel about market timing?*

TOP: I don't know of any study that suggests that over a long period of time market timers have been very successful. There are probably a couple of market timers who do very well, but they are only a handful. Historically, market timers have not done well. It is a very difficult discipline to use successfully.

TDS: *Your investment approach seems to emphasize the careful selection of value, regardless of overall market conditions. How carefully do you coordinate your purchases to general market or economic conditions?*

TOP: There are some underlying factors that suggest the mix of our portfolios, or suggest what the risk is and where we should be looking for alternative investments. We pay quite careful attention, for example, to what inflation is doing and to what interest rates are doing, because they are certainly going to affect the overall environment. Not only are they going to affect the overall economy, but they are going to affect the amount of investment alternatives that are available. So, when we are in a period with rapid growth in inflation, as was the case in the late 1970s and early 1980s, the competitive environment for equities was very difficult. Any money manager would be foolish not to at least be cognizant of that fact. Conversely, we also know that during periods of low inflation and low interest rates, that the environment can be rather conducive to investing in equities.

TDS: *How did you acquire your investment approach?*

TOP: I decided a long time ago, when I was investing for myself, that if I was going to be able to outperform the market I would be better off studying how the experts did it instead of trying to recreate the wheel. And so I do a lot of studying. I looked at how people like John Templeton and Warren Buffett and John Neff were able to achieve the kind of results they have achieved. I studied the writings of Benjamin Graham and others. And, of course, you are never able to completely appreciate all that knowledge until you begin to apply it. When I did start to apply it for clients in 1975, I was careful to maintain contact with money managers who have similar investment philosophies as my own, not only reading their literature but actually conversing with them about the existing environment to see if they had changed their parameters. What I found was that although a money manager has to be flexible, the really successful managers are absolutely consistent in the application of their investment philosophies. I think that is a very important lesson to learn. And you really only learn it through applying it.

TDS: *I find it a curious oddity that so many of the investment legends reside in locales that effectively insulate them from most Wall Street thinking.*

TOP: That's true. I don't know the reason for that, but I think that being away from Wall Street provides an environment that is much more conducive to long-term investing and to rational thinking. You're not bombarded with day-to-day announcements from the news media or from brokers that might distort your investment philosophy and really remove you from the consistency that is necessary. It is much easier to filter those things out when you are away from the melee of the crowd.LL

National Investment Services of America

Address:	815 E. Mason
	Milwaukee, Wisconsin 53202
Phone:	(414) 271-6540
Stock Portfolio Director:	Eugene Martin
Year Established:	1979
Assets Under Management:	$300 million
Minimum Investment:	$1 million
Fees:	1%
Average Annual Return Since Inception:	+20.1%
Average Annual Diff. to S & P Since Inception:	+3.9%

The following is an interview with Eugene Martin, director of stock management for National Investment Services of America.

TDS: *What are you looking for in a company?*

EM: We buy small- to medium-sized companies that have what I call the ideal unregulated monopoly—a company that is dominant in its market niche, whether because of management or product.

TDS: *How long do you typically hold your selections?*

EM: Our horizon is a two-year period. We don't like to project beyond then, but we have held stocks for as long as nine years. But ideally we like to project out two years and not go beyond that.

TDS: *Describe your selection process.*

EM: We do everything internally; we don't buy research from Wall Street. We are able to generate our own ideas using a data base of 8,000 companies and then applying certain criteria. As companies begin to pop out, we give them a closer look. We insist that a company has at least a three-year track record. And we also have a policy of not buying new issues.

TDS: *What types of numbers are you looking for in terms of price-earnings ratios, earnings growth, return on equity,* * *etc.?*

EM: We feel that the price-earnings ratio is at the crux of our philosophy because once we find a company we like we have to take them to the marketplace to see how other people have valued them. If we find a company whose PE is one-half its growth rate, that's the type of company that appeals to us. We also look for a minimum growth rate of 20% per year in terms of earnings and a minimum return on equity of 20%.

TDS: *You are buying stocks that most brokerage houses don't even cover.*

EM: I would hope so. These companies are not off-the-wall types; we do require a three-year track record, but I would dare say that though we'd never be the first investor in a company, that if we can find a company that meets all the criteria we require of it and if there are ten investors or less, and if Wall Street doesn't cover it, that's ideal for us.

TDS: *Do you attempt to time your purchases to any overview of the market as a whole?*

EM: Not really. We're a fully invested–type manager. We just don't think that over a long period of time that market timing works. Perhaps you'll be successful at it once or twice, but it's just not our style. MM

Shopping Around

If you plan to widen your search for a professional money manager, there are several courses to follow. The Investment Counsel Association of America is a professional organization dedicated to establishing the highest professional and ethical standards for its members. The complete roster of all ICAA member firms can be obtained by writing or calling:

> Investment Counsel Association of America
> 20 Exchange Place
> New York, New York 10005
> (212) 344-0999

In recent years, a new cottage industry has surfaced: talent scouts who will, for a fee, match you with a money manager on the basis of track record, risk-tolerance level, investment objective, and size of portfolio. Talent scouts monitor the performance of hundreds of managers, then distill that amount down to a workable number on the basis of results. Most scouts will charge a finder's fee, usually about $1,500. Two highly respected talent scouts are:

Michael Stolper
Stolper & Company, Inc.
770 B Street
Suite 420
San Diego, California 92102
(619) 231-0102

George Daniels
Investment Direction Associates
The Financial Center
Suite 900
Birmingham, Alabama 35203
(203) 250-5600

Less expensive methods of obtaining raw performance data are also available. For $195, CDA Investment Technologies, Inc., will provide the track records of more than 300 professional money managers, each of whom is managing $100 million or more. CDA ranks the top 20 managers for one-, three-, and five-year periods. Data is updated quarterly, and can be obtained by writing or calling:

CDA Investment Technologies, Inc.
11501 Georgia Avenue
Silver Spring, Maryland 20902
(301) 942-1700

Time Well Spent

Despite the time and possible expense involved in finding a highly competent private portfolio manager, the eventual results can be well worth the effort. The five professional managers profiled in this chapter combined for an average annual return of 20.3% over the fifty-one years of cumulative track record, beating the S & P index by an average of 5.7% per year.

A simple illustration shows just how much difference an excellent professional manager can make: Assuming you were fortunate enough to have started with a $100,000 portfolio, at the 20.3% average annual rate of return earned by the five managers listed here, your $100,000 would have grown to $634,828 (before taxes) in just ten years. If, instead, you would have earned the 14.6% average annual gain posted by the S & P, your $100,000 would have become only $390,702, or $244,126 less. And as I've noted repeatedly, there is little evidence to suggest that the average stockbroker can manage money well enough to even come within 3% per year (before commissions) of the S & P 500 over a long period of time.

Certainly not all professional money managers are as skilled as the five interviewed here. But all live in the real world of performance accountability, where only those with superior track records survive over time. It is a world where brokers are rarely seen, especially for any length of time.

CHAPTER 10

Advisory Newsletters

Despite the myriad advantages in choosing mutual funds or some form of professional money management, many investors simply cannot bring themselves to hand over their money to another person, no matter how impressive that person's record or credentials. This independent type of investor generally wants to keep control of specific investment decisions and often likes the excitement of owning individual stocks, with their attendant "stories." Many investors feel that, yes, mutual funds offer greater diversification, and, yes, mutual funds are professionally managed, and, yes, mutual funds have public track records, but—they are boring. One investor has said that buying individual stocks was "my Las Vegas, and I save the air fare."

Until relatively recently, this type of investor would either have had to rely on the advice of a stockbroker or make all investment decisions alone without any significant outside information or guidance. Whichever method the investor chose, he or she would then have had to execute the trades through a full-service broker, who would charge from 2 to 5% commission for each transaction. If this type of investor sounds suspiciously like yourself, take heart: the advent of the discount broker and the emergence of several quality investment newsletters now allows you to play individual stocks, using investment information that is both professional and free of conflicts of interest while still retaining all final investment decisions for yourself. Your decisions can then be executed through any of a number of excellent discount brokerage firms at a fraction of the cost charged by the large salesmen/brokers.

A Nice Fit

Clearly, investment newsletters and discount brokers were made for each other, and when used together wisely can produce results that approach those obtained by the finest mutual funds and professional management firms (although rarely with the same level of diversification). Investors can use one or more newsletters to obtain professional recommendations on a wide variety of individual stocks; the investor can then decide which, if any, of the recommendations to act upon, and then execute the decision through a discount broker.

When using a discounter for the first time, you will notice a refreshing change from your salesman/broker: since registered representatives of discount firms are salaried—not commission—employees, there is no sales pressure, no prying questions, no worthless advice, and no conflicts of interest to sift through. Trade executions are every bit as good, and often faster, than salesman/broker trades, and the commission savings are substantial: on most transactions you'll save about 50% by using a discount broker. The three largest firms, Charles Schwab, Quick & Reilly, and Rose & Company, all have offices in nearly every major city, along with a handful of equally competent regional discount houses.

How to Find a Good Newsletter

Finding a newsletter that will produce consistently above-average investment results can be considerably more difficult than finding a quality discount broker. Unlike mutual funds, which are tightly regulated by the Securities and Exchange Commission and are required to publish their track records regularly, investment advisory letters are only loosely controlled and are under no obligation to publish their results. Track records that are published by newsletters are often unaudited and should be viewed with deep skepticism. Virtually anyone with a few dollars to spend can publish an investment newsletter; the only requirement is that the editor be a registered "investment adviser," a regulatory distinction that can be bought from the SEC for $250 and, like the Series 7 license obtained by stockbrokers, proves nothing with respect to real investment expertise. Predictably, hundreds of letters have popped up in the last several years, largely in response to public interest arising from the 1982–1987 bull market. Many, perhaps even most, newsletters are not worth the paper they are printed on, and some can be downright dangerous. Careful selection—a most difficult assignment in an unregulated business—is the key to profitable investing through advisory newsletters. Fortunately, several independent and objective sources are available to aid in that search.

Select Information Exchange publishes a free catalog listing nearly all newsletters and describing each letter's approach, strategies, and prices. More importantly, the catalog offers a valuable trial subscription package in which investors can receive a short trial subscription to any twenty of the hundreds of letters listed for only $11.95. You can receive this catalog by writing to:

> Select Information Exchange
> 2095 Broadway
> New York, New York 10023
> (212) 874-6408

Services have also emerged that track the performance records of many of the newsletters. Among the most respected is the often-quoted *Hulbert Financial Digest*, published monthly by Mark Hulbert and William Bonner. The digest can be an invaluable aid not only in evaluating which newsletters to choose, but also as a constant source of the latest thinking and recommendations from over one hundred advisory letters. In addition to an intelligent and perceptive overview of market trends, each issue contains:

- Top six-performing newsletters during most recent month
- Top six-performing newsletters during most recent year
- Performance rankings for about one hundred newsletters, covering the following periods: one month, one year, each year since 1981
- Book review
- Advisory sentiment indicator
- List of stocks most often recommended by newsletters for purchase
- List of stocks most often mentioned by newsletters to be avoided
- Scoreboard of forecasts regarding the stock market, bond market, interest rates, and precious metals, from sixty-two leading advisory letters.

A one-year subscription to the *Hulbert Financial Digest* is $67.50. Trial subscriptions, at $37.50 for five months, are also available. Call or write Hulbert at:

> Hulbert Financial Digest
> 643 S. Carolina Avenue S.E.
> Washington, D.C. 20008
> (800) 227-1617 (ext. 459)

Five of the Best

Finally, there are the newsletters themselves. What follows are profiles of five highly respected newsletters that have consistently earned superior results for their readers. All performance figures, with the exception of those for the *Primary Trend* newsletter, are courtesy of the *Hulbert Financial Digest*, and cover the period from Hulbert's inception in July 1980 through 1988.

Growth Stock Outlook

Address:	4405 E. West Highway
	Bethesda, Maryland 20814
Phone:	(301) 654-5205
Editor:	Charles Allmon
Average Annual Return:	+14.8%
Average Annual Diff. to S & P 500:	+1.0%
Published:	monthly
Cost:	$65 for three months
	$175 for one year
	$320 for two years

The following is an interview with Charles Allmon, president, editor, and chief portfolio manager of *Growth Stock Outlook*.

TDS: *What type of companies do you buy for your portfolios?*

CA: We are looking for bonafide growth companies, both large ones and small ones. And we are very fundamental in our approach: We look at sales first, then we look at earnings, and we look very carefully at balance sheets. We have six in-house CPAs; we look at balance sheets above everything else. We're looking at current ratios*, debt-to-equity ratios*, cash levels*, return on equity, price-earnings ratios. Book value is very important to us; we're certainly not interested in companies selling at high multiples to book value. We prefer companies selling under book value. And of course we look carefully at the industry that each company operates in.

TDS: *What is your average holding period?*

CA: We are long-term holders. We believe that patience is very important. One of the things I find in this business is that patience is often more important than money. So we often hold stocks for fifteen years, or until we think they are overpriced.

TDS: *You were one of the few investment managers who correctly predicted the bear market which began in August 1987. Some reports had you sitting 80% in cash at the time.*

CA: Well, we don't use charts or Ouija boards; we just look at reality. We hadn't had a bear market in a long time. We look at underlying value anyway; we don't buy market action. If we don't see values, we're simply not going to play.

TDS: *Your investment approach is such that market action only affects stock selection to the degree that it increases or decreases the amount of values, or bargains, available.*

CA: That's exactly right. You can always find something to buy regardless of what is going on in the market.

TDS: *What are the most common mistakes the average investor makes?*

CA: There are two common mistakes made by the average investor. One, they buy baloney stories; they go to the office, they go to the club, they go to the party, and somebody says, "I just invested in the greatest thing since sliced bread. You better mortgage the house and jump in." Most of these stories are pure baloney. You don't buy a stock on the basis of a story; you look at the numbers. Then, if the numbers check out, you begin to look at the story behind the numbers. But all too often people just buy these stories and the numbers never materialize and then they lose their shirt. The second most common mistake is that the average investor tries to hit a home run in one or two stocks. That's the worst thing they can do. They should be broadly diversified; they should never put more than 5% of their assets into any one stock, and probably not more than 1 or 2%.[NN]

(Large investors wishing to benefit from Charles Allmon's investment expertise may be interested in the Growth Stock Outlook private portfolio management service. The minimum portfolio size is $175,000. Allmon also manages the Growth Stock Outlook Trust, Inc., a closed-end mutual fund* listed on the New York Stock Exchange. More information can be obtained by writing to the above address.)

The Primary Trend

Address:	700 N. Water Street
	Milwaukee, Wisconsin 53202
Phone:	(414) 271-2726
Editor:	James R. Arnold
Average Annual Return:	+20.0%
Average Annual Diff. to S & P 500:	+3.8%
Published:	18 issues per year
Cost:	$65 for 5 issues
	$110 for 9 issues
	$180 for one year
	$295 for two years

The following is an interview with James R. Arnold, editor of *The Primary Trend*.

TDS: *What type of investor would be interested in your newsletter?*

JRA: The letter is primarily for the conservative investor and for the patient investor. We are not trading oriented, our average holding period is two-and-a-half to three years. We are buying what we consider to be out-of-favor values, much like Warren Buffet or John Templeton. As an example, we are currently heavy in energy stocks, which is very contrarian. Energy stocks are totally out of favor and are tremendously underowned by the institutions. We look at that as a positive because if the institutions ever decide that they want to own them, they are going to throw a lot of money at them. So we try to anticipate major changes.

TDS: *Are you a technician or a fundamentalist?*

JRA: We use fundamental and technical analysis. We will not recommend anything unless both the technicals and the fundamentals look good. We use longer-term technical work as a screen to alert us to things that are going on in other areas of the market that we should pay attention to. We will sell something, however, on technicals. If we have a stock that has done well and the fundamentals appear to be decent, but the stock starts to deteriorate, we will sell the stock and not wait around to find out the reason for the deterioration, which might not surface until much later fundamentally.

TDS: *What is your outlook for the U.S. stock market over the next five years?*

JRA: Looking out over the next five years, we think the Dow could be selling in the 2800 area, maybe as high as 3000. There are a number of advisers predicting 3800, 4000, 5000, but we just can't see that. We like to take a historical perspective. History does tend to repeat itself, not necessarily in detail, but in general ways. So we think we can learn a lot from past history. If you look at the Dow Jones industrials, you'll notice that they've never sold to yield less than 3%, at least not for any length of time. A 3% yield has represented a ceiling on price. Even assuming a 6% growth in dividends—a very optimistic assumption since the historic compounded growth rate is 4½%—the Dow would hit the ceiling in 1990 at about 2850. If the advisers who are predicting 3800 or higher are going to be right, then you'll have to throw the history book away and I'm not willing to do that. But if the Dow does go to only 2800 over the next few years, we're still going to be making a lot of money, without worrying about 4000 or 5000.

TDS: *You've been forecasting a cyclical upturn in inflation. Why?*

JRA: We think that a major factor will be an increase in oil prices, probably brought about by Iran winning the war with Iraq, or at least chewing off a big chunk of Iraqi territory and holding onto it. Iran would then become much more influential as a member of OPEC, and they're on record as saying they want to see $30-a-barrel oil. Also, the United States hasn't learned anything over the last ten years; we haven't done anything to increase our self-sufficiency as far as energy is concerned. This is why we own so many energy stocks. They are either out of favor or underowned. Twenty-dollars-per-barrel oil would cause inflation to rise to about 5 to 5½%; $30 oil would get inflation to the 8% area. Boone Pickens [oil magnate and Chairman of the Mesa Limited Partners] thinks $20 oil is a shoo-in, and his mother didn't have too many stupid children.

TDS: *What can the average person do to improve the return on his investments? Besides subscribing to a good newsletter, of course.*

JRA: The best vehicle for the average investor is a good mutual fund. They should look at the track record, not just the latest three-month numbers that blare out at you in the newspapers. Look at how the fund has done in up-cycles and down-cycles. If a person is going to invest serious money, either find a good mutual fund that is run by good people with a good track record whose philosophy makes sense to you, or find a money management firm with the same criteria. ∞

(In addition to editing *The Primary Trend*, James R. Arnold also serves as president and chief portfolio manager of Arnold Investment Counsel, a private money management firm. The minimum portfolio size required to qualify for private management is $500,000. In 1986, Arnold launched the Primary Trend Fund, a no-load mutual fund that follows the same long-term value-oriented approach as his newsletter. Information about both the private portfolio management service and the no-load mutual fund can be obtained at the above address.)

The Prudent Speculator

Address:	P.O. Box 1767
	Santa Monica, California 90406
Phone:	(800) 258-7786
Editor:	Al Frank
Average Annual Return:	+23.8%
Average Annual Diff. to S & P 500:	+9.9%
Published:	every three weeks

Cost: $40 for three issues
                                   $200 for one year
                                   $350 for two years

The following is an interview with Al Frank, editor of *The Prudent Speculator*.

TDS: *Do you prefer to buy large- or small-capitalization stocks?*

AF: We prefer small-capitalization companies, but we will buy whatever is undervalued, including companies like Ford and Chrysler. Our list is eclectic. We choose them strictly on their undervaluedness and growth potential.

TDS: *And how do you define value?*

AF: There are about five or six principal criteria that we look at and then a couple-dozen others. We define value in terms of book value; we like to buy a stock at book value or less because very often other people will pay one-and-a-half or two times book value for a company. We also define value in terms of price-earnings ratios. We like to buy stocks for half of their average price-earnings ratios. We watch price-to-cash-flow ratios* carefully; historically, companies that trade for five or six times cash flow or less are frequently undervalued. And we look for a company's return on equity to be greater than the price-earnings ratio of the stock.

TDS: *Some of your criteria seem to interact.*

AF: Yes. There gets to be a lot of interrelationships. For example, we look at return on equity to see if it's growing and therefore can support a higher price-earnings ratio than the market is currently giving it. It is a rule of thumb that you could have a normal price-earnings ratio that equals the return on equity. If a company is returning 15% on shareholders' equity, it might support a price-earnings ratio of fifteen, although that relationship doesn't carry through forever. I wouldn't want to pay thirty-times earnings for anything, even if a company is returning 30% on equity.

TDS: *How flexible are you in applying these standards?*

AF: Very flexible. Some corporations are asset plays, selling for 25 to 50% of book value or replacement cost. Maybe they're not very exciting in terms of earnings or growth, but quite valuable as takeover candidates or turnaround situations. Then, of course, some companies are growing rapidly and are very exciting in terms of their earnings trends and sales trends. It gets to be a very complicated business. Every week we print an analysis of 500 companies with about thirty-five items that we are watching for each.

TDS: *You are primarily a fundamentalist. Do you use technical analysis at all?*

AF: For the overall market, yes. We look at the New York Stock Exchange and try to determine if it is overbought or oversold. If it is overbought we step back; if it is oversold we become very aggressive.

TDS: *Do you tell your readers when it is time to sell a stock?*

AF: We give goal prices. Because we analyze these companies from a fundamental basis, we can come up with a goal price for each stock. Absent a major market decline, we want our readers to hold their stocks until the goal price is reached. If things look dicey and a stock is near its goal price, then we might try to take some profits. But we try to get the goal price and live through the 5 and 10% corrections.

TDS: *How many stocks are on your recommended list at a given time?*

AF: It varies. After the crash there were 140. Now there are about 50. During market tops we get down to 6 or 8. That in itself is an indicator of an overvalued market.

TDS: *How do you feel about predictions or market timing?*

AF: We are not primarily a market timing letter. We offer stock recommendations for long-term portfolios. I don't believe anyone can time all the markets all the time, although some people may be able to time some of the markets some of the time. There's a code for market letter writers: Make many predictions and only repeat the ones that worked out.[PP]

MPT Review†

Address:	P.O. Box 5695
	Incline Village, Nevada 89450-
	5695
Phone:	(702) 831-7800
Editor:	Louis G. Navellier
Average Annual Return:	+39.1%
Average Annual Diff. to S & P	
500:	+22.4%
Published:	Monthly
Cost:	$195 for one year
	$325 for two years
	$425 for three years

The following is an interview with Louis G. Navellier, editor of *MPT Review*.

TDS: *What type of investor would be interested in your newsletter?*

LGN: Our letter is for the very sophisticated investor. The people we attract are very serious investors. And we are more expensive than normal because we only want the serious investor. We want people who are going to be able to afford a portfolio; we don't want people to just go out and buy one or two stocks off our list. We want them to structure a very balanced portfolio, hopefully containing ten or twelve stocks. We want our readers to have a portfolio mentality where they buy a balanced group of stocks. Our objective is to get a nice compounded rate of return over a long period of time.

TDS: *Describe your system for selecting stocks.*

LGN: What is unique about our system is that we calculate risk and return. Lots of people calculate return indicators*, but we

---

†Began operations as *OTC Insight*. Renamed *MPT Review* after editor Louis G. Navellier separated from Insight Capital Management, which had served as the newsletter's co-publisher. Figures reflect the average total return for all twelve portfolios managed by Navellier for the four-year period 1985–1988.

actually calculate risk indicators* also. Regarding the return indicators we use—the primary one is called Alpha—we divide it by the risk indicator to get a risk/reward ratio*. Basically, everything we do is risk adjusted. We want to get a good return per unit of risk. We've found that risk is a very dynamic thing that is constantly changing. So reward/risk ratios are constantly changing, too.

TDS: *Are your recommendations fundamentally or technically based?*

LGN: We are quantitative analysts. A technician doesn't look at risk; he only looks at a chart. A quantitative analyst uses a computer to base a portfolio and calculate risk. Our quantitative analysis gets us out of the blocks quickly. We monitor 2700 stocks; the top 240 hit our buy list. The next step is to try to beat our own buy list. We do that in a number of ways, including some fundamental analysis. We also run it through an asset-allocation process, which forces us to take bigger bets on our lower-risk stocks and smaller bets on our riskier stocks. That is the idea behind our twelve model portfolios.

TDS: *What size companies do you buy?*

LGN: We buy mainstream OTC and a few low-capitalization and New York Stock Exchange companies. The average price of recommended stocks has been $26 per share. We buy a lot of special situations with moderate price-earnings ratios. We don't buy high flyers.

TDS: *Do you invest independently of overall market action?*

LGN: We act semi-independently of the market. We don't try to time the market. The system is designed to beat the market. We're pretty much fully invested all the time, but our strategy does change. After a prolonged bull market our average beta tends to be very low, which means we are buying very selective stocks. The higher the market goes, the more conservative we get. Conversely, the lower the market goes, the more aggressive our system becomes. So although we are always fully invested, we are always changing the type of stocks we buy. The higher the market goes, the more risk there is; the lower the market goes, the less risk there is. We adjust our strategy accordingly.

TDS: *What is the most common mistake made by the average investor?*

LGN: Most investors are overly emotional and are trying to make too much too fast. There are some brokers who sell on greed and fear, and there are newsletters that sell on greed and fear—it's a proven marketing formula that works with the retail public because the average investor is a high-strung, emotional person who often gets a little too greedy. The public is not satisfied with 20% per year—they want more. And because they're so emotional, you should never go near the stock market. On the other hand, our newsletter is brutally analytical and somewhat cold-blooded in the way we approach the market. ⁹⁹

Outstanding Investor Digest

Address:	14 East 4th Street, Suite 501
	New York, New York 10012
Phone:	(212) 777-3330
Editor:	Henry Emerson
Average Annual Return:	††
Published:	Monthly
Cost:	$275 for 12 issues

The following is an interview with Henry J. Emerson, editor and publisher of *Outstanding Investor Digest*.

TDS: *What does your newsletter try to do?*

HJE: We simply focus on money managers with superior long-term track records. We follow what they are saying in their client correspondence and shareholder letters. We report on their

††*Outstanding Investor Digest* does not make specific recommendations; instead it interviews a select group of outstanding money managers, many of whom do give specific investment advice as well as comment on larger questions regarding the financial markets and the economy.

portfolio activity and we publish exclusive conversations with several of these managers in each issue.

TDS: *How many managers are you following?*

HJE: We focus on only the top 5 to 10% of all money managers. Currently, that number amounts to less than 100.

TDS: *What can the average investor gain by reading the latest thoughts and recommendations of the world's top money managers?*

HJE: The professional investors we follow have had a history of keeping their heads on straight while everyone else was losing theirs. These managers have a little better sense of when things are in excess and when they're not. There is certainly something to be gained by listening to certified contrarians, people who don't get caught up in the crowd. There is also something to be gained by understanding their philosophy, since their investment approach has worked for many years. You will find that the investment philosophies of many of these managers are often quite similar. Also, there is also something to be gained by understanding their insights into a particular company. I can't imagine a better source of investment ideas than the ideas of people who have been very successful for long periods of time.

TDS: *You mentioned that the investment philosophies of many of the most successful money managers are strikingly similar. In what way?*

HJE: Most of the money managers who have been successful don't pay a lot of attention to what's going on in the overall market or economy. They are not necessarily great macroeconomic thinkers; 90% of their focus is on relative value. In other words, is this stock cheap. If a particular stock is cheap, it doesn't matter what is going on elsewhere. A cheap stock makes up for a world of evils. The key is to find cheap stocks. There are cheap stocks in an overvalued market; they are just few and far between.

TDS: *How do you feel about the business of making predictions?*

HJE: Nobody has a crystal ball. Lots of people claim to have a crystal ball because that's what sells. They have this econometric model and plug in everything from the price of potatoes to what side of the bed their wives get up on. It sells newsletters; it doesn't make money. If anyone really had a model that was that accurate, do you think they'd be selling it to you and me?

TDS: *Your newsletter seems to emphasize exactly the opposite of salesmanship. You are telling investors to listen to proven professionals who have a track record of success.*

HJE: Yes. I think it makes sense in any aspect of human activity to do business with people who have demonstrated that they are good at what they do. Whether it be picking sides for a baseball game, or picking an attorney, or picking a money manager, there are people who are better than others at what they do. [RR]

Now Go Do It

Yes, you *can* do it yourself: you *can* take charge of your own investments, and you *can* finally begin to earn your rightful share of the ample profits generated by the stock and bond markets.

It will be worth it. The kinds of returns described in the previous three chapters are not reserved only for a one-in-a-million lottery winner. They are reserved for *anyone* willing to spend the small amount of time necessary to put their investment futures into their own hands.

I have attempted to show in this book the very real costs and dangers associated with trusting life savings to professional salesmen/brokers laboring under intense conflicts of interest and with little or no investment qualifications. I have also attempted to show a better way, a way in which every investor—from the rank beginner to the experienced market player—can profit from the inevitable growth in the world economy.

The strategy of capitalizing on that growth through no-load mutual funds, private professional money management, and investment newsletters is a strategy that need not intimidate anyone. An unwarranted fear of the unknown should not prevent investors from missing the extraordinary returns that are so easily available through these investment resources. I hope the information in this book will provide investors with the motivation, knowledge, and confidence they need to begin earning the investment results they deserve.

Glossary

Adjusted book value—The value of a company computed using current market values, instead of the traditional cost-minus-depreciation method.

Bank CDs—A certificate of deposit with a savings institution that carries a fixed rate of interest for a fixed period of time. Certificates of deposit can be purchased for amounts ranging from $500 to $1 million, and for time periods of from three months to five years. There is never a risk to principal, although some or all of the interest may be lost if an investor redeems the CD before its specified maturity date. The interest rate on CDs is usually fully taxable and is often comparable to the rates on government securities of equal maturities.

Bear market—A market whose underlying long-term trend is down.

Book value—An accounting term that measures the amount of shareholders' equity in a firm, i.e., the amount of assets actually owned by shareholders. Book value is determined by subtracting a firm's liabilities and preferred stock from its assets. As a general rule, most stocks trade in the open market at prices above their per-share book value.

Call option—An option that gives its owner the right to buy a certain stock at a certain price by a certain date. An IBM May 150 call would give its owner the right to buy IBM at $150 per share at any time before the third Saturday in May, when the option expires. Call options appreciate in value as the price of the underlying stock goes up.

Capital appreciation—That portion of an investment's total return that is gained solely from the appreciation in the underlying price of the security. It does not apply to dividend or interest income.

Cash levels—The amount of cash or cash equivalents, such as certificates of deposit or treasury bills, that a corporation has on hand.

Cash value—The worth of a company after subtracting all liabilities from its available cash.

Churning—The practice of excessive and pointless trading in a customer's account for the sole purpose of generating commissions.

Closed-end mutual fund—A type of mutual fund in which the number of shares that can be sold is fixed at the time the fund becomes public. Since no additional money can be put into a closed-end mutual fund after its initial offering, an investor wishing to purchase a closed-end fund would have to buy fund shares from a fund shareholder wishing to sell. Closed-end mutual funds are traded on securities exchanges, such as the New York Stock Exchange. Because the size of a closed-end fund is limited by the terms of its charter, they are popular among investors who believe that a mutual fund's performance is harmed by ever-increasing size.

Cold-calls—A prospecting technique used by stockbrokers in which individuals suspected of being possible investors are solicited over the phone, without any prior permission or notice.

Commodity price-fixing—The practice of attempting to artificially control the price of a certain commodity by increasing or decreasing its supply in the open market. The most famous attempt at commodity price-fixing was, and is, being made by OPEC, which attempts to control the price of oil in world markets by establishing production quotas for its members.

Contrarian—An investor who buys securities that are currently unpopular and out of favor with the intention of holding them for the long-term.

Corporate bonds—A type of debt security in which an investor lends money to a corporation for a fixed period of time in exchange for a fixed amount of interest.

Current ratio—A corporation's current assets divided by its current liabilities. A current ratio of two or more is evidence of a healthy liquidity condition.

Debt-to-equity ratio—The amount of debt on a corporation's balance sheet, expressed as a percentage of its total capitalization. A debt-to-equity ratio of 40% or less is generally considered an acceptable debt level, although certain industries such as banks, utilities, and insurance companies will tend to have debt ratios on an average of 60 to 70%.

Discretion—A legal term referring to the practice of granting a stockbroker permission to make trades in a customer's account without securing the client's permission before each trade.

Dividend discount model—A mathematical method of valuing stocks or bonds that attempts to measure the projected long-term return of an investment versus the certain no-risk return on long-term government bonds. Key factors in the process are the present level of dividends paid by a company, the projected growth rate in the dividends, the present level of return that could be earned in government bonds, and the premium that an investor must demand of the investment in order to make its additional risk (relative to government bonds) worthwhile.

Double bottom—The pattern of prices formed when a stock declines to a certain level on high volume, advances off of that level on declining volume, then falls back to but not below the earlier level on volume approaching but not equaling that of the previous decline. The stock then rebounds off of the low and again begins advancing on light volume.

Earnings—The profits of a corporation. Earnings are usually expressed in terms of earnings per share, which is determined by dividing a corporation's total profits by the number of common shares outstanding. If a company earned $10 million in profits in a given period and has five million shares of stock outstanding, its earnings per share would be $2.

Earnings growth—The rate of growth of a corporation's profits.

Fundamental analysis—A type of securities evaluation that focuses on numbers, i.e., a corporation's earnings per share, current ratio, debt-to-equity ratio, return on shareholders' equity, and earnings growth rate.

Fundamentalist—A securities analyst who relies on objective standards of measurement rather than interpretation of chart patterns formed by stock price movement, to make investment decisions. The fundamentalist examines current price-earnings ratios, earnings growth, liquidity, and debt ratios as well as forecasts of future trends in each category in arriving at investment strategies.

Gap—A price range in which no shares change hands. For a declining stock, a gap is produced when the lowest price a stock is traded at during a certain day is higher than the highest price the same stock is traded at on the following day. For an advancing stock, a gap is produced when the highest price the stock is traded at on a certain day is lower than its lowest price the following trading day.

Head-and-shoulders formation—A pattern formed by price movements of a stock that approximately resembles a head and shoulders, with three upward surges, the second of which goes beyond the first and third.

IRA—An Individual Retirement Account. Under current law, individuals not covered by a company retirement plan may contribute up to $2,000 or 100% of income, whichever is less, into an IRA and the amount of the contribution will be considered fully tax deductible. Those covered by a company plan may make fully deductible IRA contributions only if their adjusted gross income is below $25,000. Those with AGIs of $25,000 to $35,000 may make partially deductible contributions, and those with greater than $35,000 of adjusted gross income will not qualify for even a partially deductible IRA.

Junk bonds—Unsecured loans obtained by corporations issued solely for the purpose of financing attempts to acquire other companies. These bonds, which are sold to individual investors through brokerage firms, usually carry an above-market interest rate as well as substantially above average risk of default. They also tend to be more interest rate sensitive than government or investment-grade corporate bonds, i.e., the resale price of junk bonds tends to react with greater volatility in the resale bond market. Like all bonds, however, the resale price of junk bonds will move inversely to interest rates.

Keogh—A retirement plan for self-employed individuals that allows 25% of income or $30,000, whichever is less, to be placed in an tax-deferred account each year, with the amount of the contribution considered free from tax.

Limited partnerships—A type of business organization in which certain investors—the limited partners—contribute capital to the business but take no role in its management. The limited partners liability is limited to the amount of their investment.

Liquidity—The ability to quickly convert an investment to cash.

Long-term debt—Money owed by a corporation that comes due during a period beginning later than one year from the present.

Long-term government bonds—A type of debt security issued by the U.S. Government that carries a fixed rate of interest and a fixed maturity date, ranging from fifteen to thirty years. Like all bonds, these securities may be sold in the resale market prior to maturity at prices determined by supply and demand.

Low-load mutual funds—Mutual funds that carry sales charges of from 1% to 3%.

Market-maker securities—Securities that are sold to an investor directly from the inventory of a brokerage firm, rather than from another investor.

Market timing—An investment strategy in which investment decisions are made based upon short-term predictions of market movements.

Money market funds—A type of mutual fund that invests exclusively in short-term securities. Such funds are usually completely liquid, carry no risk to principal, and pay a fluctuating interest rate comparable to that of three-month treasury bills.

Net/Net book strategy—Current assets (cash, inventory, and receivables) minus all liabilities, both current and long-term. If a stock can be purchased at a price below this number, the shareholder would, in effect, be getting the company's fixed assets for free.

No-load mutual funds—Mutual funds that charge no sales or redemption fees.

Overnight gap—A gap in a trading range produced by a stock opening at a price either above or below its complete trading range from the previous day.

Parking—The practice of buying shares in a false name in order to conceal the identity of the real owner.

Price-earnings ratio—The relationship between a company's stock price and its earnings per share. If company X has earned profits of $2 per share and its stock is selling for $20 per share, its price-earnings ratio (also known as the PE ratio) would be 10. If its stock price were $40 and its earnings per share $2, its price-earnings ratio would be 20.

Price-to-cash-flow ratios—The price of a company's common stock, expressed as a multiple of its per share cash-flow. For example, if a company has a cash flow of $3 per share and its stock is trading for $21, the company would have a price-to-cash-flow ratio of seven.

Profit sharing—A type of retirement account in which an employer contributes a percentage of company profits to the retirement plan of an employee.

Put option—An option that gives its owner the right to sell a certain stock at a certain price by a certain date. The holder of an IBM May 150 put would have the right to sell IBM at $150 per share any time before the third Saturday in May, when the option would expire. Put options appreciate in value as the price of the underlying stock declines.

Quotron—A computer-like device that instantaneously announces the minute-by-minute price movement of thousands of stocks and bonds.

Return indicators—Any of a number of indicators which measure the return on an investment. The most common return indicator is the simple annualized total return, which combines whatever capital appreciation or depreciation has been earned in an investment to whatever dividend or interest income has been realized, then adjusts the figures to reflect a one-year holding period. For example, if stock XYZ has appreciated 30% in value over a four-year period and paid another 10% in dividends, it would have an annual average total return of 10% (30% + 10% ÷ 4 = 10%). Return on shareholders' equity (defined elsewhere in the glossary) is another standard measure of return.

Return on equity—The total profit of a corporation divided by the amount of shareholders' capital (equity) in the corporation. More simply, ROE is the measure of return, usually expressed as a percentage, earned for each $1 of stockholders' money invested in a company. A return on equity of 15% or more is considered above average, although smaller, faster-growing firms will tend to have higher ROEs than larger corporations.

Reversal patterns—A pattern of prices formed when a stock is in the process of changing its long-term trend. The head-and-shoulders formation is an example of a major reversal pattern.

Reverse stock split—A split that increases a stock's per share price while reducing the number of shares outstanding. If XYZ stock were selling for $1 per share and if shareholder John Smith held 500 shares, Smith would hold 100 shares of stock at $5 per share after a one-for-five reverse stock split.

Risk indicators—The primary measure of an investment's potential risk is its beta, which is a measure of volatility. A beta of one indicates that a stock tends to be exactly as volatile as the overall market; a beta of two would indicate that the stock, in theory at least, is twice as volatile as the market as a whole. Betas are computed on the basis of past price movements and do not necessarily predict a stock's future price volatility. To the extent, however, that beta is a generally accurate barometer of a stock's susceptibility to overall market swings, beta is a useful tool in computing one aspect of a stock's theoretical risk. For example, if a stock has a beta of two and the overall market declines 20%, that stock would be expected to decline twice that amount, or 40%. Higher beta stocks, therefore, are considered more risky than stocks with betas of one or less.

Risk/Reward ratio—The relationship between an investment's risk and its potential return. For example, if an investment carries a high risk, either by nature of a high beta or other economic or financial factors, investors will require some reason to believe that the investment's potential total return will also be above average. Without the potential for significantly above average return, investors would have no incentive for taking on above average risk.

SEP—Also known as the Simplified Employee Pension plan, the SEP is an employer-funded retirement plan that allows for maximum annual contributions of 15% of total income up to $30,000 per year.

Shareholders' equity—The amount of shareholders' money invested in a corporation. This amount represents the total value of stock originally sold to the public plus any earnings retained by the company, i.e., profits not paid out to shareholders in the form of dividends.

Stop-loss order—An order given by a customer to a broker requiring that shares of a given stock be sold if the price of the stock reaches or falls below a pre-determined point. Stop-loss orders are intended to minimize the size of possible losses, especially those which could occur quickly during the course of a trading day while a customer is not actively monitoring the movement of a stock. For example, an investor who buys 100 shares of IBM at $100 per share may wish to limit the size of any potential loss to 10%, and would place an order with a broker to sell the shares if the price of IBM stock reached or fell below $90 per share. Most stop-loss orders stay in effect for one month, or until cancelled by the customer.

Technical analysis—An approach to market forecasting that holds that since stock movements at any one moment reflect the cumulative wisdom (or lack thereof) of the entire investing world, the proper interpretation of those movements (through chart patterns) is therefore faster and more reliable in terms of forecasting future price movements than those based upon predictions of future earnings or other developments.

Technician—A market strategist who makes investment decisions at least partially based upon chart formations representing prior price movements of stocks.

Ten-times earnings—If a company has profits (earnings) of $1 per share and its stock price is $10, it would be trading at ten-times earnings.

Treasury bills—Debt securities issued by the United States Government that carry fixed rates of interest for a fixed period, usually three, six, or twelve months. Treasury bills are issued in increments of $5,000 with a minimum purchase of $10,000 and may be sold prior to maturity in the government bond resale market.

Trend channels—That area of a stock chart between two lines formed by connecting a stock's high points and its low points over a period of time. The two lines, which run roughly parallel to each other, tend to contain a stock's movement. Any sudden jump or fall by a stock to a point outside of the trading range formed by the trend channel is called a "breakout" and is considered significant by technicians.

Triple bottom—Identical to the double bottom with one more advance on light volume and one more fall back to the low price recorded twice earlier.

401k—A Salary Reduction Retirement Plan, usually set up in conjunction with a profit-sharing plan, funded by employer contributions and employee pre-tax contributions. Employee salary reduction contributions may not exceed the lesser of $7,313 or 15% of compensation.

403b—A Pre-tax Salary Reduction Retirement program for certain nonprofit organizations as defined by section 501c-3 of Internal Revenue Code. Employees of schools, colleges, nonprofit hospitals, as well as religious, charitable, scientific, and literary organizations are allowed to contribute the lesser of $9,500 or 16.66% per year into this entirely employee-funded payroll reduction program.

Bibliography

1. Schwed, Fred, Jr. *Where Are the Customers' Yachts?* New York: Simon & Schuster, 1940.
2. Stern, Richard L. "Look at the Brokers' Yachts." *Forbes*, 17 January 1983, pp. 41–42.
3. "87 Highest-Paying Careers for the 80s." *Working Woman*, October 1984, pp. 93–96.
4. Putka, Gary. "Brokerage Houses Didn't Fare Well in Survey of 1982 Performance of Investment Advisers." *Wall Street Journal*, 10 January 1983, p. 39.
5. "The 1986 Investment Challenge." *Fortune 1986 Investor's Guide*, Fall 1985, p. 99.
6. "The 1986 Investment Challenge." *Fortune 1987 Investor's Guide*, Fall 1986, pp. 140–43.
7. "The Fortune Investment Challenge." *Fortune 1988 Investor's Guide*, Fall 1987, pp. 175–91.
8. "The Fortune Investment Challenge." *Fortune 1989 Investor's Guide*, Fall 1988, pp. 217–21.
9. *Wall Street Journal.* 3 February 1989, Section C, page 1.

10. "Rating the Investment Bankers." *Forbes*, 2 December 1985, pp. 155–60.

11. "The Money Rankings of Mutual Funds." *Money*, April 1985, pp. 159–94.

12. "The Money Rankings of Mutual Funds." *Money*, October 1985, pp. 173–218.

13. *Investment Policy*. Salomon Brothers, Inc., 19 October 1987.

14. *Research Weekly*. Prudential-Bache Securities, Inc., 14 October 1987.

15. *Wall Street Journal*. 20 February 1985, p. 26.

16. Kenney, Ray. *Milwaukee Journal*, 30 April 1985.

17. Ettorre, Barbara. "Don't Let the Slam Dunks Get to You." *Forbes*, 18 July 1983, pp. 79–83.

18. Terkel, Studs. *Working*. New York: Avon, 1975, pp. 438–47.

19. Ibid.

20. Ibid.

21. "Highs and Lows of Being a Stockbroker." *Changing Times*, August 1984, pp. 49–52. Quoted by permission from Changing Times, the Kiplinger Magazine, (August 1984 issue). Copyright 1984 by Kiplinger Washington Editors, Inc.

22. "How to Sound Like a Million Dollars on the Phone." *Registered Representative*, May 1985, p. 100.

23. Forbat, Pamela Savage. "The Voice Doctor." *Registered Representative*, May 1985, pp. 45–51.

24. *Wall Street Journal*. 21 January 1985, p. 32. Reprinted by permission of *The Wall Street Journal*, © Dow Jones & Company, Inc. 1985. All rights reserved.

25. Hitschler, W. Anthony. "To Know What We Don't Know." *Financial Analysts Journal*, January-February 1980, pp. 28–32.

26. Baldwin, William. "The Impossible Dream." *Forbes*, 22 October 1984, pp. 144–51.

27. Terkel, Studs. *Working*. New York: Avon, 1975, pp. 438–47.

28. Hitschler, W. Anthony. "To Know What We Don't Know." *Financial Analysts Journal*, January-February 1980, pp. 28–32.

29. Brown, Philip, George Foster, and Eric Noreen. *Studies in Accounting Research #21: Security Analyst Multi-Year Earnings Forecasts and the Capital Market*. Sarasota, Florida: American Accounting Association, 1985, p. 56.

30. Elton, Edwin J., Martin J. Gruber, and Mustafa Gultekin. "Expectations

and Share Prices." *Management Science,* September 1981, pp. 983–84. Copyright 1981, The Institute of Management Sciences, 290 Westminster Street, Providence, Rhode Island 02903, U.S.A.

31. Dreman, David. "Tricky Forecasts." *Barron's,* 24 July 1978, p. 5. Reprinted by permission of Barron's, © Dow Jones & Company, Inc. 1978. All rights reserved.

32. Elton, Edwin J., Martin J. Gruber, and Mustafa Gultekin. *Professional Expectations: Accuracy and Diagnosis of Errors.* New York: Graduate School of Business Administration, New York University, November 1982, p. 10.

33. Richards, R. Malcolm, James J. Benjamin, and Robert H. Strawser. "An Examination of the Accuracy of Earnings Forecasts." *Financial Management,* Fall 1977, pp. 78–85.

34. Ruland, William. "The Accuracy of Forecasts by Management and by Financial Analysts." *Accounting Review,* April 1978, pp. 439–47.

35. Cragg, J. G., and Burton G. Malkiel. "The Consensus and Accuracy of Some Predictions of the Growth of Corporate Earnings." *Journal of Finance,* March 1968, pp. 67–84.

36. Fisher, Anne B. "How Good are Wall Street's Security Analysts?" *Fortune,* 1 October 1984, pp. 130–36.

37. Ibid.

38. Morgenson, Gretchen. "How Reliable is Your Broker's Research?" *Money,* December 1984, pp. 149–54.

39. Ibid.

40. Ibid.

41. Fisher, Anne B. "How Good are Wall Street's Security Analysts?" *Fortune,* 1 October 1984, pp. 130–36.

42. Morgenson, Gretchen. "How Reliable is Your Broker's Research?" *Money,* December 1984, pp. 149–54.

43. Brown, Philip, George Foster, and Eric Noreen. *Studies in Accounting Research #21: Security Analyst Multi-Year Earnings Forecasts and the Capital Market.* Sarasota, Florida: American Accounting Association, 1985, p. 38.

44. Greenwald, John. "The Forecasters Flunk." *Time,* 27 August 1984, pp. 42–44.

45. Hitschler, W. Anthony. "To Know What We Don't Know." *Financial Analysts Journal,* January-February 1980, pp. 28–32.

46. Richards, R. Malcolm, James J. Benjamin, and Robert H. Strawser. "An

Examination of the Accuracy of Earnings Forecasts." *Financial Management*, Fall 1977, pp. 78–85.

47. Fisher, Anne B. "How Good are Wall Street's Security Analysts?" *Fortune*, 1 October 1984, pp. 130–36.

48. Hitschler, W. Anthony. "To Know What We Don't Know." *Financial Analysts Journal*, January-February 1980, pp. 28–32.

49. Zacks, Leonard. "EPS Forecasts—Accuracy is Not Enough." *Financial Analysts Journal*, March-April 1979, pp. 53–55.

50. Elton, Edwin J., Martin J. Gruber, and Mustafa Gultekin. "Expectations and Share Prices." *Management Science*, September 1981, pp. 975–87.

51. Zacks, Leonard. In "EPS Forecasts—Accuracy is Not Enough." *Financial Analysts Journal*, March-April 1979, pp. 53–55.

52. Elton, Edwin J., Martin J. Gruber, and Mustafa Gultekin. *Professional Expectations: Accuracy and Diagnosis of Errors*. New York: Graduate School of Business Administration, New York University, November 1982, p. 15.

53. Fisher, Anne B. "How Good are Wall Street's Security Analysts?" *Fortune*, 1 October 1984, pp. 130–36.

54. Bamford, Janet, and William G. Flanagan. "Watch Your Assets." *Forbes*, 8 October 1984, pp. 197–206.

55. "Motivation 101 At Merrill Lynch." *Wall Street Journal*, 14 June 1984, p. 33. Reprinted by permission of The Wall Street Journal, © Dow Jones & Company, Inc. 1984. All rights reserved.

56. *Wall Street Journal*, 7 March 1985, p. 45. Reprinted by permission of The Wall Street Journal, © Dow Jones & Company, Inc. 1985. All rights reserved.

57. Powell, Bill. "The New Dealmakers." *Newsweek*, 16 May 1986, pp. 47–52.

58. Ibid.

59. Addis, Ronit. "The Honor Roll." *Forbes*, 7 September 1987, pp. 166–67.

60. Ibid.

61. Ibid.

62. Ibbotson, Roger G., and Rex A. Sinquefeld, *Stocks, Bonds, Bills, and Inflation* (SBBI), 1982, updated in *Stocks, Bonds, Bills and Inflation 1984 Yearbook™*, Ibbotson Associates, Inc., Chicago. All rights reserved.

Footnote references
(Conversations)

CHAPTER 1

A   Author's notes of interview March 1986. Signed permission authorization and accreditation of quotations on file.

B   Author's notes of interview March 1986. Signed permission authorization and accreditation of quotations on file. Anonymity requested by interview subject.

CHAPTER 2

C   Recorded interview of June 1986. Signed permission authorization and accreditation of quotations on file.

D   Author's notes of interview March 1986. Signed permission authorization and accreditation of quotations on file.

E   Author's notes of interview October 1985. Signed permission authorization and accreditation of quotations on file. Anonymity requested by interview subject.

F   Author's notes of interview November 1988. Signed permission authorization and accreditation of quotations on file. Anonymity requested by interview subject.

G   Recorded conversation of February 1986. Signed permission authorization and accreditation of quotations on file.

H   Author's notes of interview March 1986. Signed permission authorization and accreditation of quotations on file. Anonymity requested by interview subject.

CHAPTER 3

I   Author's notes of interview February 1986. Signed permission authorization and accreditation of quotations on file.

J   Author's notes of interview February 1986. Signed permission authorization and accreditation of quotations on file.

K   Author's notes of interview February 1986. Signed permission authorization and accreditation of quotations on file.

L   Author's notes of interview January 1986. Signed permission authorization and accreditation of quotations on file.

M   Author's notes of interview February 1986. Signed permission authorization and accreditation of quotations on file.

M-1   Author's notes of interview January 1986. Signed permission authorization and accreditation of quotations on file.

CHAPTER 4

N   Author's notes of interview August 1986.

CHAPTER 5

O   Author's notes of interview June 1986. Signed permission authorization and accreditation of quotations on file. Anonymity requested by interview subject.

P   Author's notes of interview March 1986. Signed permission authorization and accreditation of quotations on file. Anonymity requested by interview subject.

Q   Author's notes of interview April 1986. Signed permission authorization and accreditation of quotations on file. Anonymity requested by interview subject.

R   Author's notes of interview April 1986. Signed permission authorization and accreditation of quotations on file. Anonymity requested by interview subject.

S   Author's notes of interview April 1986. Signed permission authorization and accreditation of quotations on file. Anonymity requested by interview subject.

T   Author's notes of interview May 1986. Signed permission authorization and accreditation of quotations on file. Anonymity requested by interview subject.

U   Author's notes of interview April 1986. Signed permission authorization and accreditation of quotations on file. Anonymity requested by interview subject.

V   Author's notes of interview May 1986. Signed permission authorization and accreditation of quotations on file. Anonymity requested by interview subject.

W   Author's notes of interview March 1986. Signed permission authorization and accreditation of quotations on file. Anonymity requested by interview subject.

X   Author's notes of interview June 1986. Signed permission authorization and accreditation of quotations on file. Anonymity requested by interview subject.

Y   Author's notes of interview May 1986. Signed permission authorization and accreditation of quotations on file. Anonymity requested by interview subject.

Z   Author's notes of interview March 1986. Signed permission authorization and accreditation of quotations on file. Anonymity requested by interview subject.

AA Author's notes of interview June 1986. Signed permission authorization and accreditation of quotations on file. Anonymity requested by interview subject.

BB Author's notes of interview June 1986. Signed permission authorization and accreditation of quotations on file. Anonymity requested by interview subject.

CC Author's notes of interview April 1986. Signed permission authorization and accreditation of quotations on file. Anonymity requested by interview subject.

DD Author's notes of interview May 1986. Signed permission authorization and accreditation of quotations on file. Anonymity requested by interview subject.

EE Author's notes of interview April 1986. Signed permission authorization and accreditation of quotations on file. Anonymity requested by interview subject.

CHAPTER 7

FF Author's notes of interview October 1986. Signed permission authorization and accreditation of quotations on file.

GG Author's notes of interview November 1986. Signed permission authorization and accreditation of quotations on file.

HH   Author's notes of interview November 1986. Signed permission authorization and accreditation of quotations on file.

CHAPTER 9

II   Author's notes of interview January 1987. Signed permission authorization and accreditation of quotations on file.

JJ   Author's notes of interview January 1987. Signed permission authorization and accreditation of quotations on file.

KK   Author's notes of interview January 1987. Signed permission authorization and accreditation of quotations on file.

LL   Author's notes of interview January 1987. Signed permission authorization and accreditation of quotations on file.

MM   Author's notes of interview March 1988. Signed permission authorization and accreditation of quotations on file.

CHAPTER 10

NN   Author's notes of interview March 1988. Signed permission authorization and accreditation of quotations on file.

OO   Author's notes of interview January 1987. Signed permission authorization and accreditation of quotations on file.

PP   Author's notes of interview March 1988. Signed permission authorization and accreditation of quotations on file.

QQ   Author's notes of interview January 1987. Signed permission authorization and accreditation of quotations on file.

RR   Author's notes of interview January 1987. Signed permission authorization and accreditation of quotations on file.

Index